THEY CALLED HIM
SUPERMAN

VOLUME TWO

DEBATES OF T.W. BRENTS

Edited by Kyle D. Frank

Charleston, AR:
COBB PUBLISHING
2018

They Called Him Superman (Volume 2): Debates of T.W. Brents is copyright © Kyle D. Frank, 2018.
All rights reserved.

No portion of this book (whether in part or the whole) may be reproduced without the written permission of the publisher. Exceptions are granted for reviews, research writings, or freely distributed congregational bulletins.

Published in the United States of America by:

Cobb Publishing
704 E. Main St.
Charleston, AR 72933
www.CobbPublishing.com
CobbPublishing@gmail.com
(479) 747-8372

TABLE OF CONTENTS

THE BRENTS-HEROD DEBATE
ON CALVINISM AND SALVATION 1

THE BRENTS-FROGGE DEBATE
ON INFANT BAPTISM AND THE ROLE OF THE HOLY SPIRIT IN CONVERSION
.... 167

THE BRENTS-PENNINGTON DEBATE
ON THE IDENTITY OF THE CHURCH
.... 269

The Brents-Herod Debate
on Calvinism and Salvation

A Theological Debate

BETWEEN

T. W. BRENTS
Of the Church of Christ

And

Elder E. D. HEROD
Of the Primitive Baptist Church

HELD IN FRANKLIN, KY., BEGINNING MARCH 29, 1887, AND CONTINUING FOUR DAYS

PROPOSITIONS DEBATED.

The Scriptures teach that salvation from sin is conditional, the condition or conditions to be performed by the sinner in order to salvation or freedom from sin.

         T. W. BRENTS affirms.
         E. D. Herod denies.

The Scriptures teach the unconditional election and salvation from sin, by Jesus Christ, of all his seed or generation.

         E. D. HEROD affirms.
         T. W. BRENTS denies.

First, second and fourth days' debate reported by A. M. Growden, Stenographer, Franklin, Tenn.

Introduction

In presenting this debate to the public, a few words of explanation are deemed necessary. The subjects debated being somewhat novel, and believing that the range the discussion would likely take would bring out some thoughts not developed in any debate now before the public, I felt an anxiety to have the debate published; hence I secured the services of a stenographer, without consulting Elder Herod, and not until the debate had been in progress a day or two did he know that it was being taken down for publication. He then said he thought he ought to have the privilege of revising his own speeches. I told him he could do so, so far as correcting the grammar was concerned. When I received the reporter's manuscript, I sent a letter to him, through a friend in Franklin (I not knowing his address), proposing that if he would revise and re-write his own speeches, confining himself to the same proofs, and as nearly to the same verbiage as practicable, and bear half the expense of bringing out the work, we would divide the books, and each one sell his own. Or if he did not wish to take part in the publication, if he would revise his speeches without expense to me, I would bring out the book. If not, I would revise and correct the reporter's copy, and publish it myself. To this letter I received no reply. I have, therefore, revised the manuscript, supplying such words as were manifestly left out by the reporter, yet as far as possible bringing out the debate just as delivered.

By reason of sickness in his family, the reporter was absent on the third day. I secured the services of a number of expert penmen to take as full and copious notes as possible, so that the speeches might be reproduced by a comparison of the notes taken by the several parties, each one having taken every proof text, and the points made, and as much of the precise verbiage as possible. In this way the speeches of the third day were substantially preserved; and though it is not presumed that every word was delivered just as here presented, yet in the main the verbiage is preserved, and certainly every proof introduced and every argument will be found in this work.

All of my opening speech, and most of my fourth speech on the first proposition, was spoken from manuscript, where every word was preserved, and no time lost in turning to notes and proofs; hence these speeches will he found longer than any other speeches of the same time in delivery; but I know that these speeches are presented here exactly as delivered, without the change of a single word.

The debate was well attended throughout, and the kindest feelings prevailed, both in the audience and between the speakers; and when the parting hour came, the people seemed loth to leave the place, feeling that it was good to be there. May the publication do much and lasting good.

First Proposition.

The Scriptures teach that salvation from sin is conditional, the condition or conditions to be performed by the sinner in order to salvation or freedom from sin.

Opening Speech of T. W. Brents.

MR. PRESIDENT: —I am happy in the privilege of meeting my distinguished opponent under circumstances favorable for the examination of the word of God pertaining to the proposition just read in your hearing. It is exceedingly plain, and but few of its terms need to be defined.

Sin is the transgression of the law—God's law (1 John 3:4). Salvation, or freedom from sin, is a release from the punishment due the sinner for such transgression.

The same thought is substantially expressed in several other forms, as "Remission of sin," "Forgiveness of sin," "Blotting out of sin," "Ceasing to remember sin," "Justification," etc., etc., the difference being merely technical.

About these, I suppose we will have no controversy, as it is the great subject of pardon that concerns us, not the phraseology in which it is expressed. One more term, perhaps, I ought to define.

"A condition is that which must exist as the occasion or concomitant of something else; that which is requisite in order that something else should take effect; stipulation; terms specified."— Webster.

That God alone has power to forgive sins is well understood and admitted by all; but the issue with us: Does he pardon the sins of men on conditions to be complied with by them? Than this, no more important subject can be considered by the human race, provided I am correct. If, however, my proposition is not true, it may be that

The Brents-Herod Debate

the importance of the subject is not very great. If God unconditionally saves men without a single thought, word or deed on the part of the sinner, then he may fold his arms and go to sleep, for nothing that he can do will secure his salvation, or in any way affect his future destiny. If he must even desire his salvation in order that God may save him, then that desire is a condition and my proportion is true. If he must believe anything, or in any person or thing, in order that God may save him, then that belief is a condition and my proposition is true. If he must perform any physical act, as an act of obedience to God, in order that he may be saved, then that act is a condition and my proportion is still true. My proposition does not require me to show what the conditions are—it is simply my duty to show that there are conditions with which the sinner must comply or be lost. I may incidentally do more than this.

At the suggestion of my worthy opponent, King James' version, as it is called, is made the standard of authority in this discussion.

I would have preferred this otherwise. While I believe it, on the whole, about as good as any other version, yet I know there are manifest errors in it; and in discussions like this, it should be the great aim of all parties to get at the truth; and where there are errors in the translation, known to be such, we ought to be at liberty to correct them by any light we can get, either from critics or commentators who have given us the benefit of their labors, or by an appeal to the original for ourselves. But with all its defects in translation, we believe it sufficiently clear to enable us to understand the will of the Lord and be saved. We have agreed to be governed by it in this discussion, and to it we go for proof of our proposition.

ARGUMENT.

Much may be learned as to what God is doing and proposes to do by an examination of what he has done in ages past, and I insist that the same general principle embodied in my proposition has characterized God's dealings with man from the time of his creation until now; He has blessed and prospered him while he believed and obeyed Him; and He has cursed and punished him when he forsook Him, rebelled against Him, refused to obey Him, and violated His law. This has always been, is now, and ever will be true as long as man dwells in a tenement of clay. We find an illustration of this principle in the first law given to

ADAM IN THE GARDEN OF EDEN. —Gen. 2:16, 17.

When God placed him in the garden, He commanded him, saying, "Of every tree of the garden thou mayest freely eat; but of the tree of the knowledge of good and evil, thou shalt not eat of it, for in the day thou eatest thereof thou shall surely die." Here is a clearly implied condition—if you eat of it you shall die; if you do not eat of it you may not die, but live. Another illustration we find in the case of:

CAIN AND ABEL. —Gen. 4:6, 7.

When they made their offerings, God respected the offering of Abel, but did not respect the offering of Cain; and Cain was angry about it, and the Lord said, "Why art thou wroth? and why is thy countenance fallen? If thou doest well, shalt thou not be accepted? and if thou doest not well, sin lieth at the door." Here is the spirit of my proposition—if you do well, you shall be accepted; but if you do not well, sin is at the very threshold of disobedience. Another example we have recorded in the history of

NOAH AND THE FLOOD. —Gen. 6:5-7.

Coming down the stream of time twenty-five hundred years, "God saw that the wickedness of man was great in the earth, and that every imagination of the thoughts of his heart was only evil continually. And it repented the Lord that he had made man on the earth, and it grieved him at his heart And the Lord said, I will destroy man whom I have created from the face of the earth; both man, and beast, and the creeping thing, and the fowls of the air; for it repenteth me that I have made them." God carried out this determination, and did destroy the wicked by a deluge of water. And why did he destroy them? Was it because God had unconditionally reprobated them, and decreed the wickedness for which he destroyed them? We suppose not, for their sins grieved him at his heart. Then again, we ask why this destruction came upon them? Surely it was because they were wicked, even to every imagination of their thoughts. But Noah found grace in the eyes of the Lord (verse 8). And why did he find grace in the sight of the Lord? "For thee have I seen righteous before me in this generation." Thus, we find the spirit of my proposition. God blessed and saved Noah and his family because he was righteous in his generation, and he destroyed the residue of the human race for their great wickedness. And be it remembered that these examples are referred to in the New Testament as instructive to us. When God gave the law, in detail, to the Jews, through Moses, at Horeb, he most graphically set forth the importance of obedience and the consequences of disobedience, that the people might well understand the principles upon which he proposed to govern them. In giving

THE LAW AT HOREB—Deut. 28: 1, 2.

He says: "And it shall come to pass, if thou shalt hearken diligently unto the voice of the Lord thy God, to observe and to do all his commandments which I command thee this day, that the Lord thy God will set thee on high above all nations of the earth; and all these blessings shall come on thee, and overtake thee, if thou shalt hearken unto the voice of the Lord thy God." Then follow, in detail, the rich blessings he promised them; and to impress them with the necessity of obeying the Lord in order to enjoy his favor, he adds, "And the Lord shall make thee the head, and not the tail; and thou shall be above only, and thou shalt not be beneath; if that thou hearken unto the commandments of the Lord thy God, which I command thee this day, to observe and do them; and thou shalt not go aside from any of the words which I command thee this day, to the right hand, or to the left, to go after other gods to serve them." Then he gives the other side of the picture in the fearful fruits of disobedience. In verse 15 he says: "But it shall come to pass, if thou wilt not hearken unto the voice of the Lord thy God, to observe to do all his commandments and his statutes which I command thee this day; that all these curses shall come upon thee, and overtake thee." Then follows a list of the curses that should come upon them, until the heart sickens in contemplating the wretchedness to which rebellion and sin should reduce them; and then, as if to more forcibly impress the lesson upon them, he adds, "Moreover all these curses shall come upon thee, and shall pursue thee, and overtake thee, till thou be destroyed; because thou hearkenedst not unto the voice of the Lord thy God, to keep his commandments and his statutes which he commanded thee" (ver. 45). Thus, we see the principle of my proposition clearly set out in the covenant which God made with Israel at Horeb; and it characterizes God's dealings with man everywhere. He blesses, prospers and saves him when he believes and obeys Him; and fails not to punish him when he rebels and pins against Him. The conditions have been changed in different dispensations; but conditions there always have been, and always will he, until the God of the Bible ceases to rule.

The same principle was reaffirmed in the covenant in the land of Moab; and it was again proclaimed to Solomon at the

DEDICATION OF THE TEMPLE. —2 Chron. 7:14-22.

God said to him: "If my people, which are called by my name, shall humble themselves, and pray, and seek my face, and turn from their wicked ways; then will I hear from heaven, and will forgive their sin, and heal their land. . . . And as for thee, if thou wilt walk before me, as David thy father walked, and do according to all that I have commanded thee, and shalt observe my statutes and my judgments; then will I establish the throne of thy kingdom, according as I have covenanted with David thy father, saying, There shall not fail thee a man to be ruler in Israel. But if ye turn away, and forsake my statutes and my commandments, which I have set before you, and shall go and serve other gods, and worship them; then will I pluck them up by the roots out of my land which I have given them; and this house, which I have sanctified for my name, will I cast out of my sight, and will make it to be a proverb and a by-word among all nations. And this house, which is high, shall be an astonishment to every one that passeth by it; so that he shall say, Why hath the Lord done thus unto this land, and unto this house? And it shall be answered, Because they forsook the Lord God of their fathers, which brought them forth out of the land of Egypt, And laid hold on other gods, and worshiped them, and served them; therefore hath he brought all this evil upon them." Therefore, yes, because they forsook the Lord.

Coming down to within six hundred years of the advent of Christ, we, find God, by the mouth of Ezekiel, affirming the same great principles. (Ezekiel 18:20-28.)

"The soul that sinneth, it shall die. The son shall not bear the iniquity of the father, neither shall the father bear the iniquity of the son; the righteousness of the righteous shall be upon him, and the wickedness of the wicked shall be upon him. But if the wicked will turn from all his sins that he hath committed, and keep all my statutes, and do that which is lawful and right, he shall surely live, he shall not die. All his transgressions that he hath committed, they shall not be mentioned unto him; in his righteousness that he hath done he shall live. Have I any pleasure at all that the wicked shall die? saith the Lord God: and not that he should return from his ways and live.... When a righteous man turneth away from his righteousness, and committeth iniquity, and dieth in them; for his iniquity that he hath done shall he die. Again, when the wicked man turneth away from his wickedness that he hath committed, and doeth that which is lawful and right, he shall save his soul alive. Because he considereth, and turneth away from all his transgressions that he hath committed, he shall surely live, be shall not die."

Comment on such Scriptures as these is surely unnecessary. They cannot be made more plain than God has already made them. If you will not deem it irreverent, I will say that were God here himself this day, seeking to defend my proposition, we cannot see how language could be better selected for the purpose than is here recorded.

Please note the fact that temporal blessings are not all that are here promised; for he who obeys the commandments of the Lord, shall save his soul. Is not this conditional salvation? Note the additional fact, too, that God has no pleasure in the death of the wicked, but most earnestly entreats him to cast away his transgressions, make himself a new heart and a new spirit—turn, and live (verse 31, 32). God compels no man to obey him; but he sets before him motives vast in importance as is the destiny of the human soul to induce him to obedience, and faithfully warns him of the dreadful consequences of disobedience, and allows him to choose for himself. Deut. 11:20-28: "Behold, I set before you this day a blessing and a curse; a blessing, if ye obey the commandments of the Lord your God, which I command you this day; and a curse, if ye will not obey the commandments of the Lord your God; but turn aside out of the way which I command you this day, to go after other gods which ye have not known." Does this not look about as conditional as my proposition? A blessing if you obey; a curse if you disobey.

But again (Deut. 30:15-19): "See, I have set before you this day life and good, death and evil; in that I command thee this day to love the Lord thy God, to walk in his ways, and to keep his commandments and his statutes and his judgments, that thou mayest live and multiply; and the Lord thy God shall bless thee in the land whither thou goest to possess it. But if thy heart turn away, so that thou wilt not hear, but shall be drawn away, and worship other gods, and serve them; I announce unto you this day, that ye shall surely perish, and that ye shall not prolong your days upon the land, whither thou passest over Jordan to go to possess it. I call heaven and earth to record this day against you; that I have set before you life and death, blessing and cursing; therefore choose life, that both thou and thy seed may live." Does this look as if man has nothing to do? The two roads are open before him—life is at the end of one, and death is at the end of the other. Man is perfectly free to choose the road he will travel. God says to the sinner in the road to death, "Turn ye, turn ye; why will you die? I have no pleasure in your death, but rather that you turn, and live."

We come now to the examination of the New Testament, and though the conditions have been changed, we shall find conditional salvation meeting us at every step of our investigation. We will have to abridge and condense every proof we introduce as much as we can, and then we will not be able to present a tithe of the proof available in support of a proposition so universally taught as is the one under consideration at present. We begin our investigation with a very brief examination of

THE MISSION OF JOHN THE BAPTIST.

He was to go before the Lord in the spirit and power of Elias, to turn the hearts of the fathers to the children, and the disobedient to the wisdom of the just—to make ready a people prepared for the Lord (Luke 1:17). As it was John's God-appointed work to make ready a people prepared for the Lord, did he perform the work assigned him? If so, how did he prepare them? He gave them knowledge of salvation. How did he give them knowledge of salvation? "By the remission of their sins" (Luke 1:77). But how did they get knowledge of salvation? We suppose they got it by compliance with the conditions upon which God authorized John to offer it to them.

What were the conditions of salvation preached by John? "There was a man sent from God whose name was John. The same came for a witness to bear witness of the light, that all men, through him, might believe" (John 1:6, 7). Notice, in passing, that the object of John's testimony was that all men, yes, all men, might believe. Then it was necessary that men believe in the days of John the Baptist. But what were they to believe? "John verily baptized with the baptism of repentance, saying unto the people that they should believe on him which should come after him, that is, on Christ Jesus" (Acts 19:4). Thus, we see they believed on a Christ to come—we believe in a Christ already come; this difference—no more. Christ was the object of their faith, and he is the object of our faith to-day. But what else? "In those days came John the Baptist, preaching in the wilderness of Judea, saying, Repent ye, for the kingdom of heaven is at hand" (Matt. 3:1). Then repentance was necessary in the days of John. What else? "And there went out unto him all the land of Judea, and they of Jerusalem, and were all baptized of him in the river of Jordan, confessing their sins" (Mark 1:5). But for what did John baptize the people? He "preached the baptism of repentance for the remission of sins" (Mark 1:4; Luke 3:3). What did he preach for the remission of sins? Certainly, that baptism that belonged to, or followed, repentance. However important faith may be, there is nothing affirmed of it here; nor is there anything affirmed of repentance, only that it was connected with the baptism preached by John for the remission of sins. Suppose I say, "The coat of my friend kept me warm." What do I say kept me warm? Certainly, the coat that belonged to my friend kept me warm. Again: "The house of my friend gave me shelter for the night." What do I say gave me shelter? Certainly, the house that belonged to my friend gave me shelter. Very well. "The baptism of repentance, for the remission of sins." What is for the remission of sins? Certainly, the baptism that belonged to, or followed, repentance, was for the remission of sins. If this is not plain and conclusive, then human language, common sense and Holy Writ can make nothing so.

Then we have found believing, or faith, repentance and baptism preached by John, and when the people submitted to, or performed, these conditions, they had knowledge of salvation by the remission of their sins. Then our proposition is clearly sustained in John's ministry. They were pardoned, and had knowledge of it, and were fit material for position in the great spiritual temple to be erected in the near future by divine authority.

We come now to examine the personal teaching of Jesus, and we will begin with an examination of his ever-memorable conversation with Nicodemus, recorded in the third chapter of the gospel by John: "Jesus answered and said unto him, Verily, verily, I say unto thee, except a man be born again, he cannot see the kingdom of God. Nicodemus saith unto him, How can a man be born when he is old? Can he enter the second time into his mother's womb, and be born? Jesus answered, Verily, verily, I say unto thee, except a man be born of water and of the Spirit, he cannot enter into the kingdom of God" (vers. 3-5). That the word see is here used in the sense of enjoy, we suppose no one will doubt. The thought is, that without being born again no man can enjoy the kingdom of God. How is he to be born again? "Except a man be born of water and of the Spirit, he cannot enter into the kingdom of God." The converse of the statement is clearly implied, that if he is born of water and of the Spirit, he does enter the kingdom of God. In this kingdom is a state of salvation; out of it in a state of condemnation. Paul says: "Giving thanks unto the Father, which hath made us meet to be partakers of the inheritance of the saints in light; who hath delivered us from the power of darkness, and hath translated us into the kingdom of his dear Son, in whom we have redemption through his blood, even the forgiveness of sins "(Col. 1:12-14). Then outside of the kingdom we are subject to the power of darkness, and under the dominion of Satan; in the kingdom, we are delivered from the power of darkness, and have redemption and forgiveness of sins through the blood of Jesus.

Now we have a few very plain questions for our worthy opponent, to which we invite his very special attention; and we promise to pay our respects to his answers when he makes them:

1. Can the class of persons for whom the kingdom was established be saved without entering it? If so, how?

2. What does the phrase "born of water" mean in John 3:5?

3. Can a man enter into the kingdom without being baptized? If so, how? Nicodemus did not understand the Saviour, and hence did not believe what he said. Then said Jesus, "If I have told you earthly things, and ye believe not, how shall ye believe if I tell ye of heavenly things?" (ver. 11.) He then seeks to impress him with the importance of believing on Him. Not that he intended him to stop at believing on him, but by believing he might be prepared to attend to what he had previously taught him. And he begins with an illustration drawn from Jewish history, with which Nicodemus, as a master in Israel, was presumed to be familiar. He says: "And as Moses lifted up the serpent in the wilderness, even so must the Son of man be lifted up; that whosoever believeth on him should not perish, but have eternal life" (verses. 14, 15). As the dying Israelite had to look upon the brazen serpent on the pole in the camp, that he might live (Num. 21:8, 9), so Jesus must die upon the cross, that whosoever believeth on him should not perish, but have eternal life. Now, what is the object of, and necessity for, believing? That the believer may not perish, but may have eternal life. What can this mean? Is believing not a condition upon which depends eternal life? Will my worthy opponent say no? Will he say that looking on the brazen serpent was not a condition on which depended the life of the bitten Israelite? Was looking upon the brazen serpent any more a condition of life to the bitten Israelite, than believing on Christ is to the sinner to-day? We will listen attentively to his explanation of this.

"For God so loved the world, that he gave his only begotten Son, that whosoever believeth in him should not perish, but have everlasting life" (ver. 16). Whom did God love? He loved the world. And how much did he love it? He so loved the world that he gave his only begotten Son. For what did he give his Son? That whosoever of the world he loved, might have everlasting life, on condition that they would believe on him. Is not believing on him here made a condition on which depends the eternal life of the sinner? Will our opponent say no? Surely, we are here taught that the "world may be saved, if they will accept salvation on the conditions upon which it is offered to them. "For God sent not his Son into the world to condemn the world, but that the world through him might be saved" (ver. 17). Here the mission of Jesus is most beautifully expressed—might be saved, not shall be saved, whether they want to be saved or not. He came to provide a way by which men might be saved if they will believe and obey him, not to force salvation upon them. And the means of salvation are as free to all men as they are to any man. He came to save the world, and tasted death for everyman. Though JESUS came not to condemn the world, yet all will be condemned who refuse to believe on him. "He that believeth on him is not condemned." But what of him who does not believe? "He that believeth not, is condemned already." And why is he condemned already? "Because he hath not believed on the name of the only-begotten Son of God" (ver. 18).

Here we find belief in Jesus to be the condition upon which men may escape condemnation, and unbelief is the condition upon which men bring condemnation on themselves. "Of course, we understand the Lord to be speaking of such belief as takes God at his word, and goes right along in obedience to his commands—a belief perfected as the word of God directs. "He that believeth on the Son, hath everlasting life." Yes; the obedient believer has everlasting life in promise, but what about the unbeliever? "He that believeth not the Son, shall not see life; but the wrath of God abideth on him" (John 3:39). And again: "I said, therefore, unto you, that ye shall die in your sins, for if ye believe not that I am he, ye shall die in your sins" (John viii, 24). And still again: "If any man hear my words, and believe not, I judge him not; for I came not to judge the world, but to save the world. He that rejecteth me, and receiveth not my words, hath one that judgeth him; the word that I have spoken, the same shall judge him in the last day" (John 12:47, 48).

Here we learn that Jesus came to save the world; and we learn that the world he came to save is co-extensive with the judgment of the last day. Will all men be judged? Then Jesus came to save all men. But he who rejects him, and receives not his words, cannot be saved by him, however ample the means of salvation provided for him. The words reject and receive both imply the exercise of will in rejecting Christ and in refusing to receive his words.

"Many other signs truly did Jesus in the presence of his disciples, which are not written in this book, but these are written that ye might believe." Yes, these signs are written that ye might believe, not that you shall believe, whether you are interested yourself or not. But that ye might believe what? "That Jesus is the Christ, the Son of God, "These are written as evidence to convince the world of the truth of this grand proposition, that all men might believe it. But what if they do believe this? "And that, believing, ye might have life through his name" (John 20:30, 31). Yes, might believe, and might have life by believing. This expresses the thought most beautifully. Now I want to ask my worthy opponent this question: After all these signs are recorded, if a man refuses to believe the proposition set out here, that Jesus is the Christ, the Son of God, is there a possibility for him to get eternal life through his name? If so, how? And if not, why not? I will not anticipate his answers, but will wait till he makes them.

Peter says: "To him give all the prophets witness that, through his name, whosoever believeth in him shall receive remission of sins" (Acts 10:43). Here we have the same style, except the phrase remission of sins is substituted for the word life, by which, doubtless, the same thought is intended; and it seems to me that, in the plainest terms possible, remission of sins in the name of Jesus Christ is made to depend upon belief in him as a condition to be complied with by those whose sins are remitted at all. Will he who does not believe on him get remission through his name? If so, how? They are condemned already. "Be it known unto you, therefore, men and brethren, that through his name is preached unto you the forgiveness of sins; and by him all that believe are justified from all things from which he could not be justified by the law of Moses" (Acts 13:38, 39). Here we have forgiveness of sins in place of the phrase remission of sins, which means the same thing; and all that believe are justified, thus plainly making belief a condition of justification.

Paul says: "I am not ashamed of the gospel of Christ, for it is the power of God unto salvation to every one that believeth, to the Jew first, and also to the Greek" (Rom. 1:16). But the gospel is God's power to the salvation of no one, whether he be Jew or Greek, who does not believe it. Truly then salvation is conditional, as the power of God to salvation is rejected by the unbeliever.

"The word is nigh thee, even in thy mouth, and in thy heart; that is, the word of faith which we preach; that if thou shalt confess with thy mouth the Lord Jesus, and shall believe in thine heart that God hath raised him from the dead, thou shalt be saved; for with the heart man believeth unto righteousness, and with the mouth confession is made unto salvation" (Rom. 10:8-10). Here we have confession with the mouth, and belief in the heart, in the plainest terms possible, made conditions of salvation. If this language does not show these to be conditions, then I respectfully submit that human language can show nothing to be a condition of anything. To this passage I solicit the special attention, of my worthy respondent. Will he say that belief and confession are not here shown to be conditions of salvation? If he will say they are not, will he be so good as to construct a sentence that will express the thought without using the very word condition?

On one occasion a young man came to Jesus, and said: "Good Master, what good thing shall I do that I may have eternal life" (Matt. 19:16)? Had my proposition been untrue at that time, it occurs to me that JESUS would have answered something after the following style: "There is nothing that you can do that you may have eternal life; for eternal life is not dependent on conditions to be complied with by man." Not thus understanding the subject, however, the Master told him what to do that he might have treasures in heaven.

On the day of Pentecost, when Peter convinced the people that God had made that same Jesus whom they crucified both Lord and Christ, "They were cut to the heart, and said unto Peter and the rest of the apostles, men and brethren, what shall we do?" Do for what? To obtain pardon, or remission of sins, as the answer plainly shows. 'Peter said unto them, repent and be baptized, every one of you, in the name of Jesus Christ, for the remission of sins" (Acts 2:38).

Here remission of sins, in the case of these believers, is made to depend on the additional items of repentance and baptism. The preposition for unites repent and be baptized on one side with remission of sins on the other. Remission of sins is the object for which and to which the actions expressed in both verbs look as the end in view. Connected, as they are, by the conjunction and, they cannot be separated, Whatever one is for, the other is for. The relation of one to the remission of sins is the relation of both. Then, if we can find the relation of one we will have found the relation of both. Peter says: "Repent and be converted, that your sins may be blotted out" (Acts 3:19).

Then, as repentance is required that sins may be blotted out, and as baptism sustains the same relation to remission, expressed by the one preposition occurring but one time, it follows that baptism is to be performed in order that sins may be blotted out. From this conclusion, there is no appeal. Then, as the Pentecostians believed before they asked what to do, it follows that faith, repentance and baptism were conditions of pardon then, and are so to-day.

That repentance is a condition is already plain enough; but to make assurance doubly sure we will present further proof. Jesus said: "Except ye repent, ye shall all likewise perish" (Luke 13:2). And Paul said: "The times of this ignorance God winked at, but now he commandeth all men everywhere to repent; because he hath appointed a day, in the which he will judge the world in righteousness by that man whom he hath ordained" (Acts 17:30, 31). Then without repentance sinners will not be ready for the judgment, but will surely perish.

When the rest of the apostles heard Peter's defense for going in among the uncircumcised, "they held their peace and glorified God, saying, Then hath God also to the Gentiles granted repentance unto life" (Acts 11:18). Then repentance is unto life, looking to life, in order to life, a condition on which life depends. But the people at Pentecost, inquired what they must do. Peter told them what to do for remission of sins. Now we respectfully ask our esteemed opponent if he would answer the same inquiry now as Peter did then? If not, why not?

The Philippian jailer said to Paul and Silas: "Sirs, what must I do to he saved" (Acts 16:30)? Now, in this question we have the very issue presented in my proposition, What must I do to be saved? Will my worthy opponent say whether this question does not cover the ground in controversy here? How would he answer such a question if put to him to-day? Something after the following style. I imagine: "What must you do? Do nothing. What can you do to be saved? Just nothing at all; for your salvation is not dependent on conditions to be performed by you; salvation is not of works, lest any man should boast." But did the inspired teachers so treat the question? No, indeed; but they answered it: "Believe on the Lord Jesus Christ, and thou shalt be saved, and thy house. And they spake unto him the word of the Lord, and to all that were in his house." Thus, all the conditions of salvation were presented and attended to the same hour of the night. When the Lord appeared to Saul and convinced him that he was Jesus, Saul said: "What shall I do, Lord? And the Lord said,..Arise, and go into Damascus, and there it shall be told thee of all things which are appointed for thee to do" (Acts 22:10). And a man was sent to him who told him to arise and be baptized, and wash away his sins, calling on the name of the Lord (ver. 16). Now here are four examples recorded, where those competent to answer were asked what the inquirers must do, and in no case were they told that they could do nothing: but in every instance they were told what to do in order to be saved. Now will our esteemed opponent tell us how any man, believing in unconditional salvation, as he does, can ask such a question as, What must I do to be saved? or in faith do anything to be saved? or tell any one else what to do to be saved? We suppose he will give us an explanation of these matters, and we will await his answer. We respectfully ask that it be full and explicit.

The Brents-Herod Debate

In the commission given by Christ to his apostles after he arose from the dead, and before he ascended to heaven, he said: "Go ye into all the world, and preach the gospel to every creature. He that believeth and is baptized shall be saved; and he that believeth not shall be damned" (Mark xvi 15, 16). Here we learn that the salvation promised in the gospel was intended for every creature in all the world who would accept it on the conditions stipulated. In the plainest terms possible, we are told that, of every creature in all the world, he that would believe the gospel and be baptized should be saved. If this language does not establish my proposition, then no proposition can be established by any language that may be employed. It is not necessary that I stop to show that belief and baptism sustain the same relation to the salvation promised, for if either one is a condition necessary to the enjoyment of salvation, then salvation is conditional and my proposition is established.

But suppose I say to a man: "Dig me a cistern, and wall it up with brick, and I will give you one hundred dollars." The specifications are all made, the proposition accepted and reduced to writing. The man makes the excavation according to the specifications, and demands the money for the job—can he get it? Has he complied with the contract? He was to dig the cistern and wall it up with brick; he has dug the cistern, but has not put a brick in it—is he entitled to the pay? Assuredly he is not. Very well, He that believeth and is baptized shall be saved. The man believes, but has not been baptized—is he saved? Is he not in the same condition of the man who had not put a brick in the cistern, when, by the contract, he was to wall it up? But what of those who do not believe? He that believeth not shall be damned. But why did not the Lord add, "and is not baptized shall be damned"? Because if he did not believe he would not be baptized, nor would it do him any good if he were to be, "for without faith it is impossible to please God." Baptism without faith would be about like walling up the cistern without digging it. You say that would be impossible; even so is scriptural baptism without faith impossible. The style is, "He that believeth and is baptized." "If thou believest with all thine heart thou mayest" One of those to whom this commission was given said to the disciples scattered abroad: "Which sometime were disobedient, when once the longsuffering of God waited in the days of Noah, while the ark was a preparing, wherein few, that is, eight souls, were saved by water. The like figure whereunto even baptism doth also now save us, (not the putting away of the filth of the flesh, but the answer of a good conscience toward God,) by the resurrection of Jesus Christ" (I Peter 3:20, 21).

Here we are told that baptism saves us, and not only so, but it now saves us. In what sense does baptism save us? Surely it is not the power that saves us, but it is a condition, upon compliance with which God saves us. We have seen that in the commission under which Peter acted, he was charged to preach the gospel, and Jesus promised that he that would believe and be baptized should be saved; and Peter could have meant nothing else than that baptism saves us as a condition, in harmony with the commission given to him by the Master. And it must save us from the punishment that is due us on account of our sins, as there is nothing else from which it can or does save us. It cannot refer to a future salvation, for it now leaves us. It does not save us from temporal calamity, as insult, persecution, sickness or death, for the baptized man is still subject to them. Then if it does not save us from the punishment due us on account of our past sins, will our opponent tell us from what it does save us?

Isaiah, through the light of prophetic vision, says: "In that day there shall be a root of Jesse, which shall stand for an ensign of the people, to it shall the Gentiles seek" (Isa. 11:10). Again: "Seek ye the Lord while he may be found, call ye upon him while he is near: let the wicked forsake his way, and the unrighteous man his thoughts: and let him return unto the Lord, and he will have mercy upon him; and to our God, for he will abundantly pardon" (Isa. 55:6, 7).

Jesus says: "Ask, and it shall be given you; seek, and ye shall find; knock, and it shall be opened unto you: for every one that asketh receiveth; and he that seeketh findeth; and to him that knocketh it shall be opened" (Matt. 7:7, 8).

Here we learn that we are to seek the Lord, but we must seek after the due order. David said: "Ye are the chief of the fathers of the Levites: sanctify yourselves, both ye and your brethren, that ye may bring up the ark of the Lord God of Israel unto the place that I have prepared for it. For because ye did it not at the first, the Lord our God made a breach upon us, for that we sought him not after the due order" (1 Chron. 15:12, 13). Here we learn that we must seek the Lord's favor after the due order; find the due order is God's order. We must seek in God's appointed way. When we ask, we must ask in harmony with God's revealed will. James says we ask and receive not because we ask amiss. We must ask in faith, too, for "without faith it is impossible to please him: for he that cometh to God must believe that he is, and that he is rewarder of them that diligently seek him" (Heb. 11:6). Belief is an indispensable condition, without which none can come to God. But we must believe that he is a rewarder of them that diligently seek him. Here we have another question for our friend. Does he believe that God will reward a man, however diligently he may seek him, unless he is one of the eternally and unconditionally elect? Will he tell us?

But we will hear Paul on this matter of seeking the Lord. He says: "God that made the world and all things therein, seeing that he is Lord of heaven and earth, dwelleth not in temples made with hands; neither is worshiped with men's hands, and though he needed anything, seeing he giveth to all life, and breath, and all things; and hath made of one blood all nations of men for to dwell on all the face of the earth, and hath determined the times before appointed, and the bounds of their habitation; that they should seek the Lord, if haply they might feel after him, and find him, though he be not far from every one of us" (Acts 17:24-27).

Here we learn that God made of one blood all the nations of men that dwell on all the face of the earth; and that he intended them to seek the Lord and find him. And every one that seeks him will find him if he seeks him in God's appointed way. But we need not seek him or call on him until we are willing to obey him.

"Though he were a Son, yet learned he obedience by the things which he suffered; and being made perfect, he became the author of eternal salvation unto all them that obey him" (Heb. 5:8, 9).

The eternal salvation, of which Jesus is the author, is for them, and only them, that obey him. And it is not for some of them only, but it is for all of them. Every one. Obedience to him is the condition upon which all men may attain to eternal salvation, and it is attainable to no one who will not obey him. If there was not another sentence in the Bible bearing upon the subject, this one is enough to establish my proposition beyond even respectable quibble. Will my worthy opponent give us a plain, unambiguous exegesis of this passage? It is surely worthy of his most serious attention.

(Time expired.)

Elder Herod's First Reply.

BRETHREN MODERATORS, LADIES AND GENTLEMEN:—I am equally proud that I have the opportunity and pleasure of addressing so large and respectable an auditory of people as there is now before me. I have listened with patience to every word of my brother and during the entire talk, my mind was ruminating, and, for the life of me, I have to decide that after the hour's talk he has failed to make a single reference to the written statement in his proposition. When I present myself before you to discuss a question, it will be knowing that anything presented before a jury that is not relevant to the question would be rejected. The judge would reject everything that was not in accordance with the testimony. I am now going to announce to this people that I expect to be here four days, and at the close of the affirmation I expect to prove all I say, and to confine myself to every word that is uttered in my proposition. I shall use no time in calling attention to foreign questions.

It now becomes necessary for me to announce the proposition. He has affirmed that salvation from sin is conditional. The moment we state that, we arrive at the point where it is necessary to stop and ask a question, for I know that you will listen to me. Conditional is to perform conditions. My brother assumes that the sinner is to comply with conditions. What is to be accomplished by compliance with conditions? He says, salvation from sin. I submit what is his duty now, to devote his whole time to show that the salvation of sinners is in their own hands. A large amount of testimony has been read, but not one out of the fifty passages has any relevancy to the proposition. He goes back to the law, and shows what God's promises and blessings and threatenings are. He would impress the idea that when we comply or obey, we have a free passport to heaven. I repeat that not a single word he read contains a single promise for heaven, or a threat of hell. They are saved from the calamities to which they had become obnoxious. Now, why bring that to prove that salvation from sin is to be perfected by the sinner?

Another point—salvation from sin is conditional, the conditions to be performed by the sinner. About six times in his discourse he has gone to a second party—somebody to administer baptism. Does he want half a dozen Saviours? I ask, how many questions am I to understand that he is going to bring before this audience for salvation, depending on three or four acts, and every one to be performed by the sinner? A man cannot get an administrator, and unless he goes into the water he is out. He cannot save anybody out of the water.

I call your attention to the testimony that God has given on the subject of salvation. I will reply to every word.

Salvation from sin—who is the sinner? He says you need salvation if you are a sinner. He says you must perform the conditions. Notice the conditions: Belief in the Lord Jesus Christ. Is belief the cause? or the effect? If belief is the effect, what is the cause? What constitutes belief? I say, legal gentlemen, you are qualified to answer—you are faithful and impartial. What chances have you in that man's case? What control have you in the testimony, if it is to be doubtful? None at all. Do you control the testimony? or does the testimony control you?

Unless he can bring the sinner to God, how can God save him? There must be an influence or cause— belief is an effect—there must be a cause. I appeal to you all, without regard to your religious views, what is the cause? It is testimony. Who gives the testimony? I can answer that fast enough. The sixth chapter of John. The words are the words of Jesus Christ. Now, I remember, he says that "all that the Father giveth me cometh unto me." "No man can come to me except the Father which hath sent me draw him; and I will raise him up at the last day. It is written in the prophets, and they shall be all taught of God. Every man therefore that hath heard, and hath learned of the Father, cometh unto me" (John 6:44, 45). I got that testimony from God. "He that cometh unto me I will in no wise cast out" (John 6:37).

Proverbs of Solomon 16:: First, I want to quote a declaration in Romans 10: Paul says: "With the heart, man believeth unto righteousness. How can I believe anything without the force of testimony? We want two passages to answer each other. Read the passage. "The preparations"—in the plural—"of the heart in man, and the answer of the tongue, is of the Lord. Just think! God is to prepare the heart—is to furnish the answer for the tongue. With the mouth, confession is made unto salvation. It is plain enough to be seen that it is unconditional. He must show that man is a free agent He must submit to the proposition that God controls it, or that he does not. The testimony carries your mind to the verdict. The proverbs have said the preparations of the heart in man is from the Lord. Does a man believe before the preparation, or after? He would have you believe after, in order to get into Christ. I will not bring a large amount of evidence on the question, for he will fail in making even an attempt to answer. He said he would not anticipate me. I am not afraid of that. He will not attempt to answer me.

There is an Old Testament Scripture which says: "Look unto me all ye ends of the earth, and be ye saved, for I am God: and beside me there is none other." My brother has told you that every man is capable of saving himself if he complies with the conditions. I translate from the Old Testament to the New Testament Scripture. I submit a problem that will not be solved. I said,

The Brents-Herod Debate

after he said salvation was conditional, that the winner controlled the condition, thus buying his salvation. Read how the apostle disputes that idea. You will be startled when you think of the importance to be attached to the Scriptures I am introducing. Acts 4:11, Peter said: "This is the stone which was set at naught of you builders." How many of you believe the Bible? "The same is become the head of the corner." You will tell me that Jesus is the sinner's Saviour, and then that the sinner saves himself. Let that settle the question on this subject. If this is true, I have no right to stand here and announce salvation in the name of Christ. But I am just reading God's word now. "The name has become the head of the corner, neither is there salvation in any other." He has as many Saviours as sinners. I want you to look at the facts as I read them, as he has brought his testimony into the question. Now, Bro. Herod, I have no right to bring up a sinner unless he has no name. He seemed to make it as plain as could be. It looked nice, but would not save from sin. I want him to make a point, and find a sinner that has no name; then he can save himself. First part of the paragraph, "Neither is there salvation in any other." Do you carry salvation in your pockets? I did not think there was a man who would deny Jesus Christ in that way. I have quoted a part of the passage. I call attention to the second part, and then you get the reason of my reference. Listen to the apostle (Acts 4:12): "Neither is there salvation in any other, for there is no other name given among men whereby we must be saved." Didn't he tell you that you could get it without him? No credit reflected on Christ. I am now giving you a plain statement on the subject. I intend to cover the whole ground. You cannot put a condition of salvation that sbuts the door for everybody. I am going to talk plain, and treat all with due courtesy. I am now going to close the paragraph and sbut the door, and if my brother can tell who it is outside of the name of Christ that is a Saviour I shall learn something I never knew before. "For there is no other name given among men whereby we must be saved but the name Christ Jesus." Did Paul preach conditions? No sir. I am on the defensive, and I say that the testimony is irrelevant to the statement of his proposition. He has taken them from their proper channel.

Read Acts 4:, next 1 Cor. 2: I want to say to you that I have a Saviour. Let us hear the first verse. Everybody listen to the language: "When I came to you, I came not with excellency of speech, or of wisdom, declaring unto you the testimony of God; for I determined not to know anything among you but Jesus Christ, and him crucified." Set down a pen, and make a note. Yes, but you say that is troublesome. I appreciate an argument when I hear it, and he is better able to make it than I am. I give testimony—listen to the facts: "Declaring the testimony of God;" "I determine to know nothing but Jesus Christ and him crucified." Legal gentlemen and intelligent audience, I leave it to you—I want to hear that again. "For I determined not to know anything among you but Jesus Christ and him crucified. "Every saint and sinner he gets to heaven will sing awhile to themselves, and then awhile to the Lord. Are you willing to sit here and hear him say that the Bible knows no Saviour but a frail being?

The apostle does not stop, but continues further: "And I was with you in weakness, and in fear, and in much trembling, and my speech and my preaching was not with enticing words of man's wisdom, but in demonstration of the Spirit and of power." That your faith and hope may stand on conditions! I would not preach it—it was not a part of the paragraph at all. It gives room for a third party to glory. "That your faith and hope might be in God." If your faith and hope are in your hands, and depends on what you have done, then the Lord is valueless. The apostle refers back to what the Lord came into the world for. My brother, give Christ the praise.

The first announcement was from the prophet Isaiah, that glad vision of Christ when he made his advent into the world, and the object of this advent. Where did he come from? He came from heaven. What for? My brother will say he came to tell them to save themselves. If that is Bible teaching, I accept it; but if it is not, we ought to reject it.

The first chapter of Matthew, commencing with the New Testament. Not on a telephone or a telegraph but through an angel to these lower grounds of sin. A dispute has come about the name of the stranger—it had to be settled. "Thou shall call his name Jesus, for he shall"—redeem his people from original sin! Make a way possible for them to save themselves from their sins! That would be nice.

I have offered a $10 Bible to any one who would show it, but no one has ever got it. I call your attention to the reading. I am coming up to one of the strong points in the Lord's testimony. Will you accept his testimony, or the testimony of my opponent? What is it you determine to believe—him or the Bible? "Thou shall call his name Jesus, for he shall save his people from their sins" I submit it to the legal gentlemen, if Christ with that announcement, after he made the agreement to save them, should say I did all I could to save them but they would not let me. Now listen, because I am talking about the passage, I remember, "Let God be true, or every man a liar. "The angel said that he WOULD save his people from their sins if he saved them, is he requiring a second payment for the same debt by their saving themselves? Would God receive satisfaction, and then ask a second payment on the part of the sinner for the same debt, in acts of obedience, in whatsoever way?

The Bible says Christ came to save them. Did the prophet tell them anything about what he was to do? Dan. 9:: Now everybody listen. Daniel is going to prophesy in regard to the coming of Christ, in removing the sacrifice, and hence for a purpose. He says:

"Seventy weeks I have determined upon my people," to give them a chance to save themselves! Pretty clever. I give you a chance to make fifteen dollars. Pretty good to give you a chance to make it. What about those seventy weeks? "To finish the transgression, to make an end of sin, and make reconciliation, to bring in everlasting righteousness," and say, Do certain things and I will seal it to you! Belief—God—Preacher—Water! God is the saviour of the family! Everybody listen, and I will read passages to show. I am well enough posted in the rules of discussion as to the rights of my opponent and my duties. Make an end of sin—seal up the vision of the prophets—bring in everlasting righteousness—and if you have his righteousness it will do; but if you come without it, you are a rag-shop, and the fire will burn it up.

I now call your attention to another passage of the prophecies— Isa. 72:: "Surely, they are my people." What! "Children that will not lie—so he was their Saviour; in all their afflictions he was afflicted, and the Angel of his presence saved them; "and yet you tell me it depends on us to save ourselves, or else we are subject to an endless fire.

I want my life to be spent in honoring the Lord Jesus. If I have a friend, I want to remember him.

Now I want to consult the apostle Peter, third chapter. He says the sinner is to give up his sins by obedience. What is the language? "Who his own self bore our sins in his own body on the tree?" He (Brents) says they are on you, and they will stay on till you get them off. I cannot come two hundred miles, and assemble with you here to listen to these questions. I say there is nothing in that I call your attention to Peter's language. I submit it to you. Listen: "Who, in his own body bore our sins on the tree of the cross." How long ago? Almost nineteen hundred years ago. He had the sins of his people on him. You cannot get away from the conclusion. How came they there? I am ready to respond on the testimony of the Bible. I am not going to spend my time on a proposition unless I can prove it. How came they to be borne in the Lord's body? Let me give the answer. Isa. 53:6: "All we like sheep have gone astray. We have turned every one to his own way, and the Lord hath laid on him the iniquity of us all." What did that say? They were sinners, and needed salvation. What occurred therein the record given? Try God's love on that subject, Remember, I am in the defensive. I read chapter and verse. How did he bear the sins in his body? All we, like sheep, have gone astray; each one had turned to his own way, and the Lord hath laid on each one his sins, and adopted conditions for him to do, to get free from his sins! Now, everybody listen to this. I am giving forcible language. I transposed it, now I will give the force of the paragraph. What is it? All we, like sheep, have gone astray, each one turning to his own way; and I said by certain conditions we could be made free, and my brother is the exponent of these conditions. He has not a particle of the Lord Jesus about it. Suppose he admits it, and says this was original sin, and that then we have actual sins and transgressions-how can you get rid of your own sins? By three or four steps. Don't you know that it would land you in hell just as certain as if you had a mill-stone about your neck. I am willing that the record shall determine the question. I will devote a moment to prove it, I will discuss this point. If your actual transgressions were not included, it would be equal to a mill-stone about your neck. Heb. 9:: "Almost all things in the law were purged from sin." If the blood of Christ is to purge from sin, and he forgives, where is there any relation in what is done to obtain from Christ what he died for—for the actual sins and transgressions—and to say that the accepting or rejecting him decides it all? Has he died in vain? A stub of a sinner dies, and makes his way to an endless hell, when God is trying to save him! I would not worship such a God. In order to put away sin, a system of conditions has been introduced, and you must obey these conditions; and where is the blood, for there is no remission without it? Is not that a grand idea? I come back to that pin I put down: "And the Lord hath laid upon him." Who will be responsible for the adulterers and liars, and drunkards? If it were a legal question, I would refer you to the law, and let that settle and decide it. "And the Lord hath laid upon him the iniquity of us all, and by his stripes we are healed." Is it the stripes, or the obedience, that heals?

Now let me call your attention to another passage. I have now found the Saviour laden with the sins of his people. They are charged to his account; what did he do with them? Now, Paul, I want your testimony. Hebrews 9:, what is said about that question? "Now once in the end of the world hath he appeared, to put away sin by the sacrifice of himself. "Would he not mock the miseries of the sinner if he did it not? The assertion is that he put them away. I return now to the question that I anticipated. What are you going to say? I see men here that have heard me preach for seven years or more, and all will bear testimony that I preach Jesus Christ as the Saviour from sin. Christian duties never save from sin. I read in the epistle as to the amount of sin put away. Titus says, in treating of that subject, "Who gave himself for us," that he might offer salvation upon terms and conditions for all who would accept it! If he had said that, there would not have been a discussion here now.

In place of that, I give it in the language of the apostle, and hence I must begin where the apostle takes up the question. "Who gave himself for us, that he might redeem us from all iniquity." My brother says that he came to all the world, and died to save it. I emphasize the word "world" as well as you do. I have no secrets, religiously. Read that passage again. It is of interest and importance to every one who would know the Bible facts in denial of the proposition. You will find me there till he has done. I came here to stay four dine. "Who gave himself for us, that he might redeem us from all iniquity, and purify unto himself a peculiar people zealous of good works."

The product of salvation is to bring salvation. I am defending Jesus Christ to-day. My brother is defending the sinner. I am proving what Christ did for the pinner. I have a passage that says he gave himself for us, that he might redeem us from all iniquity. I will settle it before I have done with this discussion. I want the benefit of these passages in the after speeches. I want to see how it was done. I am now going to use water. I hope that when the proper time comes he will talk about the water, because there is a washer-woman or washer-man, and something is to be cleansed. I reckon neither he nor I have had a place in that water yet.

(Time expired.)

Dr. Brents' Second Speech.

Mr. president: —I am now to reply to the speech which was made by my worthy opponent in the forenoon. I will not treat him as he treated me. I made a speech of an hour in condensed scriptural argument, and I gave chapter and verse for every position taken, and asked his special attention to a number of them; and to not one single one of them did he even allude—not one. He did not take hold of a single passage, and attempt to show that it did not teach what I claimed for it. I asked him a number of plain but respectful questions, to which I had a right to expert his attention in his speech; but to not one of them did he make any reply whatever. Does he call this debating? Near the close of his speech, he said he was going to set up a theory to wipe my speech all out. Now I respectfully submit that this kind of work is better calculated to make infidels than Christians. When I make an argument drawn from unmistakable proofs from Holy Writ, and call on him, in respectful style, to meet and answer it, but in place of answering it he goes off to hunt passages from the same Bible which seem to teach something else, it brings the Bible into conflict with itself. If it be a book of contradictions, if cannot be an emanation from God. It must be consistent with itself in all its parts, or it cannot be worthy of its Author and the confidence of men.

I thought debating consisted in the affirmant laying down his premises, and supporting his positions by such proof as he deemed sufficient for the purpose; then the respondent takes up the proofs adduced, and shows that they do not teach what is claimed for them; this done, then it is in order to set up an adverse theory. I respectfully suggest that the course pursued by my worthy opponent is not debating at all.

He says that, according to my theory, a man's salvation is in his own hands; and also that I had no Jesus in my speech. Though I quoted much from the mouth of Jesus, and showed by many passages that there is no salvation without faith in Christ, yet I had no Jesus in my speech—no Jesus in my proposition!

When I first sent my proposition to him, it read, "Salvation from sin by Jesus Christ is conditional" He objected to this, and worded for me the present proposition, leaving out the words Jesus Christ, though he left them in his own. Did he do this in order that he might throw it up to me in debate? I reckon not, surely.

I have showed time and again that there is no salvation out of Christ, in this or in the Jewish dispensation. He died "for the redemption of the transgressions that were under the first testament, that they which are called might receive the promise of eternal inheritance" (Heb. 9:15). The efficacy of his blood looked backward and forward. Every offering made under the old testament was made efficacious by the blood of Christ.

But he says there was no promise of heaven or threat of hell "back there." Paul says they drank of that spiritual rock that followed them; and that rock was Christ. Is there no heaven in drinking of Christ? What becomes of the great cloud of witnesses named in Heb. 11:, who all died in faith, and of whom the world was not worthy? Abraham, Isaac and Jacob were mentioned among them. What became of them? "Many shall come from the east and west, and shall sit down with Abraham, and Isaac, and Jacob, in the kingdom of heaven" (Matt. 8:11). No heaven for them! Ezek. 18:27: God says, he that "doeth that which is lawful and right, he shall save his soul alive." God swore that those whose carcasses fell in the wilderness in unbelief, should not enter into his rest (Heb. 3:16). What becomes of them?

He scoffs at the idea of the sinner having his salvation in his own hands. I did not say he has his salvation in his own hands; but I do say he must comply with the conditions upon which salvation is offered to him in the gospel, or be lost. Because a sinner avails himself of the means God has provided for his salvation, does he reject God, Jesus Christ, or anything else that has anything to do with salvation? God gives us bread—but does that destroy human agency in the production of bread? God does his part, and requires us to do our part. God gives the soil, warmth, light, moisture, none of which man could do for himself; but man can prepare the soil, plant the seed, cultivate and gather the crop—and thus he gets bread; but if Eld. Herod refuses to do anything to make or get bread—because God gives it to him, I guess—if his friends do not provide for him he will be likely to go to bed hungry. God has provided salvation for man on conditions; "but he that believeth not will be damned." But more of this after a while.

If man has no agency in his own salvation, who is to blame if he is not saved? He is as passive as a block of marble, and certainly had no power to have it otherwise. He says sins were pardoned long ago—will he tell us when? I guess he will go back before the foundation of the world was laid. Then there is no such thing as pardon of sin now at all. Will he tell us whether or not there in any such thing as pardon for sinners to-day? We will have more to say about this when he takes position on it.

If it was all fixed up before time began, the sinner not having even to accept any means of salvation, then again I ask, Who is to blame if a man is not saved? Will Jesus Christ say in the judgment, "Depart from me, ye workers of iniquity?" No, sir; no works of his had anything to do with his destiny, for he never had a chance to be anything else but what he is. God never loved or provided for him—Jesus never died for him; he has not, nor did he ever have, any interest in the blood of Jesus, and yet God will confine him in the rude flames of an angry hell forever—for what? Just to see his writhings and contortions I suppose! He said he would not worship a God whose purposes could be thwarted by a "stub of a sinner;" but here is a picture of the God he does worship. I wish to vindicate the character of the God I worship against such an imputation. The darkest picture of savage cruelty and the inquisition of Rome sink into pleasantry before it. They would speedily end, but the punishment of the damned never; and all fixed up four thousand years before he was born, and that by a merciful God, without giving him any chance to avoid such a destiny. Is this the God of the Bible? It cannot be.

If man has nothing to do in his own salvation, why did God mock him, saying, "Look unto me all ye ends of the earth, and be ye saved, for I am God, and beside me there is none else." Why did he set life and death before him, and tell him to choose, when he could not choose? Why did Jesus say, "Come unto me all ye that labor and are heavy laden, and I will give you rest," when there was no chance for him to come? Why did Jesus Christ command his apostles (I reckon there is Christ in this, as he is speaking) to "go into all the world, and preach the gospel to every creature," when he knew that only the chosen few could be benefitted? Why did he promise salvation to those who would believe and be baptized, when only the elect could be saved? Indeed, even they had been saved from before the world began; hence salvation could not be promised those who were already saved. Why did he threaten with damnation those who refused to believe, when all who are lost had been lost before time began, and were bound to remain lost, believe or not believe.

But the theory of conditional salvation requires the agency of a second party. Well, your theory did not even require the sinner himself, for it was fixed up four thousand years before he was born. If my friend had been away back in the days of the Jews, when a clean person had to officiate for the unclean, he would have said, "Not so, Lord; we want no second party." When the angel appeared to Cornelius, saying, "Send to Joppa for Peter, who shall tell the words by which you shall be saved," he would have said, "Stop! though you are an angel fresh from the throne of glory, there must be no second parties in this business." When the Lord appeared to Saul, who cried, "Lord, what wilt thou have me to do?" the Lord said, "Go into Damascus, and there it shall be told thee what thou must do," my friend would have objected stoutly, for he would have been alarmed at the introduction of second parties.

He wants to know if belief is a cause or an effect. Well, it is the effect of testimony, but way be the cause of salvation. Effects become causes in thousands of cases. Faith is the belief of testimony. God given the testimony, but it is man who believes it; hence faith comes by hearing.

But he thinks if man has to do anything, it robs God of the glory. Does my friend think himself robbed of parental glory, when his son trustingly, promptly, and faithfully obeys him?

He went to John 6:: "All that the Father giveth me shall come to me; and him that cometh to me I will in no wise cast out." But, does this say anything about whether they were given conditionally or unconditionally? Not a word. But let us read further: "No man can come to me, except the Father which hath sent me draw him; and I will raise him up at the last day. It is written in the prophets, "And they shall be all taught of God. Every man, therefore, that hath heard, and hath learned of the Father, cometh unto me." That, is the way men are taught of God. The gospel is preached to the people; they hear and learn of Jesus; they accept salvation on the terms stipulated, and God's way come to him.

He scoffs at the idea that man is a free moral agent. Well, I insist if man is not free, he is not responsible. He cannot be responsible for that in which he has no agency. God would cease to be a just God if he were to damn a man for not obeying him, when he never had a chance to obey him. If a man is not of the elect, is there any chance for him to make himself elect? Will my worthy opponent answer? If a man not elected should give all his goods to feed the poor, do everything in his power, even go on his knees three times a day, is there any chance for him to be saved? All, but you tell me he has not the requisite love. Well, who is to blame for that? Is there anything he can do to change himself, or make God love him, when God, before the world began, determined he would not love him or he loved by him?

This very fact that Jesus commanded the gospel to be preached to all, offering salvation to alt who would believe and obey, is evidence, high as heaven, that man can accept the salvation offered; and this evidence is made certain by the fact that he is threatened with punishment if he refuses to believe it.

He quotes Acts 4:32: "For there is none other name under heaven given, among men, whereby we must be saved," that is, no other than the name of Jesus Christ. He insists that if the sinner has to do anything, be is saved in his own name. To make the matter conclusive, he says, "Until I find a man without a name, there is no chance to find a man who can be saved on conditions." Paul, Cornelius, Crispus, Gaius and Lydia all had names, and were saved by believing and obeying the Lord. The name of Christ gives authority to the commission under the New Covenant; the blood of Christ fills its place; Jesus Christ as the Saviour, fills his place. The idea that because a man is saved by the name of Christ, that nothing else has anything to do with it, would annul the blood of Christ, and every other agency connected with man's salvation. The man who thus reasons has a cloud over his eyes, sure enough.

He quotes: "Beside me, there is no Saviour." In a certain sense there is no Saviour but God. God alone has the power to forgive sins. Certainly, but does he forgive sins conditionally or unconditionally? God saves through Jesus Christ, his Son, who died for all men; but when he assumes that he saves unconditionally, he assumes the whole question in debate. He assumes what he ought to prove. Just a few scintillations of truth from the word of God would be in order along here.

"But there is no other name given among men, whereby we can be saved." But how do we get into the name of Christ? (Acts 10:48). This man had a name, and was saved through the name of Jesus Christ. Peter said: "Can any man forbid water, that these should not be baptized, which have received the Holy Ghost as well as we? And he commanded them to be baptized in the name of the Lord." "When they heard this, they were baptized in the name of the Lord Jesus" (Acts 19:5). Thus, we come in contact with the name of the Lord Jesus where there is salvation.

But he says man cannot save himself. In the sense of pardoning himself, he cannot in the sense of instrumentality, he can. He asks: "How many saviours does he have?" He makes everything connected with salvation a saviour. Had my friend been in the house of Cornelius when they were about to baptize him, he would have said, "No, Peter; there is but one Saviour." And, worse still, had he been in Jerusalem on the day of Pentecost, when Peter exhorted the people to save themselves from that untoward generation, he would have brought charges against Peter for talking about men saving themselves. James says: "Brethren, if any of you do err from the truth, and one convert him; let him know that he which converteth the sinner from the error of his way, shall save a soul from death" (Jas. 5:19, 20). Take care, James, Eld. Herod will get after you for talking about any one saving a soul.

"We get salvation without the name of Christ. "He says I said so. I never said that a man could be saved without the name of Christ in this world, and I have never been in another yet. The gentleman makes inferences for which I would not like to be responsible

But he goes to 1 Cor. 2:1-5: "And I, brethren, when I came to you, came not with excellency of speech or of wisdom, declaring unto you the testimony of God." The apostle was able to confirm what he preached among the Corinthians by miracles and divers gifts of the Spirit, that their faith should not stand in the wisdom of man, but in the power of God. And now what has all that to do with conditional or unconditional salvation? Had he quoted, "In the beginning, God created the heavens and the earth," it would have been just as appropriate. But he talks about the crucifixion of Christ, and his paying the debt. If all the elect were saved before the foundation of the world, what good did the crucifixion of Jesus do? And if he paid the debt, where does the grace, mercy and forgiveness of God come in? If Jesus paid all, then God forgives nothing; and away goes this much-talked of grace. He has wiped it all out at one brush.

He says, "When those who accept the terms get to heaven, they will sing a while to their own glory, and then awhile to the glory of God." Well, he will not be able to give glory to anyone for saving him, for he was never lost. He cannot give glory to Jesus Christ as his Saviour, for Jesus came to save the lost; and if he were eternally and unconditionally elected to salvation, then Jesus never came to save him.

But he says none will be lost for whom Christ died. Paul says: "Destroy not him with thy meat, for whom Christ died" (Rom. 14:15).

And again: "And through thy knowledge shall the weak brother perish for whom Christ died" (1 Cor. 8:11).

Now here is a square issue between my friend and the apostle. He says that none can perish for whom Christ died. Paul was of a very different opinion, it seems.

I propose to show that he has gone squarely into universalism. He says none will be lost that Christ came to save, or for whom Christ died. We read: "And that he died for all, that they which live should not henceforth live unto themselves, but unto him which died for them, and rose again" (2 Cor. 5:15). "That he, by the grace of God, should taste death for every man" (Heb. 2:9). "And he is the propitiation for our sins, and not for ours only, but also for the sins of the whole world" (1 John 2:2). See also 1 Tim. 2:4-6; 2 Pet. 3:9; Titus 2:11, and Rom. 5:31-18.

The gentleman says that all for whom Christ died will be certainly saved. I have shown that he died for all men; therefore all men will be saved, and Universalism is true, according to Mr. Herod. I turn him over to Universalism. This is quite an improvement on the position he has been occupying. God is not willing that any should perish, but that all come to repentance and live. The only reason why all are not saved, is because they will not obey God, that they may be saved. But if God is not willing that any should perish, why will not all be saved, if there is nothing required of anyone. (Time expired.)

Elder Herod's Second Reply.

BROTHERS,. MODERATORS, LADIES AND GENTLEMEN: — It has again fallen to my lot to present myself before you. I arise with the same astonishment that I did this morning. I had all the time been expecting that pretty soon after we had defined our proposition, our worthy friend would have come right down to business, and showed some conditions for salvation from sin. Not a single one who has listened will fail to remember perfectly well that he has been playing off in the bush about conditions and free agency. Free agency may exist, and his proposition be not true at all, for the reason that he avers that he is proving conditions. Why doesn't he read where Christ has laid down the same rule that he has been attempting to find by zig-zagging it around? I was about to call his attention to water. He says that water sustains the same relation to salvation that repentance does. I call his attention to it. I will put the Saviour and water together (Ephesians, chap, 5:) The admonition is to the husband as to what Jesus Christ has done. "Husbands love your wives, as Christ also loved the church and gave himself for it." Past tense. After you have gone through and built up by faith and repentance, you have not learned much. What was the object of giving himself for the Church? "That he might sanctify and cleanse it by the washing of water by the Word. "Does he mean that the sinner is cleansed and sanctified by the washing of the word, or does he mean that Christ will do it? I am quoting the language of the inspired apostle to the Gentiles, and I want everybody to take the force of the language that he has left on record, addressed to that church: "Even as Christ loved the Church and gave himself for it." Could he love that which did not exist? We'll see soon who is the Universalist. I am flattering myself on dumping him over into Universalism directly. The same apostle says; "He has given him to be head over all things to the church, which is his body." It was a universal Christ. I am willing to accept that universalism.

He fixed up a kind of temporary relation after the acts of obedience are performed. Listen to the apostle as he gives a description of the relation as it exists between Christ and the Church. That body is made up of many members — what is the real relationship existing? Members of his body, of his bones and flesh. Members one of another. How near is the relation? So near, that if one member suffers, they all suffer; if one is in pain, they all are in pain; if one rejoices, they all rejoice. Now I have got the object of his love. If my friend wants to know how they are brought to Jesus Christ, in the 31st chapter of Jeremiah, the prophet answers the question:

"Yea saith the Spirit, I have loved them with an everlasting love, with loving-kindness I have drawn them unto myself. That was flesh of my flesh, and bone of my bone, and no man hates his own flesh." Now he tells why it is that he gave himself for that church, and the object that was communicated by the guilt, and by the death of Jesus. If I don't show the Church clean without the assistance of a washerwoman, then I will confess I am wrong. Christ loved the Church and gave himself for it, that he might sanctify and cleanse it with the washing of water, by the word. Was that cleansing it by the hands of a Herod, or the hands of my worthy opponent? Does the sinner cleanse himself, or does Christ cleanse him?

He makes a great deal of fun of a man's being saved by the Christ, who is a full and complete Saviour. He shall have the pleasure of answering this passage, and unless he can do it, he must acknowledge that he has swamped his own proposition. "Even as Christ loved the Church and gave himself for it," to give it a chance to sanctify and cleanse itself by obedience! Now, my friends, what do you think such a Bible as that would be? Suppose it says he might sanctify and cleanse it by the washing of water by the word, then he says Jesus Christ will wash them if they obey, or do something to hire him. They can't be free without the act of Jesus Christ, and I insist that his proposition has no Jesus in it. It is no more than the women who held the clothes of the man, saying, "We will eat our own bread, only let us be called by thy name."

You look astonished. I don't wonder at it. He says the Bible contradicts itself if my position is true. If he acknowledges what he did acknowledge, that Christ is the Saviour, he contradicts himself, and what is the use of discussing this question. Answer the passage, and tell whether it was water that came out of the throne of God, or Adam's water beneath the sun. The waters above the firmament were divided from those beneath. This is the point. I will consider another passage. A great many blessings depend upon conditions—we are arguing the question of salvation or freedom from sin. Is it the result of a condition? A plain paragraph in King James' translation. I want everybody to listen to this question. Eleventh chapter of Romans. Brother Brents just wasn't to read what Paul said, and if the apostle Paul had been in the place of my brother, he would not have said this, with all due respect; for I have not got down below the platform of a gentleman, and I don't want to get above.

I now introduce and read a paragraph out, and then I am willing to leave the question to this respectable congregation, to see the force when connected and compared with this proposition and argument. "So then it is not of him that willeth, or of him that runneth, but of God that showeth mercy." Is that true? Why, Paul, did you put in these words if it is conditional? How in it? When the sinner gets salvation, does he get it as a reward of his labor? Did you buy your salvation? [pointing to Dr. Brents] Now again I quote from Paul's letter to his son (Second Timothy). Decide this question as to whether the affirmative is true or the opposite. What did you say, sir, to the eldest son? "Be thou partaker of the afflictions of the gospel" who has called us with a holy calling just as soon as we complied with the conditions.

Where is your Bible? You profess to be book folks; I want to know whether it is in there or not. I now read the passage without transposing. See that everybody gets the benefit of the wording before he gets done. I will know about the conditions of salvation.

I now call your attention to the first chapter of Second Timothy, second and third verses: "Be thou a partaker of the afflictions of the gospel, according to the power of God, who hath saved us and called us with a holy calling, not according to our works, but according to his own purpose and grace, which was given to us in Christ Jesus before the world began." This is the best place in the world to have settled this matter in favor of my brother's theory, and we would not have been here to-day discussing this question. "Saved us and called us just as soon as we believed and obeyed." I have heard that ever since I was a little boy. When was it? Let us determine as to the period. Let us read the passage and see if there is a clue to the answer of the question. "Not according to our works, but according to his own purpose and grace, given to us in Christ Jesus," but manifest in these last times by the appearing of our Saviour, if we obey him. Is that there? Why preach it then. I will have to read it again—they have shaken their heads at me. I don't mean any harm by transposing. I wish to get your minds on it, and then you will get the substance. Now I read the passage, and read it right, and dismiss it, and call your attention to another: "According to his own purpose and grace which was given us in Christ Jesus before the world began, but is now made manifest by the appearing of our Saviour Jesus Christ." Is it true, or is it false? I am in no hurry. I came here to stay four or five days with the people. That Bible is a terribly big book. I have the credit of keeping to the subject. I never turn out of my way for another. I am too old for that. I want to get all that is in this passage, and get you to see that if the Bible is true, the theory of my friend is false. "According to his own purpose and grace which was given us in Christ Jesus before the world began, but is now made manifest by the appearing of our Saviour Jesus Christ, who hath abolished death, and hath brought life and immortality to light through the gospel."

I must invite your attention to the fifth chapter of Romans, and then I call your attention to the presentation of the question on legal grounds, and carried out as any legal question would be. "Moreover, where sin abounded, grace did much more abound;" if you will obey. If there is a doubt on the mind, we have a right to the benefit of the doubt. Let me read what is there, because by this process your attention is directed to the fifth chapter of the Roman epistle. Moreover, the law entered that the offense might abound. Why not read that salvation from sin is conditional? It has not a particle of Jesus Christ in it; and he cannot go into the waters of baptism without a second party. I want you to see the force of the language, for the honor and glory of Jesus Christ our Saviour. I want you to determine the question. This will settle it.

I now appeal to the fifth chapter. I am perfectly willing that everybody note it. "For as by one man's disobedience many were made sinners, so also by the obedience of one shall many be made righteous." Now, I want every sinner in the house to look at it. Allow me to read it again, and then take it home with you and consider it till tomorrow morning at nine o'clock. "By the obedience of one shall many be made righteous." Do you believe it now? Is it by the obedience of everyone for himself? It ought to read that way to suit my friend's proposition. Is it not by the righteousness of Jesus Christ imputed to many that the many were made righteous? I know by your bright smiling faces that you all see that now. Did you ever know that the Book read that way before? If you did not, it is a good thing that you have learned it now.

(Time expired.)

DR. BRENTS' THIRD SPEECH.

MR. PRESIDENT: — I come before you this morning to resume the discussion begun yesterday. My opponent has not yet deigned to notice my introductory speech of yesterday. He is indeed a singular respondent. He says he is in the defensive. It is well he has told us that. I am sure no one would have found it out had he not told us. No one from hearing his speeches would have concluded that he was here to reply to me. He has not noticed a single passage introduced by me—not one. He has said I introduced not a single passage of Scripture to prove conditional salvation. This, no doubt, made a strange impression upon those who heard my opening speech. I am glad that he has not the privilege of deciding that question for you, but each one who hears us has the privilege of deciding for himself. From yesterday's experience, I have lost all hopes of converting him — he can't see anything. He can't see that I have introduced a single proof of my proposition yet. I need not restate my arguments—they are as yet unassailed. All I have to do is to follow him and show up the absurdities with which his speeches abound. He says I can't draw him into the bushes away from the proposition. Well, the people will decide as to who goes into the bushes. It is his duty to follow me and answer my arguments if he can. Has he attempted to do this? Who, then, has been beating the bush? He has learned a few passages that are in a groove in which he runs; and there he sticks. I wish I could get him to answer me in some way.

There were some things in his first speech which I wish to notice. He quoted Matt. 1:21: "He shall save his people from their sins." What does he want with this? It says not a word about conditional or unconditional salvation. He shall save his people from their sins! Yes, certainly, but how? That is the question. Has he forgotten it? Who are the people that he saves? I showed yesterday that he became the author of eternal salvation to all them that obey him. Not another one. He talks about "transposing." That is a new name for it; but let me try my hand at it. He became the author of eternal salvation to the elect, whether they obey him or not. How does he like that? He is the author of eternal salvation to all who obey him, elect or not elect. He is able to save to the uttermost all who come to God by him, but he does not propose to save any others. Hence salvation is conditional.

But he quotes: "He bore our sins in his own body on the tree. "Yes, but how did he bear them? "He died for our sins according to the Scriptures" (1 Cor. 15:4). For whom did he die? He tasted death for every man. He is the propitiation for our sins, and not for ours only, but also for the sins of the whole world. He is just as much the propitiation for every man as he is for any man — he bore the sins of every man just as he bore the sins of Elder Herod himself. We got back about nineteen hundred years yesterday. I suppose he will get back to creation, or beyond that, soon. I want to say now, once for all, that so far as this discussion is concerned, it does not matter when the plan of salvation or scheme of redemption was fixed up, whether before the foundation of the world, or yesterday, unless we look at its bearing on the question of conditional or unconditional salvation. The time of its conception will amount to nothing. We want to know whether or not its provisions were conditional. This is the question. And I defy him to show any provisions made for his own salvation, either before time began, or at any other time, which are not as free to any man who will comply with the conditions as they are to Elder Herod himself.

He says I have talked about Christian duties, but Christian duties never save anybody. John says if we confess our sins, he is just and faithful to forgive us our sins. Was that said to the Christian? Yes, certainly. "If we say that we have not sinned, we make him a liar, and his word is not in us." The purest Christian on earth needs pardon for his sins every day he lives; and thank God provisions are made in the plan of salvation for such pardon; if not, there is no hope for the salvation of any one who lives. There is nothing in my proposition confining it to the alien. I have a right to examine the subject of salvation, or freedom from sin, anywhere in any class to whom salvation applies.

But he says he could make a Bible with conditional salvation in it. The gentleman need give himself no trouble to do that. Here is one, of which God is the author, with conditional salvation streaming through it from one side to the other. He says he could make a Bible with conditions. I would like to see one he would make — it would be a gem, I'm sure.

I come now to notice his yesterday evening speech. He was astonished that I did not put in one passage to prove conditional salvation. I have scarcely ever had a debate in which this stereotyped phrase does not open every speech. The people will decide this for themselves. I let it go for what it is worth, and it is worth nothing except to fill up time. I suppose he used it as tilling, for I am sure be did not expect any one to believe it.

He introduced Ephesians 5:26, 27: "Husbands love your wives, even as Christ also loved the Church, and gave himself for it; that he might sanctify and cleanse it with the washing of water by the word." He ought to have kept away from this passage surely. He asks, "Did Christ love the Church before it was a Church?" Did you love your wife before you married her? — before she was your wife? He thinks Christ loved and saved him before the foundation of the world, and if he is part of the church he must have loved his part a good while before it was a Church. He asked me if the sinner cleanses himself, or does Christ cleanse the sinner. I answer that Christ cleanses the Church by cleansing the material that is put into it. And how does he cleanse it? "With the washing of water by the word." That is, with the washing of water authorized in and required by the word. Ananias told Saul to arise and be baptized and wash away

The Brents-Herod Debate

his sins, calling on the name of the Lord. Here is the washing that cleansed Saul from sin, and I suppose the same kind of washing cleansed the Ephesians.

He says he understands my position. I don't think he does; but whether he does or not, I am here to state my own position, and if he would allow me to do this, he might be able to put in his time profitably in answering my arguments.

In connection with the washing of water by the word, he dropped a thought that ought to have been further developed. He talked about Adam's water and Christ's water. If they are as muddy as his exegesis of this passage, they are unfit for use, surely. What kind of water floated the ark and covered the earth? What kind of water was it that John baptized Jesus and the multitudes in? What kind of water was at Enon near to Salem, where John was baptizing? In what kind of water did Philip baptize the eunuch? What did he mean by Adam's water and Christ's water? and what has that to do with conditional or unconditional salvation?

He made a most singular remark to this effect: If Christ is the Saviour, and my proposition is true, then the Bible contradicts itself. Is not that strange? Christ is the Saviour, but how does he save?— conditionally or unconditionally? He gave the commission saying, "Go ye into all the world and preach the gospel to every creature; he that believeth and is baptized shall be saved." Are not these conditions? He is the author of eternal salvation to all that obey him. Will he also save those who do not obey him? If not, then is not salvation by Jesus Christ made to depend on obeying him? I am glad to know, my dear friend, that this people can see things that you cannot see.

He says if man can obey or not obey as he chooses, then he is a free moral agent. Yes, and if he is not a free agent, he is not responsible. If he is not free, who is responsible for his damnation? If he has power to choose life or death; if when the gospel is preached to him, he is a free agent, and can accept or reject salvation as he chooses; then I can see sense, reason and justice in the punishment of the sinner. But if the sinner is not free, and God punishes him for what he could not avoid, then is he a monster, and not the God of the Bible. Suppose a father to chain his son to a post or pillar with fetters that the son cannot break, then the father very kindly invites the son to come to him. The son replies: "Father, I cannot come. I am bound by this chain. Please loose me, that I may come." The father knows the boy has told the truth, but still he commands him to come. The boy more earnestly pleads with his father to loose him, that he may come; instead of which the father tells him: "If you don't come to me. I will kill you" The boy says: "Father, I respect your authority, I have always obeyed you, and would now if I could. Oh, loose me, that I may honor your authority and come to you." The father raises his gun and kills the boy. What would you say of such a man? You would say he is not fit to live, but ought to die, and if there be one place in the infernal regions hotter than all others, he ought to be consigned to that place.

Now, what does my friend think of this for the character of the God he worships? Before time began, God, Jesus and the devil seem to have had a confab in eternity. As yet there is no world, no man—no anything. God reveals to his Son and the devil his purposes of making the earth, and making the human race to inhabit it; and that in some form, after they are once created, they will forever exist. Their destiny becomes matter of concern, and God agrees that he will give his Son a select few for his inheritance; and they are personally designated to be his, on condition that he will give his life for them. But these are only a small portion of the number of persons God intended to create; what destiny is provided for the larger portion? The devil becomes heir to them without any conditions whatever, and they are personally and definitely known, each one of them. Time is born, and man is created as contemplated. The devil's party begin to remonstrate; but there is no remedy. God never loved them; Jesus never died for them; there is nothing but a home in hell that awaits them, let them do as they may. Now if this is not substantially my friend's theory, he will please correct me; I don't want to misrepresent him, and he has not fully developed his theory yet. I repeat, his theory makes God a monster.

If all the cruelty of earth were boiled down into one item, it could not equal the cruelty of God in this picture. This is his God, not mine.

But it is not of works. What is not of works? The plan of salvation was not of works "By grace are ye saved." Certainly: but upon conditions, or without conditions? The system of salvation was conceived in infinite wisdom. The means were provided; Jesus consummated them; and man accepts them, and is saved; or he rejects them, and is lost. If not saved, His because he will not be saved; and his unending wail will be, God is just, though I am lost. — "The grace of God that bringeth salvation, hath appeared unto all men. "Though man is saved by grace, salvation is none the less free to all who will accept it. God had a right to stipulate the terms, and it is not our business to debate the question as to why he did not save us this way or that way. It is our business to accept salvation on any terms upon which we can get it.

But my friend quoted Titus 3:5: "Not by works of righteousness which we have done, but according to his mercy he saved us, by the washing of regeneration, and renewing of the Holy Ghost." "Not by works of righteousness which we have done"—well, then, it was some other way; "according to his mercy"—yes, it was an exercise of great mercy to save us on any terms. But according to His mercy he saved us—how? By the washing of regeneration and renewing of the Holy Ghost. What is the washing of regeneration? First, what is regeneration? Generate means to beget; re as a prefix, means again; regenerate, then, means to beget again. Man has been begotten once; he must be begotten again—and this is regeneration. The gospel is the incorruptible seed with which man is begotten; he believes, and is begotten—regenerated; but he is not saved yet, for he is saved by the washing of regeneration, that is, the washing that follows, or grows out of, regeneration. The baptism of repentance—that is, the baptism that belongs to, or follows, repentance. Very well; the washing of regeneration is that washing that belongs to or follows regeneration that saves us. Perhaps Peter knows what washing it is that saves people. After telling us that in the days of Noah eight souls were saved by water, he says: "Baptism doth also now save us." Baptism is the washing of regeneration by which we are saved according to God's mercy, and not by any works of our own devising. Surely this is an unfortunate proof-text for our friend. It proves my proposition exactly. He should have kept away from it, by all means. He need not tell us that this is spiritual washing, for the renewing of the Holy Spirit is mentioned in addition to the washing.

The plan of salvation could not have been devised by man—it was through mercy. Man could not have conceived the plan, and furnished the means for the production of bread; but, according to his mercy God gives us bread by giving the soil, the light, the heat, the air, the rain; and then we prepare the soil, plant the seed, cultivate the crop, and the result is we get bread; but he that refuses to work, and expects God to fill his pantry with bread, will be likely to go without bread, unless it be given him by some one more wise than himself.

(Time expired.)

Elder Herod's Third Reply.

Bro. Moderators, ladies and gentlemen: —I am again permitted to be before you for thirty minutes, and I am still somewhat astonished by my venerable old brother.

(Brents: I am glad my wife is not present to hear that; it would be bad for you if she were here.)

Herod: He labors strenuously to show that the passage of Scripture he refers to proves that salvation is the result of conditions performed by the sinner. He has owned up to it; it was by grace. He has made that noble confession. He complains that he has introduced passage after passage to prove conditional salvation, and that he has time and again invited my attention to them, and asked me to reply. I have replied to every passage that had an immediate reference to the facts stated. I am well apprised of that, and so are you. You quote from the first four books of Moses as though they had anything to do with this proposition. What kind of a dispensation was that? Was it a gospel dispensation, or a law dispensation?

I repeat again, did that law covenant promise eternal salvation? or did it furnish a single threat of eternal damnation? I want to notify him that we are not under law; for by the deeds of the law shall no flesh be justified—cursed is every one that continueth not in all things written in the book of the law to do them. But he hangs the salvation of this entire audience on his conclusion that we are still under the law of Moses. I blush at it. There are some things in his speeches that I propose to reply to. Listen at the next record given by the apostle in his letter to the Galatians. In this epistle he asks if life could be gained by the law, and if it could, why was it not by law? And yet my worthy opponent has proposed salvation to one and all upon the legal principle; and just says; "If you accept terms and comply with conditions, you can have life; and without complying with them you cannot." The inspired apostle says it cannot be.

He's got some conditions, though. I believe yesterday evening he was willing to admit that belief was the effect of a cause, and that the cause was the testimony. Does the juror control the testimony, or the testimony control the juror?

He afterward said that "an effect may become a cause." It can't reach back, but it may reach forward; therefore it can't be a cause of salvation. I give the answer, and that without any trouble. I will give him something to reply to. What is the product of an effect? The apostle tells you so plain, that there can be no mistake about it. He says: "Created in Christ Jesus unto good works, that we should walk in them." Belief is the product of faith, and faith is produced by evidence, and evidence by the existing facts. Every one sees that belief is a result of causes produced by the existence of facts. That is a settled conclusion to that subject. If I can read his position out of the Bible, I will reply to it; I never try to reason it out.

Sixth chapter of John—I don't want to turn to it; it doesn't make a bit of difference to me; I know it. I may miss a citation, but I never miss the words. I call attention, now, to the sixth chapter of John. What is the question? It is about the cause of belief—yes, the cause of belief. Sixth chapter of John's gospel: "They said unto him, What must we do to do the works of God?" My brother would give half a dozen conditions. What did God say? I am addressing myself to an intelligent audience. Do you want a Bible solution to the problem between myself and my opponent? Are you ready to read a plain answer to the inquiry. Listen: "This is the work of God, that you believe on him whom he hath sent." He says it is volition of your mind. Now he turned right round, a moment ago, and said: "For by grace are ye saved through faith, and that not of yourselves; it is the gift of God."

I remember to have asked as old a minister as my friend about this once; he said it was the act of the creature. He said, in his remarks, that faith was not the gift of God. I now call your attention to a passage that will settle it—Heb. 10: If he will read the Bible, he will find that my little groove spreads over the whole Bible between this and to-morrow night. "Lay aside every weight, and the sin that doth so easily beset us, and run, with patience, the race set before us, looking unto Jesus, the author and finisher of our faith." Listen to the apostle in this same letter to the Hebrews, in the next chapter: "Now faith is the substance of things hoped for, the evidence of things not seen. "Faith is what produces the evidence, and the evidence produces the belief."

Now I raise another question in connection with this language. I have been calling your attention to the question, What is faith, when it is entertained by the sinner—where he got the substance? Is it original with him, or does it come from somewhere else? Listen to a Bible answer to the question. It is called the faith of Jesus Christ —not the faith of Brents or Herod—the faith of Jesus Christ; and hence it is the "substance of things hoped for, the evidence of things not seen." He will not say any more that I don't reply.

I was astonished about him going to Mark. He went there for the commission, and he has labored on it to show you that there are conditions in it. I am going to read it, and I want the people to see the conditions. Listen to the language of our Lord Jesus Christ. I will show the report of that committee, and show that Dr. Brents or Herod cannot labor under that commission in the present age of the world. Go into all the world, and if the truth is preached, he says that he that is not baptized will be. They had received the baptism of John. You see he can't keep away from the water. I will now read the commission till I come to the finality. He may sift it with all the ingenuity and skill that he may have on that subject. "And these signs shall follow them that believe. In my name shall they cast out devils; they shall speak with new tongues; they shall take up serpents, and if they drink any deadly thing, it shall not hurt them; they shall lay hands on the sick, and they shall recover." Do you reckon Dr. Brents could take a dose of strychnine and survive it? I call your attention to his own passage, and before we get through with the discussion he will not complain of my not replying to him. Believers and those that were baptized could do these things—why? Because miracles were with them, but they have ceased.

"Elder Herod failed to show that salvation is unconditional!" Is a man to prove himself not guilty of anything? I thought he was here to prove that salvation is conditional. He even went far enough to tell you how to get it. He ought to be able to prove it—it cannot be his way and mine both.

The answer to his great question is to be able to show salvation consummated by Christ without a condition performed by the sinner (second chapter of the epistle to the Ephesians.) I am now going to read to you for the purpose of calling attention to the work performed by the Lord Jesus Christ, the eleventh verse of that chapter. I am sure I am correct when I say second chapter, eleventh verse: "Wherefore you being in time past Gentiles in the flesh, who were called uncircumcision by that which is called the circumcision in the flesh made by hands; that at the time ye were without Christ, being aliens from the commonwealth of Israel, and strangers from the covenants of promise, having no hope, and without God in the world."

Were they not recognized as sinners? Everybody says they were. How were they recovered from that condition?

He says by acts of obedience—faith, repentance and baptism. Now read to where, the apostle says: "At that time you were without Christ, and strangers from the covenants of promise, without God, Now ye are in Christ Jesus, who sometime were far off; but are now nigh." How did they get nigh? By the blood of Christ. That brought them up. If it was sufficient to bring them up to a state of election, the act of belief could not affect that. Look at the conclusion that the apostle has arrived at: "Who hath broken down the middle wall of partition and made of twain one new man. For by him we both have access by one Spirit unto the Father. Now therefore ye are no more strangers and foreigners, but fellow citizens with the saints, and of the household of God." There is a volume, but not a condition.

In the Colossian letter, we see that the Saviour performed the work there. I have heard of a people who had a form of godliness, but who denied the power. "For in him dwelt all the fullness of the godhead, bodily, and ye are complete in him, which is the head of all principality and power; in whom also ye are circumcised with the circumcision made without hands, in putting off the body of the sins of the flesh, by the circumcision of Christ. If it is baptism to be understood here, then it must be done at the hands of the Lord Jesus Christ, and not at the hands of Brents or Herod.

We read further: "Buried with him in baptism, wherein also ye are risen with him through faith in the operation of God." I want him to note that, and read the passage that has water in it, and what the Saviour has done. Water baptism will be right in its place. The last chapter of Luke I want next. If you are saved from your sins, it is the result of your industry—I protest against that.

I want everybody to listen to the plain and forcible words on that occasion: "Then opened he their understanding, that they might understand the scriptures, and said unto them, Thus it is written, and thus it behooved Christ to suffer and to rise from the dead the third day, and that repentance and remission of sins should be preached in his name among all nations, beginning at Jerusalem."

Remission of sins in the name of the Saviour. He has insisted that you can choose, even to the defiance of God himself. Your bright faces show the interest you have in this issue. I have transposed—he doesn't seem to like the term, "that remission of sins should be preached in the name of the sinner."

(Time expired.)

Dr. Brents' Fourth Speech.

MR. PRESIDENT:—Before replying to the speech just closed, I propose to finish up the advance argument left off yesterday. If I do not present it now, and wait until my next speech, then he can reply, when I will have no chance to reply to his reply.

I was speaking on the subject of obedience and calling on the name of the Lord for salvation, and I had taken the position that no man need call on the Lord until he is willing to obey him. In support of this, I read Heb. 5:8, 9: "Though he were a son, yet learned he obedience by the things which he suffered; and being made perfect, he became the author of eternal salvation unto all them that obey him." According to the gentleman's position, obedience has nothing to do with the eternal salvation of which Jesus is the author. He says he believes in Christian duties as much as any one does; but what good does all the duties he preaches to saint or sinner do, in securing his salvation? Just none at all. Indeed, if his theory is true, his preaching can do no one any good, and the world would do just as well if he and I and every other preacher were to stay at home; and if I believed as he does, I would stay at home. If I did not believe I could be instrumental in turning men and women from sin to righteousness, that they might thereby make their calling and election sure, I would never leave my home to get into a pulpit again. James says: "Let him know, that he which converteth the sinner from the error of his way shall save a soul from death." But Elder Herod is afraid to try that, lest he makes another Saviour. He would be alarmed at trying to save a soul.

Jesus says, "Why call ye me Lord, Lord, and do not the things which I say?" (Luke 6:46.) And again, "Not every one that sayeth unto me, Lord, Lord, shall enter into the kingdom of heaven; but he that doeth the will of my Father which is in heaven" (Matt. 7:21), None but the saved can be citizens of the kingdom of heaven, and none but those who do the will of the Father can enter the kingdom; hence we conclude that doing the will of the Father is an indispensable condition of salvation. Will my worthy opponent say that a man can be saved without doing the will of the Father, either as saint or sinner?

But we must be willing ourselves. Jesus said to the Jews: "Search the scriptures, for in them ye think ye have eternal life, and they are they which testify of me; and ye will not come to me that ye might have life" (John 5:39, 40).

Life was set before them, but they would not come to Jesus, through whom alone they could get it. When beholding the dazzling splendor of Jerusalem, and contemplating the desolation to which it would be reduced in consequence of the wickedness of the people, Jesus says: "O Jerusalem, Jerusalem, thou that killest the prophets, and stonest them which are sent unto thee, how often would I have gathered thy children together, even as a hen gathereth her chickens under her wings, and ye would not. Behold, your house is left unto you desolate" (Matt. 23:37).

Does not this show that the wickedness of the people brought destruction upon themselves and their city? And they would have been saved had they heeded the oft-repeated admonitions of the Saviour. Their own obdurate if in prevented them from accepting the salvation offered them. So, it has ever been. If men have not been saved, it has not been because they could not be, but because they would not obey God, that they might be saved. If men are not saved to-day, it is not because they cannot be saved; but because they will not comply with the conditions upon which God proposes to save them.

But why are men condemned? We have already heard Jesus say, in the plainest terms, that "he that believeth not is condemned already, because he hath not believed on the name of the only begotten Son of God;" and "he that believeth not the Son shall not see life; but the wrath of God abideth on him." But we will hear him further on the subject of condemnation.

"Marvel not at this; for the hour is coming in the which all that are in their graves shall hear his voice, and shall come forth; they that have done good, unto the resurrection of life, and they that have done evil, unto the resurrection of damnation" (John 5:28-29), Does this need comment or explanation? They that have done good shall be resurrected to life, and they that have done evil shall be resurrected to condemnation. Was ever language more plain? They that have done good, either in coming into the kingdom, or as citizens of it. Why do not all do good? Simply because they will not.

On this subject Jesus further says: "I was a-hungered, and ye gave me meat; I was thirsty, and ye gave me drink; I was a stranger, and ye took me in; naked, and ye clothed me; I was sick, and ye visited me; I was in prison, and ye came unto me. Then shall the righteous answer him, saying, Lord, when saw we thee a-hungered, and fed thee? or thirsty, and gave thee drink? When saw we thee a stranger, and took thee in? or naked, and clothed thee? or when saw we thee sick or in prison, and came unto thee? And the King shall answer and say unto them, Verily, I say unto you, inasmuch as ye have done it unto one of the least of these my brethren, ye have done it unto me. Then shall he say also unto them on the left hand, depart from me, ye cursed, into everlasting fire prepared for the devil and his angels; for I was a-hungered, and ye gave me no meat; I was thirsty, and ye gave me no drink; I was a stranger, and ye took me not in; naked, and ye clothed me not; sick and in prison, and ye visited me not Then shall they also answer him, saying, Lord, when saw we thee a-hungered, or athirst, or a stranger, or naked, or sick, or in prison, and did not minister unto thee? Then shall he answer them, saying, Verily I say unto thee, inasmuch as ye did it not to one of the least of these, ye did it not unto me. And these shall go away into everlasting punishment; but the righteous into life eternal" (Matt. 25:35-46). Here again we learn that obedience to the will of the Lord gives entrance into life eternal, and neglect of duty sends them into everlasting punishment, whether it be with regard to entering the kingdom or the discharge of duty in it. Then are not rewards and punishments conditional?

"And to you who are troubled, rest with us, when the Lord Jesus shall be revealed from heaven with his mighty angels, in flaming fire, taking vengeance on them that know not God, and obey not the gospel of our Lord Jesus Christ; who shall be punished with everlasting destruction from the presence of the Lord, and from the glory of his power; when he shall come to be glorified in his saints, and to be admired in all them that believe" (2. Thess, 1:7-10). On whom will he take vengeance when he comes? Those who know not God and obey not the gospel. In whom will he be glorified? His saints who believe on him, and have obeyed him, and thus escaped his vengeance.

Finally, we propose to show that the final judgment will be based upon the very principle contained in my proposition. Indeed, we have already seen that the wicked will go away into everlasting punishment, and the righteous into life eternal; that they that have done good shall be resurrected to life, and they that have done evil will be resurrected to damnation; and that Jesus Christ will take vengeance on them that know not God and obey not the gospel: and we insist that these Scriptures are sufficient to settle this question forever. But our resources are ample, and we can afford to be liberal. We therefore invite your attention to Rom. 2:4-11: "Despisest thou the riches of his goodness and forbearance and longsuffering; not knowing that the goodness of God leadeth thee to repentance? But after thy hardness and impenitent heart treasurest up unto thyself wrath against the day of wrath and revelation of the righteous judgment of God; who will render to every man according to his deeds: to them who by patient continuance in well doing seek for glory and honor and immortality, eternal life: but unto them that are contentious, and do not obey the truth, but obey unrighteousness, indignation and wrath, tribulation and anguish, upon every soul of man that doeth evil, of the Jew first, and also of the Gentile; but glory, honor, and peace, to every man that worketh good, to the Jew first, and also to the Gentile: for there is no respect of persons with God. "This is too plain to need comment, God will render to every man according to his deeds, not according to the eternal decree of election which settled his destiny before time began. Paul enters into specifications—to them who patiently continue to do well, He will render eternal life; but unto them who are contentious and do not obey the truth, but obey unrighteousness, He will render indignation and wrath; and it matters not whether he fails to obey the truth in coming into the church or after he is in—the principle is the same.

John says: "I saw the dead, small and great, stand before God; and the books were opened; and another book was opened, which is the book of life, and the dead were judged out of those things which were written in the books, according to their works. And the sea gave up the dead which were in it; and death and hell delivered up the dead which were in them; and they were judged, every man, according to their works" (Rev. 20:12, 13), Every man was judged how? According to the eternal and immutable decree of election? What a ridiculous farce such a judgment would be! But they are judged according to their works. Those who have obeyed the gospel will enter upon the enjoyment of eternal life in a glorious immortality; but those who will not obey the gospel will go into everlasting fire prepared for the devil and his angels.

Once more John says: "And, behold, I come quickly; and my reward is with me, to give every man according as his work shall be. I am Alpha and Omega, the beginning and the end, the first and the last. Blessed are they that do his commandments, that they may have right to the tree of life, and may enter in through the gates into the city "(Rev. 22:12-14). The Lord says my reward is with me to give to every man as his work shall be. They who do his commandments here will have right to the tree of life, and be permitted to pass through the pearly gates into the city where God, Jesus, angels, and all who have washed their robes in the blood of the Lamb, will ever be. Will they who have not done his commandments enter in as well? If not, salvation from sin is conditional, the condition or conditions to be performed by the sinner, in order to salvation or freedom from sin.

"Let us hear the conclusion of the whole matter: Fear God, and keep his commandments: for this is the whole duty of man. For God shall bring every work into judgment, with every secret thing, whether it be good, or whether it be evil" (Eccl. 12:13, 14).

Having closed our advance argument, we come now to notice the speech of the gentleman to which you have just listened. He introduced Luke 24:45-47: "Then opened he their understanding, that they might understand the scriptures; and said unto them, Thus it in written, and thus it behooved Christ to suffer, and to rise from the dead the third day; and that repentance and remission of sins should be preached in his name among all nations, beginning at Jerusalem. "He asks, "Did he say that remission of sins should be preached in the name of the sinner?" He can get but one idea into his head at a time. I may ask, Did it require remission of sins to be preached in the name of Christ, without repentance? Is not repentance a condition upon which remission depends? But, according to his idea, there was no use preaching remission to any but the elect, for it could do others no good: why mock them by offering them that which was never intended for them?

Where was this preaching to begin? At Jerusalem. Then let us go there and see how it began. Peter was inspired—filled with the Holy Spirit sent fresh from heaven; preached the wonderful things concerning Jesus Christ—that God had made him Lord and Christ. When the people heard this, they were cut to the heart, and cried out, "What shall we do?" "Do for what? For that remission of sins that was to be preached here in the name of Jesus. My friend would have answered, "Do nothing—just nothing at all. Remission of sins is not conditional." But the inspired preacher did not understand the matter that way, and hence did not answer that way. He said: "Repent and be baptized, every one of you. in the name of Jesus Christ, for the remission of sins." That is the way repentance and remission of sins was preached at Jerusalem in the name of Jesus. [Then turning to Elder Herod] Do you preach that way now? [Elder Herod—" Yes. "] Beautiful consistency! What is the use of telling them to repent and be baptized for remission, if remission is not conditional?

He says I went back to the first five books of Moses as if we are still under that law. I went to those books and to the Old Testament to show the principle upon which God has always dealt with man—that he blessed and saved him when he believed and obeyed him, and cursed and punished him when he rebelled against him. I stated this plainly when I introduced those passages, and all understood it but Elder Herod, He cannot understand anything.

He next introduced Eph. 2:8-10: "For we are his workmanship, created in Christ Jesus unto good works," etc. Why does he not read the twelfth verse? Does it ever occur to him that the Bible is not a book of contradictions, especially that it does not contradict itself right in the same connection? Let me put in the twelfth verse for him. "That at any time ye were without Christ." When were the eternally elect without Christ? This is the last passage in the Bible to which he should have gone. "Being aliens from the commonwealth of Israel." When were the eternally elect aliens? "And strangers from the covenants of promise." When were the eternally elect strangers from the covenants of promise? "Having no hope. When had the eternally elect no hope? "And without God in the world." When were the eternally elect without God in the world?

But he says, "Faith is the gift of God," and he quotes this passage to prove it—that is, the eighth verse: "By grace are ye saved through faith; and that not of yourselves: it is the gift of God." Yes, what is the gift of God? Elder Herod says the faith. Then it should have read, "This is the gift of God," for he refers to that which is last introduced. By grace are you saved through faith, and that salvation not of yourselves: it is the gift of God. As further evidence that faith is the gift of God, he quotes: "This is the work of God, that ye believe on him whom he hath sent" (John 6:29). Let us lead the preceding verse: "Then said they unto him, What shall we do, that we might work the works of God?" What was the question? Did they want to know what God was to do in or for them? No, but what must we do, that we may work? This is the work of God, that who believe? That ye believe. If a man does a work for another as instructed and commanded by him for whom he works, it is not his own work, but the work of him for whom it is done. So it is the work of God to believe on Jesus because God has commanded it. Paul says faith comes by hearing, and hearing by the word of God. That is enough to settle that. He introduces Col. 2:11: "In whom also ye are circumcised with the circumcision made without hands, in putting off the body of the sins of the flesh by the circumcision of Christ." Did Christ's literal circumcision put off their sins? Surely not. The circumcision of Christ is the circumcision authorized by Christ to put off their sins. How was it done? "Buried with him in baptism, wherein also ye are risen with him through the faith of the operation of God, who hath raised him from the dead." "He that believeth and is baptized shall be saved." These were buried with him in baptism and were risen with him, and thus had put off the sins of the flesh by complying with the conditions ordained for that purpose.

He told us yesterday that he had a Saviour without water. He then spoke of Adam's water and Christ's water. Did he not see his inconsistency? If Christ has water, he has no Saviour without water. Then he has a plan of salvation without any water in it. Then he has a Christ and a plan of salvation not known in the Bible. Jesus Christ was baptized in the Jordan, and he commanded every creature in all the world who would be saved by him, to be baptized.

I did not put water in the plan of salvation. If I had made the plan of salvation I might have made a bungle of it, as he does in applying Scripture. I am a child of mortality, needing salvation by the blood of Jesus, and I am willing to take salvation through his blood on any conditions he will offer it to me.

He says the commission by Mark is not applicable to us now. Does he not know that it is Mark's record of the same commission he quoted from Luke? He asks me if I will take a dose of strychnine; and in the next breath he answers his own question by saying there were miracles with that commission once, but they are done away now. Does it follow that because the miracles are done away, the commission is done away also? He says it had reference to those baptized by John. Did John go into all the world and preach the gospel to every creature? I thought John's mission was confined to the Jews; but does he intend to give up the question as to John's ministry by admitting that he that believed and was baptized was saved in John's day, but is not now?

(Time expired.)

Elder Herod's Fourth Reply.

BROS. moderator, ladies and gentlemen: —I arise to respond to the last half hour's speech of my worthy opponent. I remember where I was when my time expired. I was upon the last chapter of Luke's record of the Lord Jesus Christ. I came down to the point where it says repentance and remission of sins are to be preached in his name among all nations. My brother says he accepts that. The very moment he accepts the language of the Lord Jesus Christ himself, that moment he forever puts a lock upon his own mouth. If you were a jury, I would be willing to take this to you. If my brother transfers the name to a second party, then the first party is responsible for the second party. It is under the control of a poor, fallible sinner. Jesus got just so far, and he could get no further.

Peter had fully recognized all that was involved in the proposition in the second chapter of Acts. Sinners, on Pentecost, asked, "What must we do?" Repent. Why, that's a condition; if you get that away, stick a pin right there, and step right back to where we get that question answered so plainly. Where did they get the promise of repentance? Do you remember? John says. "I indeed baptize you with water unto repentance, but he that cometh after me is mightier than I, whose shoes I am not worthy to bear; he shall baptize you with the Holy Ghost and with fire." Now I submit as to how many promises that were to be consummated, the promise of three things—repentance, baptism of the Holy Ghost, and of fire.

Repent—you have the promise of repentance. But we take it to the eleventh chapter of Acts: "Then hath God granted unto the Gentiles repentance unto life." Where did repentance come from? From the same source that remission of sins comes from. The Lord Jesus Christ has incorporated this, and he [Brents] has not yet learned it. I want him to study it before he commences the discussion of another question like this. "Granted repentance!" When did he do that? Before Peter went over there, or after? After he went there and obeyed! I intend to sift till everything that ought not to be there is driven out. "When they heard this they held their peace and glorified God, saying, Then hath God granted unto the Gentiles repentance unto life." I will be with him to the edge of the water, and if he doesn't find it, I want him to acknowledge it.

I now call your attention to Cornelius. The angel came and told him to send to Joppa; some one should tell him words. What did the angel do? Told of the experimental relation that had been made down there, and I would be glad if you would go down. Says Peter, "I am not going; the Gentiles are heathens; they are unclean." He did not know that God had been there—he has got to get in before God! Let us see what the narrative discloses. I have read every chapter and verse in regard to the question of baptism. I call upon him to answer the question, or say that I have been noticing it all the time. Tell Peter to go down. Peter was on the house-top, hungry. He fell into a trance, and there appeared something like a sheet, with the corners joined, and all manner of unclean beasts were in it; and he heard the words, "Rise, Peter; slay and eat." The Lord can't do anything for them till the preacher gets there and tells them the conditions of salvation! He says that a man has his part to do, and will be lost if he doesn't do it. A man was crossing a river once; the ice broke, and he slipped in; the ice pushing against him, he commenced to pray one of his shortest prayers, "Lord, help!" The ice moved off, and he said, "That will do, Lord; I can get out myself now."

See the force of the argument? It makes the preacher the viceregent of God. It puts you into the hands of my brother, and not one of you can enter the kingdom of heaven without the preacher there. He has failed, surely. "Got to discussing election"—what do you mean by that? That death and hell were cast into the lake of fire. I am answering now the point I was upon about the vision of Peter. "Rise, Peter; slay and eat—go down to Cornelius." "Have you obeyed the gospel down there? Can't come, unless you have. That is just simmering it down to facts. "Can't come, unless you have obeyed!" No preacher had ever preached a sermon in that country; and there is no chapter and verse that he can quote that I have not read time and again. What was the voice? "Rise, Peter; slay and eat." What did Peter say? "Nothing common or unclean hath at any time entered into my mouth." "What God hath cleansed call not thou common or unclean." God cleansed them before a minister ever went amongst them.

My friend has spent his time wandering about in the law. The moment we come to the real issue of the case, he comes back to the second chapter of Acts: "When they heard this, they were cut in their hearts." "What shall we do?" Peter answered them—that was his business. He says that baptize and repent was in order to remission of sins. He says that you ought to understand that he has thoroughly established his proposition. Perhaps you have got better light than I have; it doesn't look that way to me, however.

I have submitted a question as to whether repentance and baptism were in order to, or because of. If it is in order to, I want him to answer a number of questions as to the meaning of Bible words. For is the word. He says it means in order to; I say it means because of. What did Peter tell them—because, in the rendering of this passage he holds his entire theory. Peter said, in addressing himself to the brethren (1 Pet. 1:)—I am going to read out till I get to the plain question, and then go back to Pentecost; sinners are redeemed, every one can see that—"not with corruptible things, as silver and gold." How, then, were they redeemed? By the precious blood of Christ. He was their Saviour before the foundation of the world, by their belief in Christ, whom God raised from the dead. They were saved—was it for or because of? If it was in order to, God could not have loved those people without two things—Dr. Brents or somebody to administer baptism, and a pool or branch in order to baptism.

Was there a minister to administer baptism that day? Was there a Jordan, or branch, or pool? If it is there, read it to these people, and let them see it, and let them not go away mystified about the question.

Wouldn't it be a miracle? Dr. Brents holds a meeting of a week, and he immerses a hundred, and no one ever said a word about Dr. Brents, or the branch, either

I was amused when he got to Titus. You see how a man will read a passage, and leave out the subject at issue. He introduced it as though I had introduced it as a proof-text. He has assumed that Elder Herod has to prove that his proposition is true. In Titus, I will see why there is no baptism there. If he will show me where it is, or where the preacher is mentioned, I will give him a ten dollar Bible. I want him to establish it. Titus 3:5: Tell him you are not going. Dr. Brents said you could do as you pleased about it. I can bring out his own weapons, to break his own head with them. He attaches something to it that I say is not in it. He says that unless you do something, you will be damned. Titus says it is not by works of righteousness. I would never have got that up. He has told us that baptism must be administered. He finds this passage just in accordance with what he has preached all the time! Read it out, sir! "Not by works of righteousness which we have done." He wanted you to believe that a little grace was there. He reminds me of a Katydid—one says Katy did, and the other says Katy didn't. The recovery of sin! I criticize the remarks of my worthy opponent. I have no doubt I will always esteem him hereafter. "I say it is not by works of righteousness." He got down to the mercy of God then. He wanted you to believe that there was a preacher down there who checked them in. I wouldn't want to be in a dry country where there is no water, if his theory is true. There is no plan to save them in parts of this continent.

You will all see how you have obeyed. The fact is sent to Paul's son Titus, "who saved us by the washing of regeneration and renewing of the Holy Ghost, which he shed on us abundantly, through our Lord Jesus Christ." He was the washer-woman. "Adam's water," he says I call it; when Christ operated with water, and it came out of the throne of God.

There is a reference to the apostle Peter in the tenth chapter of Acts, at the house of Cornelius: "And while I yet spake, the Holy Ghost fell on all them that heard the words." And can any man forbid water? What for? To save these people by water! We put a poor sinner in our hands, and your souls are in our hands. We've got you, and we could get all the money you have, at that rate.

What puts away sin? His blood cleanses from all sin. He has passed out of death into life, John says, because he loves the brethren—because he believes. That doesn't militate against your duties. I am honoring the Lord in this. Water is found, and I am speaking on this question—you can't mistake it—in such a miraculous affair as this on the day of Pentecost, if you had been administering baptism and could find water enough to baptize them; and you would say it was for the remission of sins.

Freedom from sin is a part of his proposition. I am now going to get the word, and show you how freedom comes. I will cover the entire ground.

(Time expired.)

Dr. Brents' Closing Speech.

MR. President: —Elder Herod says if Jesus proposes salvation to a sinner on conditions, he transfers the saving power to a second party, and is himself no longer responsible for the salvation of anybody. He freely, graciously, and mercifully offers salvation to the whole world on conditions. Transferring, indeed! is that transferring any thing? I can see no transferring about it. If the elect were saved before the world began, I would like to know if there is any responsibility to transfer. Repentance is a condition. Yes, Peter commanded the Pentecostians to "repent and be baptized" (Acts 2:: 38). "Repent ye, therefore, and be converted." What for? That your sins may be blotted out (Acts 3:19). But he attempts to evade this by quoting Acts 11:18: "Then hath God also to the Gentiles granted repentance unto life." Does he propose to show by this that Peter was wrong in commanding persons to repent? If these passages antagonize each other, how shall we decide which is right? The apostles glorified God because he had granted to the Gentiles the privilege of repenting. They had long been aliens from the commonwealth of Israel, strangers to the covenants of promise, having no hope and without God in the world, and it was quite a source of joy to be allowed salvation on any terms. But Peter told the Pentecostians to repent because their sins were pardoned! In his next discourse he told the people to repent, that their sins might be blotted out. Did he preach one doctrine one day and another the next day? Jesus said to the wicked, "Except ye repent, ye shall all perish?" Does that look like a gift? If repentance is a gift from God to man, directly, and man never repents because God has failed to give him repentance, who is responsible for his not repenting? Will God punish man for his own neglect? But John baptized the people unto repentance. Well, does that help him any? Does the fact that two conditions change places, if such were the fact, prevent them from being condition? John baptized with the baptism of repentance, and also unto repentance. He baptized with a baptism growing out of a resolve to amend the life, and unto a life in keeping with that resolve; and all this was for or in order to the pardon or remission of sins.

But I am not done with Acts 2:38 yet. I fully analyzed this passage in my opening speech, and I need not repeat it here. Every child capable of parsing a preposition knows that remission of sins is the object of the relation created by the preposition for, and to obtain which they are commanded to repent and be baptized. That your sins may be blotted out. If the wisdom of heaven were concentrated in a single sentence, it could not be more plain—"repent and be baptized"; not that they are, but that your sins may be blotted out. We have a similar sentence in Matt. 26:28 to the one in Acts 2:38: "This is my blood of the new testament, which is shed for many for the remission of sins." I claim nothing for it, but without a violation of our agreement I may say it is exactly the same in the Greek. Was the blood of Jesus shed because the sins of the world, for whom he died, were already remitted? Perhaps my friend may think so—he may have them remitted long before the world was. Then for what was the blood of Jesus shed? If this is true, there is no such thing as pardon now at all. Will my friend tell us whether there is any such thing as remission of sins now, or not? We would be right glad to have his position on this subject, if he will give it to us. I believe in the blood of Jesus. It was shed for the remission of sins; but we get the benefits of that blood in his own way, and we have no right to debate the question with him still. We are baptized into his death, or into the benefits of his death, from which we arise to walk in newness of life.

But to get rid of baptism as a condition of pardon to the Pentecostians, he took the long, threadbare dodge that there were no administrators, nor water in Jerusalem to baptize the converts. This was indeed rich, coming from a Baptist, and one of the straightest sect at that! The record says, "As many as gladly received his word were baptized. "Does he believe it?" And the same day there were added unto them about three thousand souls. Does he believe that? Had he taken the trouble to

The Brents-Herod Debate

make the calculation, he could have proved, by absolute calculation, that they could have been baptized in half the time. Had he examined the testimony he could have found acres upon acres of water there. But he can make grimaces and frowns, and tickle the audience half to death; and he thinks the people are laughing at his shrewdness, when they are really laughing at his antics and pretty looks. [Here a point of order was raised, and it was decided that any good-humored pleasantry was admissible.] We are discussing questions that have to do with the eternal destiny of man, and there is no reason why we should not discuss them with the same seriousness and dignity that would characterize a sermon in the house of God. I have not tried to create any mirth, nor do I think I will. I want my argument to stand or fall on its merits. I do not need such clap-trap to support my proposition. Nor does any man resort to such things as long as he has anything else with which to support him.

He says Cornelius was a Christian man, and worshiped God before he ever heard a sermon, from Peter or any one else. If he was he was not a saved man, for the angel told him to send for Peter to tell him words by which he should be saved. He says if I had been there I would have told him conditions. I would not know how to tell him conditions without using words. If Cornelius was saved before Peter went there, he was saved without hearing the gospel or having any faith in it. Peter alluding to this very matter, said: "God made choice among us that the Gentiles, by my mouth, should hear the word. of the gospel and believe." Then, up to that time he had not heard the gospel or believed it Peter began with their own prophets, and proved that Jesus was the Son of God—in short, told the words by which he was to be saved, not by which he had been saved. Suppose I go to see a neighbor, and find him very sick. I tell him to send for the doctor, who will give him medicine by which he shall be cured. The sick man shouts, "I am well, I am cured!" Cured how? "Did you not tell me the Doctor would give me medicine by which I should be cured? Yes, you did, and I know I am well." You would think the man crazy—demented; and you would apply ice to his head and hot applications to his feet to create a diversion of blood from the brain.

Next, my friend says, according. to my teaching Peter would have said to the men who went after him, "Have you obeyed the gospel down there? If not, I can't go with you." No, sir; Peter was sent for to preach the gospel to them, that they might obey it. The gospel is the power of God to salvation, and it was that Cornelius and friends might hear, believe, and obey the gospel, that Peter was sent for. We send for the doctor to cure the sick; and the doctor never inquires if they are well down there—if they are, they don't need the doctor. But now, my dear sir, if Cornelius was a Christian man and was saved unconditionally before he sent for Peter, what did he want with Peter? The gospel was then, as it is now, God's power to salvation to every one that would believe it. It was necessary that Peter go and preach it to them, that they might have a chance to believe and obey it. But if Cornelius, and every one else who was or is saved at all, was saved from eternity, then the gospel had nothing to do with it—there was no gospel when that arrangement was made, nor has there ever been any use for it. If Cornelius was saved before he ever heard the gospel, he did not need the gospel, and every one else can be saved as he was; and hence the gospel is of no use to any one, and the gentleman may go back to Indiana, and no longer trouble himself to preach a gospel that is of no use to any one, even admitting that he preaches the gospel.

But he quotes, "What God hath cleansed, call not thou common or unclean;" and he says the Gentiles were already cleansed, and he makes cleansing mean salvation; and hence he proves that they were saved before Peter went there. But if he is right, the angel was wrong when he told Cornelius that Peter would tell him words by which he should be saved. There is no dodging this. This expression was undoubtedly to show Peter that the Gentiles were no longer to be denied the privileges of the gospel. If he is correct, they were saved, and yet without hope and without God in the world. They were saved, and not a people of God. This was strange salvation.

But we are redeemed by the blood of Christ. Yes, his chosen few were redeemed, but no one else. I say all were redeemed alike. He is the propitiation for the sins of the whole world. We are saved by grace, by Christ, by his blood, by his name, by faith, by works; and even baptism saves us. His idea is a very strange one—if the blood of Christ cleanses from all sin, nothing else can have anything to do with it. Suppose I say I live by breathing, by eating, by sleeping, by exercise—it is all true; but it is not true that I live by any one thing to the exclusion of everything else. Salvation by the blood of Christ excludes nothing else connected with salvation. If a man is saved at all, all the elements of salvation are presumed to be present, whether mentioned or not. A place for everything, and everything in its place. "God so loved the world that he gave his only begotten Son, that whosoever believeth in him might not perish, but have everlasting life;" and in this sense we may say we have no chance of salvation but by grace—God through Christ provided the means. We are saved by the blood of Christ. The blood of animals could not take away sins, hence Christ died for the redemption of the transgressions that were under the first testament, as well as for our sins today, and through his blood we have the only sin-offering that could forever take away sin. But we are saved by the name of Christ. In his name there is power and authority. By his authority salvation is proclaimed to the world—in his name, demons and evil spirits were cast out. Paul said to the spirit of divination, in the name of Jesus Christ, "Come out of her," and he came out the same hour; and there is no other name given by which we can be saved. We are to do all in his name; but does that exclude human agency? Every thing we do as obedience is done in his name—that is, because he commanded it; hence we are saved by grace, by the blood of Christ, by his name, and by obedience to the gospel, but by no one item to the exclusion of other things commanded by divine authority. "By grace are ye saved through faith; and that not of yourselves: it is the gift of God;" and my friend insists that faith is the gift of God. Faith comes by hearing—hearing the testimony. "These things are written that ye might believe, and that believing, ye might have life through his name."

He goes to Titus 3:5 again. I have already explained this, so that I suppose every one here understands it except Elder Herod. He has a false theory in his head, and he must have a false construction of this and many other passages to sustain his theory. If he would shape his theory by the Bible, in place of making the Bible bend to suit his theory, he would perhaps see things very differently. As long as he looks at the Bible through a perverted theory, he will not be likely to understand it. According to his mercy he saves us. Certainly not by works of righteousness which we have done, but according to his mercy. No man can deserve salvation. It is only according to his mercy he saves us; but how does he save us according to his mercy? By the washing of regeneration and renewing of the Holy Spirit. This beautifully chimes in with John 3:5: "Except a man be born of water and of the Spirit, he cannot enter into the kingdom of God." I have invited him to tell us what this means, but he has not done it. Now it is too late for him to tell us, As I could not reply to him. It has been my custom to present, in my last speech on a proposition, a resume of the entire argument; but he has not noticed or attempted to reply to my affirmative argument presented in my first speech. He has not taken up a single passage presented in that speech and attempted to show that it does not prove what I claimed for it; hence that speech stands unimpeached, and it was wholly unnecessary that I should repeat it. On this proposition, we have really had no debate, except as I have taken up his proofs and replied to him. He has not replied to me, or tried to do it; and I think he has had good reasons for not attempting it. He could not reply, for the reason that my positions are true and admit of no reply. My arguments have been founded upon the rock of God's eternal truth, and he saw very clearly that it would be madness and folly to hurl the shafts of error against them, to be broken into atoms in his hands; hence he very shrewdly kept away from them.

(Time expired.)

Elder Herod's Closing Reply.

BROS. moderator, ladies and gentlemen: —I am again before you, according to the rule, to close the discussion of the first proposition. The custom has generally been that the affirmant should have fifteen minutes at the close to sum up the testimony, but he has no right to introduce new matter.

(Brents): "I never heard of such a custom, nor was I ever at a debate—my own or any other—where such a custom prevailed. There is no such custom where I have been."

(Herod): Owing to the rule by which we have agreed to be governed, it becomes my duty to make the closing speech upon the present proposition, and as a matter of course I need not introduce any new matter. Much more has been introduced to review than I could review, were I permitted to do so in two hours.

I expect to commence about where I closed in last speech. I want to call the attention of the congregation to the utter failure of my friend to do what he promised to do—to establish, by testimony, that there was a single proof of the baptism of the Pentecostians. I know that there was water there; and he finally said that he had abundance of historical proofs that there was water there—that he could establish the fact by living witnesses. If that is the way we are to prove or to determine the question, it would do; but I think if he called certain ones, it would be seen that the proof must come from King James' version. I do not object to the opinion of a lady or gentleman; but we don't propose to determine the question by their opinion. His word is that water baptism was administered there, and he showed that its many as gladly received Peter's words were baptized; but there was a baptism promised for that occasion that did not have any water in it I tell you that, if water baptism was in order to the remission, then remission of sins was because of baptism; now can you tell me what use the blood of Christ would be? Just ponder that in your minds for a time. Please find a place for it.

Every one can see, because my Brother would readily acknowledge what I introduced yesterday from the epistle to the Hebrews, that "without the shedding of blood there is no remission." You are independent of the blood of Christ. You can go to hell or heaven, which you please; and you are free agents, as he says, you need not go to either place. I am summing up now. If you are a free agent, you need not go. We should look to the force of a conclusion. I speak to the ladies and gentleman—it would be deleterious to your best interest. He says you can just go to heaven, or you can let it alone. The way to go there is to do good. Do you desire me to show you the result of your proposition? "There is none that doeth good; no, not one." I take the position that he occupies—

if you want to go there, do good; then I turn right around, and read, "there is none that seeketh after God. There is none righteous; no, not one." Here a deluge comes on every one of you.

I am not mistaken. I said that the blood of Jesus Christ cleanses us from all sin. It will, if we will let it! You have to get up and apply it! Your God is an utter failure. You see the cause of it yourself. He died to save you, and if you are not pardoned you will be lost. I now submit the force of such an argument.

In the ministry of the grace of God (Acts 10:, 11:), he said Bro. Herod ought to have got them up. There was not a gospel sermon preached over there, you see. Just to see where the force of the proposition would be by the force of the passage upon which he relies, he said, "Send now to Peter." Now, was it my acts that you me to do? If you will repent, and get some one to baptize you, I will save you. I recognize this question as having more importance connected with it than any other in the city of Franklin today. Is it the purpose of God, or not? That is the issue. I try to honor God and glorify him. I have had passage after passage up here that has not been answered. Then he comes to Acts 2: He turns round in a personal attack on my beauty—I have never heard it called in question before to-day.

I love gentlemen and love ladies, and I will never inflict the judges with the painful necessity of calling me to order for personal insinuations. I want to get your minds off this to the proposition.

Let us carry out the argument further. I will remember the rule that it governs my action in this matter. I call your attention to some other facts now. We have had up almost every passage now that would seem pertinent to this point. The conclusion I have just referred to, that repentance and remission of sins shall be preached in his name. He advances and translates them, and comes down to Acts 2: It implies that they were baptized with water! It can't be settled with that kind of logic.

He said that Peter said that baptism was to save. I will tell what he did say, that he commanded them to be baptized at the house of Cornelius. He commanded them to be baptized in the name of the Lord Jesus. We have that up again. I want Peter to give the exposition. It was the first accession ever made from the Gentile world. In the third chapter of his first letter, he says: "When once the long-suffering of God waited in the days of Noah, while the ark was a preparing, wherein few, that is, eight souls, were saved by water, the like figure whereunto baptism doth also now save us." Where does the sin lie?

(Brents): "I introduced this passage and I made my argument on it in my first speech; he has not attempted to answer it until now. Under our rule, I submit that he cannot do it now unless be gives me time to rejoin."

(The moderators decided that he might quote without comment.)

I will therefore only quote the passage as I have introduced it. Peter said it saves; I am only calling it up to look at it in the light in which it has been raised. "The like figure whereunto even baptism doth also now save us (not the putting away of the filth of the flesh, but the answer of a good conscience toward God) by the resurrection of Jesus Christ." That is it. Every one can see it, and I am satisfied to let it pass off in the matter that has been in review on this occasion.

We next propose to show that the passage in Timothy is to show that to save from sin, no act that we can perform will serve. To Paul's son Timothy, on the question of getting rid of sin, he says, "Who gave himself for us." Now, what for? Every single one of you answer the question alike. If he gave himself for us, he had an object in doing it: and that raises the question as to what that object was. I repeat the language of the apostle to the Gentiles —if I can't show you why, then it was useless—"That he might redeem us from all iniquity."

Yes; but he says you can't get the benefit of that unless you go to work. I want everybody to listen to the force of the argument that is found in the verse of his own passage—" Who gave himself for us, that he might redeem us." Now, if God did that, is it left for you and me to do? And he says you can't show where God saved any one, without that one doing something for himself. 11. Timothy: If he hadn't challenged me in his last speech, I have no idea I should have referred to it. To his Son: "A partaker of the afflictions of the gospel according to the power of God; who hath saved us, and called us with a holy calling, not according to our works, but according to his own purpose and grace, which was given us in Christ Jesus before the world began; but is now made manifest by the appearing of our Saviour Jesus Christ."

Now I submit the question, Did salvation take place before it was revealed, or afterward? The answer of everyone is, it could not have been revealed unless it had been an existing fact; and I read the paragraph showing the object and the end to be accomplished by the epistle. "Who hath saved us and called us with a holy calling, not according to our works, but according to his own purpose and grace which was given us in Christ Jesus before the world began." Was any thing done before that? No; nothing till you do it! Now, my friends, I know that I have not much more time; I must make a few brief remarks, and close. "The Scriptures teach that salvation from sin is conditional, the conditions to be complied with by the sinner, in order to obtain salvation or freedom from sin." Has one passage out of fifty had any reference to salvation from sin?

I have introduced more than forty passages to show that Christ is the Saviour; and I repeat, and have done so all the time, that the proposition must fail for want of Scripture testimony. It is a struggle between human salvation and the salvation of Jesus Christ.

I want to know the conclusion. How are we to go away from here with nothing but a sneer for Jesus Christ? You come to us in our sins, who have never saved any one at all. Contrast it with your experience, and I will be satisfied with the conclusion.

The brother has endeavored to prove his way of salvation. I have submitted the finality of the question. Take it, and ponder it; try it by the Bible; and if you have come to the conclusion, by Scripture testimony, that it is no longer true that Jesus Christ is the way to heaven, or that he is the way to hell both, I fall by the testimony of the Bible, "Neither is there salvation in any other name given among men, whereby we must be saved."

If by the acts of all these men everyone saves himself, why didn't the Lord stay in heaven and enjoy the communion with his Father, instead of suffering, and dying, and rising a victorious conqueror? These are the conclusions to be settled by the Bible. If I was convinced that his theory is true, I would never name the Lord Jesus Christ again. I would tell you that it is in your own hands, and if you ever get to heaven it will be, not unto Jesus be all the glory, but unto man—poor, frail man. He will be entitled to the glory of his own salvation.

(Time expired.)

Second Proposition.

The Scriptures teach the unconditional election and salvation from sin, by Jesus Christ, of all his seed or generation.

Opening Speech of Elder Herod.

BROS. MODERATOR AND JUDGES, LADIES AND GENTLEMEN! —I am before you this morning for the purpose of attending to the affirmative argument, and in presenting myself before you as an affirmant to-day our portions have changed. For the past two days my worthy opponent has been affirming and I have been defending; to-day and to-morrow I am to affirm and he is to defend. And I frankly confers that I am to affirm what is taught in my proposition. I am to prove my proposition by the Scriptures. No other proof is admissible here. I want no other, for I need no other; and I shall not introduce any other.

It would hardly be worthwhile for me to announce the proposition, but I will read it:

"The Scriptures teach the unconditional election and salvation from sin, by Jesus Christ, of all his seed or generation."

Not a lady or gentleman that has heard this proposition but readily sees my duties upon this occasion. And I am fully aware that this great subject under discussion is of vast importance. You all see its importance, and the expressive anxiety on your faces shows that you are all intensely interested in a subject of so much importance as the one under investigation this morning.

1. Is salvation a fact?
2. If salvation is a fact, is there a Saviour?
3. If there is a Saviour, who is it?
4. Who is to be saved, and from what are they to be saved?

All the passages I shall introduce shall be upon the subject. I intend to stick to the subject under discussion. I will not ramble about like my worthy opponent has been doing on his proposition. I intend to confine myself to the subject, and then I shall not have time to introduce one-half of the testimony that might be introduced on this occasion. I acknowledge that I ought to give chapter and verse for all my proof. This is right, and I always want to do right.

With this I now proceed to introduce my proof, and I will begin with the twenty-third Psalm of David. I will read it all, and I want everybody to give attention to the reading, for it is just what I want, to prove my proposition. Now listen—let all listen:

"The Lord is my shepherd; I shall not want. He maketh me to lie down in green pastures: he leadeth me beside the still waters. He restoreth my soul: he leadeth me in the paths of righteousness for his name's sake." Was it for the sinner's name's sake? or for the Lord's name's sake? I know you all see this now. I will read on: "Yea, though I walk through the valley of the shadow of death, I will fear no evil: for thou art with me; thy rod and thy staff they comfort me. Thou preparest a table before me in the presence of mine enemies: thou anointest my head with oil; my cup runneth over. Surely goodness and mercy shall follow me all the days of my life: and I will dwell in the house of the Lord forever."

Is not this the truth? Do you not believe it? Respond in your own hearts if David did not tell the truth. This is the most solemn thought I ever contemplated. I never saw a people more attentive than you are at this moment. If David told the truth, and God followed him all the days of his life with mercy, then I ask if he did not have a God without conditions.

I now proceed to introduce additional proof from the same author. Psalm 33:11-13. Everybody listen to the reading. I will not be in a hurry. I will begin with the 11th verse I could read all this without looking at it, and read better than I can with one eye, for that is all I have.

Psalm 33: I cannot read it all, it would be too tedious: "The counsel of the Lord standeth forever, the thoughts of his heart to all generations. Blessed is the nation whose God is the Lord; and the people whom he hath chosen for his own inheritance. The Lord looketh from heaven; he beholdeth all the sons of men." Here we find a people chosen by the Lord for his own inheritance. When did this choosing take place? I turn to Eph. 1:3-11, and I find the answer to be before the foundation of the world. I will read it to you. Now listen everybody to the reading:

"Blessed be the God and Father of our Lord Jesus Christ, who hath blessed us with all spiritual blessings in heavenly places in Christ: according as he hath chosen us in him before the foundation of the world." Now stop right there. Does the Bible read that way? Yes. I will read it again: "According as he hath chosen us in him before the foundation of the world." Well, I never knew the Bible read that way before. Well, it reads just that way whether you knew it or not. "According as he hath chosen us in him before the foundation of the world, that we should be holy and without blame before him in love: having predestinated us unto the adoption of children by Jesus Christ to himself, according to the good pleasure of his will, to the praise of the glory of his grace, wherein he hath made us accepted in the beloved; in whom we have redemption through his blood, the forgiveness of sins, according to the riches of his grace; wherein he has abounded toward us in all wisdom and prudence; having made known unto us the mystery of his will, according to his good pleasure which he purposed in himself; that in the dispensation of the fullness of times he might gather together in one all things in

Christ, both which are in heaven, and which are on earth; even in him: in whom also we have obtained an inheritance, being predestinated according to the purpose of him who worketh all things after the counsel of his own will."

I now submit this question. By whose purpose—by the good pleasure of whom—by the counsel of whose will, was all this accomplished? Now, is this all done by the good pleasure of the sinner's will? No, it is done by the good pleasure of his will, the Lord's will, and is not the result of any act performed by the sinner, either directly or indirectly.

We now call Peter to the stand. What do you know about it, Peter? Whom are you going to talk to? and what are you going to talk about? Let us read. Now listen, everybody, to the reading: 1 Pet. 1:1, 2: "Peter, an apostle of Jesus Christ, to the strangers scattered throughout Pontus, Galatia, Cappadocia, Asia, and Bithynia, elect according to the foreknowledge of God, the Father, through sanctification of the Spirit, unto obedience and sprinkling of the blood of Jesus Christ; grace unto you, and peace be multiplied."

Now I want everyone in this house to know that I am for obedience. I believe in obedience; but I want to know when the obedience comes. Does it come before or after election. Election produces obedience. Peter says we are elected unto obedience. Obedience has nothing to do with the election.

I now go to 1 Pet. 2:9: Why do I want this? Because Peter is talking about just what I am talking about. Now this gives him good time to note it down. Now, then, listen to the reading of the passage:

"But ye are a chosen generation, a royal priesthood, a holy nation, a peculiar people; that ye should show forth the praises of him who hath called you out of darkness into his marvelous light"

I now have your attention upon these words, "chosen generation," "a peculiar people," "a holy nation." Now take these in connection with what the Psalmist David said, as quoted before:

"The counsel of the Lord standeth forever, the thoughts of his heart to all generations. Blessed is the nation whose God is the Lord; and the people whom he hath chosen for his own inheritance."

I now want to call your attention again to these words—what are they? The royal, chosen generation of Christ, Paul says, that they were chosen in Christ before the world was, and David says they were his inheritance; will he get them? My friend says, "Yes, if they will let him;" as if God were going to let a little stub of a sinner about three feet high, capsize God, take him prisoner, and thwart his purposes as easily as a man can change the hands on the face of a clock. I would scorn to worship such a God as this. God has a chosen generation—an inheritance; and it does not take the efforts of Herod or Brents to go about administering the ordinances to bring them to him.

They charge me with being a Calvinist. I am so far from believing the doctrine of Calvinism that I despise it—I scorn it. But my opponent will say that these, in time past, were not a people. Well, where did they come from? Where did this long race of Adam come from? One will say, "I make myself." Well, if I were to say that I made myself, you would think me a fit subject for the lunatic asylum. But what was I talking about? I stay with the subject. Where did all these bright and smiling faces come from? I want you to take all this down; I want you to take it all home with you. Where did they come from? They came from Adam. We were all once in Adam. Let us read Gen. 5:1, 2. Listen to the rending:

"This is the book of the generation of Adam. In the day that God created man, in the likeness of God made he him; male and female created he them, and blessed them, and called their name Adam in the day when they were created."

Did God say anything to them about getting religion, or about multiplying or replenishing heaven or hell? I will get some to hell before I am done—you need not be uneasy about that; many will go there. Adam was to multiply and replenish the earth—not one word about heaven or hell.

Now let us see. I call your attention right over to the New Testament—Matt. 1:1. Now you have it all fixed in your mind about Adam. He came from the dust of the earth, and will go back to dust. Can any one return to that in which he has never been? But what are the words of this book? "The book of the generation of Jesus Christ." My opponent has, for the last two days, been talking about men and women going to heaven! Jesus was the product of the angel; men and women are the product of Adam. Now, if the product of Adam be like him, will not the product of Christ be like him? Did they not come from where he came from? Peter says, "Ye are a chosen generation "—not Adam's generation, but the generation of Jesus Christ. Now we go to Isa. 48:9-11: "For my name's sake [not the sinner's name sake] will I defer mine anger, and for my praise will I refrain for thee, that I cut thee not off. Behold, I have refined thee, but not with silver; I have chosen thee in the fun ace of affliction. For mine own sake [not the winner's sake], even for mine own sake, will I do it; for how should my name be polluted? and I will not give my glory unto another."

Now I ask you if I would be justified in getting up here and saying, "He will do it, if you will do something?" He said it was for his own sake, and not for the sinner's sake, or for the sake of anything done by him If you had to do something, it would be, "I have hired the Lord to save me." I have read of some who made merchandise of the gospel, going round peddling it out as you would sell patent medicine; and when you do it, you make the gospel contemptible.

Now I want Rom. 11:27-29: "For this is my covenant unto them, when I shall take away their sins." So I have the words, "take away sins." This means salvation. The next has reference to the elect; and I call the attention of everybody to the leading. Listen, now: "As concerning the gospel, they are enemies for your sakes; but as touching the election, they are beloved for the fathers' sakes; for the gifts and calling of God are without repentance."

I call attention of everybody to the conclusion of the last paragraph, for it is an exact refutation of everything that has been presented by my worthy opponent for the last two days. Paul says the gifts and calling of God are without repentance—not bought by repentance.

Let us now go to Rom. 11:1-8: "I say then, Hath God cast away his people? God forbid. For I also am an Israelite, of the seed of Abraham, of the tribe of Benjamin. God hath not cast away his people which he foreknew. Wot ye not what the scripture saith of Elias? how he maketh intercession to God against Israel, saying, Lord, they have killed thy prophets, and digged down thine altars; and I am left alone, and they seek my life. But what saith the answer of God unto him? I have reserved to myself seven thousand men, who have not bowed the knee to the image of Baal. Even so then at this present time, also there is a remnant according to the election of grace. And if by grace, then is it no more of works: otherwise grace is no more grace. But if it be of works, then is it no more grace: otherwise work is no more work. What then? Israel hath not obtained that which he seeketh for: but the election hath obtained it, and the rest were blinded (According as it is written, God hath given them the spirit of slumber, eyes that they should not see, and ears that they should not hear;) unto this day."

He reserved seven thousand to himself, and even so at this time I have reserved a remnant according to the election of grace. A remnant reserved, how? According to what you have done? That is the way my opponent would have it. It is by grace, and Paul says if it is by grace it is not by works. Which will you believe, Herod, or Brents, or the apostle Paul? I would ask you to believe the apostle. He talks of freedom of will—free agency. Their wills did not exist then, and had nothing to do with it. They had no agency in the matter.

Now I want Romans 9:6: "For they are not all Israel which are of Israel." Note this, for it has the whole proposition in it. Now, I want you to tell me just what that seed is. Well, I will read it to you in the seventh and eighth verses of the ninth chapter of Romans. All listen to the reading: "Neither, because they are the seed of Abraham, are they all children: but, In Isaac shall thy seed be called. That is, they which are the children of the flesh, these are not the children of God: but the children of the promise are counted for the seed." Well, that is plain enough about the seed; now we want to know about the promise and the election. "For this is the word of promise, At this time will I come, and Sarah shall have a son. And not only this; but when Rebecca also had conceived by one, even by our father Isaac; (for the children being not yet born, neither having done any good or evil, that the purpose of God according to election might stand, not of works, but of him that calleth,) it was said unto her, The elder shall serve the younger. As it is written, Jacob have I loved, but Esau have I hated."

You talk about the children of Adam being the children of God! Paul says the children of the flesh are not counted for the seed, but in "Isaac shall thy seed be called." My proposition talks about a seed, doesn't it? and about an election? Here I have them both, all plain and easy enough, and no trouble about them.

Now, I want a little more from Romans 11:5, 6. "Even so then at this present time also there is a remnant," not according to the election of grace, but according to what they do. Does it read that way? It ought to say that, to prove my friend's position; and if it had said that, we would not have been here today in this debate.

But let us read it as it is, without transposing it. "Even so then at this present time also there is a remnant according to the election of grace. And if by grace, then it is no more of works: otherwise grace is no more grace. But if it be of works, then it is no more grace: otherwise work is no more work."

Strange and astonishing that all this was addressed by the apostle to a church, and still it means by works, just the opposite of what the apostle so clearly teaches. "So, then, it is not of him that willeth, nor of him that runneth, but of God that sheweth mercy" (Rom. 9:16). Now, does everybody believe this? My friend thinks that the sinner must will and run, too, if he is ever saved. His will must be consulted, and he must get his own consent, and then he must run to the pool or branch and get a second party to shew mercy by putting him in, or there is no salvation for him!

I now call attention to Rom. 8:33, and my object in calling attention to this is because the word elect is found in it. "Who shall lay anything to the charge of God's elect? It is God that justifieth." Why can we not complain because of the election? Because it is God that justifieth, and no man has a right to complain at what he does. Has he not a right to justify whom he will? It is not only God that justifieth, but it is Christ that condemneth. He brought them down with him; and he will bring them up with him in the resurrection. If I don't prove that he will bring them up, I will give of the question. To do this, I want 2 Tim. 2:8-11: "Remember that Jesus Christ of the seed of David was raised from the dead according to my gospel; wherein I suffer trouble as an evil doer, even unto bonds; but the word of God is not bound. Therefore, I endure all things for the elect's sakes, that they may also obtain the salvation which is in Christ Jesus with eternal glory. It is a faithful saying; for if we be dead with him, we shall also live with him."

My brother thinks that unless they have done something there will be no resurrection for them.

(Brents): "Will you please give me the chapter and verse again of the Scripture last read? I failed to get it."

(Herod): "Yes, sir; it is 2 Tim. 2:8-11."

(Brents): "Thank you, sir."

(Herod): "You are welcome. That is my pride, to be ready to give chapter and verse at any time."

Now listen, everybody, for I am not done with that yet. I now want Titus 1:1-3: "Paul, a servant of God, and an apostle of Jesus Christ according to the faith of God's elect, and the acknowledging of the truth which is after godliness, in hope of eternal life, which God, that cannot lie, promised before the world began; but hath in due time manifested his word through preaching, which is committed unto me according to the commandment of God our Saviour."

The apostle here speaks of God's elect; and his elect had a faith; and they had hope of eternal life; and God, that cannot lie, promised it to them before the world began. Now there had to be an elect people before the elect could have faith or hope either. The faith did not produce the election, but the election produced the faith. The hope of eternal life did not secure the election, but the election produces the hope of eternal life. The election was first; then faith, hope and love followed, as the fruits of election.

My worthy opponent would reverse all this order of things, which had its origin in divine sovereignty. He would try to make you believe that things which man does secures 'the election;' but the inspired apostle did not understand the subject as my worthy friend seems to teach it. Being guided by wisdom from on high, he had clear conceptions of the purposes of our heavenly Father, and could not go wrong. Now, will you believe Herod, or Elder Brents, or the inspired apostle? I advise you to believe the apostle.

Now you see I stick to the subject. I don't beat the bush around, and give you my explanations and opinions; but I read it to you right out of the book. If I had not read it right out of the Bible, you would not have been so interested as you are at this moment. This is a great question, and you are all interested when I read it in the word of God, so that you can all understand it, Herod might make a mistake, but the apostle Paul made no mistakes, he could not make mistakes, as Herod and Brents are liable to do. I advise everybody to believe him.

(Time expired).

Dr. Brents' First Reply.

Mr. president:—I am here to deny the proposition under discussion, and in this attitude it becomes my duty to reply to the speech of the affirmant, to which you have just listened. This I propose to do. I will not treat him as he did me on the previous proposition. He seemed to feel under no obligations to meet a single argument I made, or to show that my proofs did not prove what I claimed for them.

He did not attempt to define his own proposition, or a single term in it. His first proof was the twenty-third Psalm, which he read entire, and what he read it for or intended to do with it, I was entirely unable to see.

There is not a single word in it about election, either conditional or unconditional. He speaks of the marked attention given by the audience to the reading. I guess they were straining their imagination to discover what connection this Scripture had with his proposition. If he will magnify his argument until I can see it I will with much pleasure attend to it.

He next introduced Psalm 33:11-13, in which the Psalmist speaks of a people chosen by the Lord for his inheritance, and then went to Eph. 1:3-11 to prove that this people were chosen in Christ before the foundation of the world. If I were to admit all he claims for these passages, the admission would do him no good, for he does not pretend to claim, and certainly did not attempt to prove, that the election was unconditional. This he must do, or fail to sustain his proposition; and I now challenge him to show any provisions made for his salvation, or the salvation of any other man, that were not made for all men on the same conditions on which he may he saved himself; whether the provisions of salvation were made before the foundation of the world, or at any other time. Does my opponent mean to say that God unconditionally elected a certain portion of the human family to salvation before the foundation of the world?

(Herod.—"No, no.")

Then you give up your proposition, for this is just what you are here to prove. But let us read the passage and emphasize the pronouns we and it, indicating the persons of whom the apostle was speaking:

"Blessed be the God and Father of our Lord Jesus Christ, who hath blessed us with all spiritual blessing in heavenly places in Christ: according as he hath chosen us in him before the foundation of the world, that we should be holy and without blame before him in love: having predestinated us unto the adoption of children by Jesus Christ unto himself, according to the good pleasure of his will, to the praise of the glory of his grace, wherein he hath made us accepted in the beloved: in whom we have redemption through his blood, the forgiveness of sins, according to the riches of his grace; wherein he hath abounded toward us in all wisdom and prudence; having made known unto us the mystery of his will, according to his good pleasure which he hath purposed in himself: that in the dispensation of the fulness of times he might gather together in one all things in Christ, both which are in heaven, and which are on earth: even in him: in whom also we have obtained an inheritance, being predestinated according to the purpose of him who worketh all things after the counsel of his own will; that we should be to the praise of his glory, who first trusted in Christ. In whom ye also trusted, after that ye heard the word of truth, the gospel of your salvation: in whom also, after that ye believed, ye were sealed with the Holy Spirit of promise" (Eph. 1:3-13).

Now if the we and us chosen in Christ before the foundation of the world include all the elect, and the entire elect first trusted in Christ, then who were the ye who also trusted after they heard and believed the gospel? To this question we invite the special attention of our friend, and we most earnestly request him not to forget to attend to it.

In the 8th, 9th and 10th verses we have a pointer to the solution of the trouble; "Wherein he hath abounded toward us in all wisdom and prudence; having made known unto us the mystery of his will, according to his good pleasure which he hath purposed in himself." He hath made known unto us the mystery. Yea, and what was the mystery? "That in the fulness of times he might gather together in one all things in Christ." Now, then, to whom did he make known this mystery? "By revelation he made known unto me the mystery: as I wrote afore in few words; whereby, when ye read, ye may understand my knowledge in the mystery of Christ, which in other ages was not made known unto the sons of men, as it is now revealed unto his holy apostles and prophets by the Spirit." Then these holy apostles and prophets were the persons chosen before the foundation of the world, to whom God abounded in all wisdom and prudence, and to whom he made known the mystery of his will. But what was that mystery? "That the Gentiles should be fellow heirs, and of the same body, and partakers of his promise in Christ by the gospel" (Eph. 3:3-6). This shows what he meant when he said (1:10) that in the dispensation of the fulness of times he might gather together in one all things in Christ, and the apostle prosecutes his argument to its culmination in chap. 4:4-C, which we read, and paraphrase as we read: "There is one body," made up of Jews and Gentiles, "and one Spirit," in this one body, which is the temple of the Holy Spirit, "even as ye are called in one hope of your calling." The Gentiles were without hope, but now they have hope in common with the Jews. "One Lord," who died for all, whether Jews or Gentiles; and "one faith, required of all in this one Lord who died for all; and "one baptism," required in the commission to be administered to all nations in the name of the Father, and of the Son, and of the Holy Spirit; and "one God and Father of all," whether Jews or Gentiles, for though the Gentiles were once without God in the world, the same Lord is rich unto all that call upon him, and in every nation he that feareth God and worketh righteousness is accepted with him.

In the second chapter, verses 12 and 13, Paul says that the Ephesians were once "without Christ, being aliens from the commonwealth of Israel, and strangers from the covenants of promise, having no hope and without God in the world; but now, in Christ Jesus, ye who sometime were far off are made nigh by the blood of Christ," Now, will my worthy opponent harmonize this language from the second chapter, with his construction of Paul's language in the first chapter. When was it that those elected in Christ Jesus before the foundation of the world was laid were without Christ, without hope, and without God in the world? Please don't forget to explain this, for this people want light along here.

He next went to 1 Pet. 1:1-3, where Peter speaks of persons who were "elect according to the foreknowledge of God the Father, through sanctification of the Spirit unto obedience and sprinkling of the blood of Jesus Christ;" and insists that the election preceded the obedience unto which they were elected. Well, we suppose all who are elected at all are elected unto obedience—but is this proof that they had done nothing before election? In the ninth verse, Peter speaks of their salvation as the end of their faith; and in the 22nd verse he says they had purified their souls in obeying the truth. Does my friend believe that God elects persons to salvation whose souls are not purified? We have a very similar expression from Paul (2 Thes. 2:13), where he says, "God hath from the beginning chosen you to salvation through sanctification of the spirit and belief of the truth." Did Paul preach one gospel and Peter another? We suppose not. Then belief of the truth is something that has to be done by the sinner that he may be chosen or elected to salvation. He must believe the truth and purify his soul in obeying it, in order to be chosen.

But our opponent next goes to 1 Pet. 2:9: "Ye are a chosen generation, a royal priesthood, a holy nation, a peculiar people that ye should show forth the praises of him who hath called you out of darkness into his marvelous light;" and he feels strong in the words "chosen generation," though he finds not a word about how they were chosen, whether with or without conditions. This he ignores all the way through.

But he is most unfortunate in the selection of his proofs—every one that bears upon the subject at all is against him. In this quotation he saw trouble ahead, and tried to anticipate me. I asked him a number of questions in my opening speech without anticipating his answers. If he would be kind enough to let me state my own positions, I would be obliged to him. He might find employment in stating his own positions, if he could be induced to take any. If he could be induced to reply to my arguments after I have made them myself, it would be a decided improvement on his past course.

He read, "Which in time past were not a people, but are now the people of God; which had not obtained mercy, but now have obtained mercy" (ver. 10). Then he went to Gen. 5:1, and talked about the generation of Adam, as though those who were not a people, and had not obtained mercy, were the seed of Adam, and his chosen generation were not. But we cannot let the gentleman escape so easily. The very same persons who were the chosen generation of the ninth verse, were those who in time past were not a people, but then were the people of God of the tenth verse. Now I want to know when the eternally elect in Christ were not the people of God—will he tell us? I want to get close to him here. I am willing to fight it out over this passage selected by himself. Will he meet me in a close grapple over it? It is not enough to say they came from Adam—who did not come from Adam? Did he not come from Adam? Whether these came from Adam, God, or the devil, the same persons, the very same, who constitute the chosen generation, had, in time past, been not a people, but then were the people of God; who had not obtained mercy, but then had obtained mercy. When had the eternally and unconditionally elected in Christ not obtained mercy? Will he tell us? I predict that we will not hear from him main on this passage. We shall see.

He scouts the idea of men and women going to heaven or hell, and quotes the first section of the first verse of Matthew, "The book of the generation of Jesus Christ." He says the generation of Adam — were those generated by Adam. Men and women came from Adam —were made of dust and will go back to dust; and he seems to think that the generation of Jesus Christ were begotten by him literally like Adam's generation were begotten by him. I hope he will develop his theory more fully along here, for as yet it is about as clear as well-stirred mud. Because Matthew introduces his gospel with an account of the genealogy of Jesus Christ, and gives the names of his ancestry, that it might be seen that he came of the lineage predicted by the prophets in confirmation of his divine character, he seizes upon the words, "The book of the generation of Jesus Christ," and reasons that it means children literally begotten by Jesus Christ independent of all connection with men and women. I have heard many perversions of Scripture, but this construction of Matt. 1:1 puts the cap-atone on the climax of all the absurdity I ever heard before. Does he not see the names of men in the generation of Jesus Christ following right along after the words he quotes? Were not Abraham, Isaac and Jacob men? and does he not see their names following the generation of Jesus Christ quoted by him? Jesus Christ was son of man as well as Son of God. He selected men to preach the gospel to men and women, and when the Samaritans believed Philip preaching the things concerning the kingdom of God and the name of Jesus Christ, they were baptized, both men and women. What a waste of labor for men and women to trouble themselves about being baptized, as they return to dust, and that is the end of them! How do you know? Elder Herod says so, and he knows.

He says the elect are God's inheritance, and then asks, with a sneer, "Will he get them? Yes, if they will let him! A little stub of a sinner, three feet high, capsizes God, takes him prisoner, and thwarts his purposes." This settles it!!

Does he mean that God will force salvation on the elect, whether they are willing or not? Jesus Christ commanded the gospel to be preached to every creature in all the world, and promise salvation to them who would believe and obey it—was he mocking them by offering them that which they could not accept? He threatened to damn every one who would not believe; and yet, if Elder Herod is right, they are sure to be damned, whether they believe or not--unless they were elected to salvation before the foundation of the world. The will of man has nothing to do with it. Jesus says, "Come unto me, all ye that labor and are heavy laden, and I will give you rest." Mr. Herod says, "Yes, if you are of the elect; none others can come. God never loved any others; Jesus never died for any others. No others have any interest in his blood or any chance to be saved by it." God says, "Whosoever will, let him come." Elder Herod says no little stub of a sinner can be consulted in God's arrangement. Jesus says, "Ye will not come unto me, that ye might have life: how oft would I have gathered you together, but ye would not;" but Elder Herod asks, "Can a sinner thwart God's purposes?" ALL this is the merest clap-trap. God never purposed to save any one contrary to his will, or a rebel against him. He is the author of eternal salvation to all who obey him—yes, all who obey him—but not another one. Jesus is able to save to the uttermost, those who come to God by him; but they must come—he is not going to conscript them into his service, that he may save them.

Elder Herod says if the Bible had read in a certain way as he "transposed" it, he would not have been here in this debate with me. Well, why is he here debating with me? If he is right, no heresy of mine can endanger the salvation of any one, nor can any truth he has learned be instrumental in saving any one.

But it seems to me that the devil outsharped the Lord on Elder Herod's theory. God fixed up the matter before the world was or man existed. He gave his Son a small, select, party, on condition that the Son would give his life for them; and he gave the devil the far larger portion "free," on the ground of pure favoritism. Do you call this ridicule? Not so. If it does not, in all earnestness, correctly represent his theory, then I confess my inability to understand him. Why does he go about preaching this doctrine? If it is true, his preaching can do no good, nor can his silence do any harm. The salvation of every person (I must not say man or woman) who will be saved at all, was saved before time began, and all others will be damned in spite of any thing they can do; not for any fault of their own, but because there never was any provisions made for them—they never had opportunity to be saved.

But he says, "It is God that showeth mercy." Certainly it is. Who else can show mercy? No one expects mercy from the devil; but does God show mercy on conditions to be complied with by man, or does he show mercy unconditionally? This is the issue between us.

My friend represents me as thinking that unless men and women have done something, they will not be resurrected. Well, he do n't believe men and women will be resurrected at all, do or not do. He says they came from Adam, were made of dust, and will return to dust—and that ends the Adam man. Paul says, "As in Adam all die, even so in Christ shall all be made alive" (1 Cor. 15:22). I believe it; does he?

But I am not quite sure that I understand him. He seemed to imply that I think there will be no resurrection for him who does not obey the gospel. If this is not what he means, I can see no propriety in his reference to the subject at all. I have already quoted Jesus as saying that they who have done good will be resurrected to life, and they who have done evil will be resurrected to damnation. This clearly shows that men will be raised, whether they obey the gospel or not; but it also shows that unless they have done good (which includes obeying the gospel), they cannot be saved or raised to life. This crushes into nothingness his whole theory of unconditional salvation.

But he next refers us to Isa. xlviii, 9-11: "For my name's sake will I defer mine anger, and for my praise will I refrain for thee, that I cut thee not off. Behold, I have refined thee, but not with silver; I have chosen thee in the furnace of affliction. For mine own sake, even for mine own sake, will I do it: for how should my name be polluted? and I will not give my glory unto another."

If he had read the next verse, he would have found that this was spoken of "Jacob and Israel, my called." Not to Jacob personally, for he was long before dead. The first verse in this book shows it to be "The vision of Isaiah, the son of Amos, which he saw concerning Judah and Jerusalem." Yea, these Jews—descendants of Jacob—were God's chosen—God's elect; but does my friend intend to say that they were all saved? Paul says, "They did all eat the same spiritual meat, and did all drink the same spiritual drink; for they drank of that spiritual rock that followed them and that rock was Christ" (1 Cor, 10:3, 4). This shows that they were elect at that time- If my friend denies it, I will prove it by a number of plain, unequivocal expressions of Holy Writ. What went with them? Will Elder Herod say they were all saved? If he will, I will prove that they went to hell by thousands. Let us read further:

"But with many of them God was not well pleased: for they were overthrown in the wilderness. Now these things were our examples, to the intent we should not lust after evil things, as they also lusted. Neither be ye idolaters, as were some of them; as it is written, The people sat down to eat and drink, and rose up to play. Neither let us commit fornication, as some of them committed, and Jell in one day three and twenty thousand. Neither let us tempt Christ, as some of them also tempted, and were destroyed of serpents. Neither murmur ye, as some of them also murmured, and were destroyed of the destroyer. Now all these things happened unto them for examples: and they are written for our admonition, upon whom the ends of the world are come. Wherefore let him that thinketh he standeth take heed lest he fall."

Now, did all these elect who had drank of Christ, the spiritual Rock, go to heaven? How wariest thou?

"For some, when they had heard, did provoke: howbeit not all that came out of Egypt by Moses. But with whom was he grieved forty years? was it not with them that had sinned, whose carcasses fell in the wilderness? And to whom swear he that they should not enter into his rest, but to them that believed not? So we see they could not enter in because of unbelief" (Heb. 3:16-19).

Thus, we find that God swore that these unbelievers, whose carcasses fell in the wilderness, should not enter into the rest prepared for the people of God, their election notwithstanding. And these very people were the seed of Abraham through the line of Isaac: yet we are told that salvation is not conditional!

But we are next referred to Rom. 11:28, 29: "They were beloved for the father's sake." Yes; is there anything strange about that? Did you never love any one because you loved his father? Who were the fathers for whose sake they were beloved? Abraham, Isaac and Jacob. Is there any proof of his proposition in this? "But the gifts and calling of God are without repentance." Will he say that a sinner can get salvation without repentance? The gifts and calling of God are without repentance as to

God, but not as to the sinner; for the Lord has said that the sinner that does not repent will surely perish.

But we are next referred to seven thousand that God had reserved to himself. Yes; but why were they reserved? For the best of reasons—"They had not bowed the knee to the image of Baal." If they had worshiped that image, they would have gone as the others went. But why were there only seven thousand of God's elect left? There had been millions of them. When they crossed the Red Sea there were about three millions; now only seven thousand. That is where Elisha made his complaint. The others had killed God's prophets, digged down his altars, and gone into idolatry. But "even so at this present time also there is a remnant according to the election of grace." Yes, a remnant—what does that mean? A remnant implies a small part of what once was. The whole Jewish nation were God's elect once; but when God proposed the abrogation of the Jewish polity and the election of a people on the principle of faith in Christ, only a remnant accepted the new arrangement; and they were, by Paul, called the election, in place of the notion, as before, and the rest were blinded in unbelief, and for their unbelief were broken off, as the natural branches of the olive tree. Does this prove unconditional salvation? Nay, verily: but just the opposite. The effects of idolatry and unbelief were never more clearly seen than here on God's elect.

He next introduced Rom. 9:7, 8: "Neither, because they are the seed of Abraham, are they all children; but in Isaac shall thy seed be called. That is, they which are the children of the promise are counted for the seed." Well, what has this to do with unconditional salvation? I suppose just nothing at all. The children of Abraham by Hagar and Keturah were born after the flesh as other children, but God gave him Isaac by promise when he and his wife were past age, and it was through him that his seed was called.

But how do we become children, and heirs of this promise? "For ye are all the children of God." How? Unconditionally? No; but "by faith in Christ Jesus," And how are they all children of God by faith? "For as many of you as have been baptized into Christ have put on Christ." That Is the way they became children of God by faith. In faith they were baptized into Christ, and thus put him on. Then "there is neither Jew nor Greek, neither bond nor free, there is neither male nor female, for ye are all one in Christ Jesus; and if ye be Christ's, then are ye Abraham's seed, and heirs according to the promise" (Gal. 3:25-29). Thus, we become children of God, the seed of Abraham, and heirs according to the promise; but this is just the opposite of unconditional election, I want my friend to notice this, and show the fallacy of my reasoning, if he can; but I guess he will give it no attention, for I have been most unfortunate in securing his attention to anything.

He reminds us that it is God that justifieth. Certainly; who else can do it? But as God justifies, does it follow that he does it unconditionally? This is the issue. My friend assumes just what he has undertaken to prove.

He quotes 2 Tim. 2:10: "Therefore I endure all things for the elects' sakes, that they may also obtain the salvation which is in Christ Jesus, with eternal glory." Well, he must have quoted this simply because it has the word elect in it, for it certainly has no bearing on the subject of conditional or unconditional salvation. But any passage seems to be satisfactory to him if it has the word elect in it, without regard to how or for what the parties were elected. May I, with becoming modesty, remind him that unconditional salvation is the matter in hand just now?

(Time expired,)

ELDER HEROD'S SECOND SPEECH.

BRO. MODERATOR, JUDGES, LADIES AND GENTLEMEN:—I appear before you to continue the affirmative argument begun in the forenoon. But before I begin my argument I desire to call your attention to one thing that my opponent said in his speech this morning. I confess it alarmed me some. He said that twenty-four thousand of Adam's race were gone to hell. I thought that the judgment was yet in the future, but he has them already judged and in hell now. If he has any passage of Scripture that says so I hope he will produce it, and read it to us—I have not seen it. I do not think there is such a passage, and I don't think he can prove what he says. If he cannot prove it by the Bible, he ought to acknowledge his error and take it back. I would not give much for a religion that has to be scared into the people.

But he says if salvation is not conditional there is no use of preaching, and he asked me what I preached for. And he has asked the same thing two or three times. I will read my answer right out of the Bible, and then I will pay no more attention to it.

I read Ephesians 4:8-12: "therefore he saith, When he ascended up on high, he led captivity captive, and gave gifts unto men. (Now that he ascended, what is it but that he also descended first into the lower parts of the earth? He that descended is the same also that ascended up far above all heavens, that he might fill all things.) And he gave some, apostles; and some, prophets; and some, evangelists; and some, pastors and teachers; for the perfecting of the saints, for the work of the ministry, for the edifying of the body of Christ."

Again, I read Isaiah 40:1,2: "Comfort ye, comfort ye my people, saith your God. Speak ye comfortably to Jerusalem, and cry unto her, that her warfare is accomplished, that her iniquity is pardoned: for she hath received of the Lord's hand double for all her sins."

This is my authority for preaching. I am commanded by the Lord to comfort his people by telling them what the Lord has done for them.

He seems to be very glad that I referred to Ephesians. Now I want to know which preceded, the hearing the gospel or their salvation? They were chosen in him before the foundation of the world. Hearing the gospel had nothing to do with their salvation. They were first elected—saved—and were God's people, then they heard and believed the gospel.

Now I want to read Matthew 24:31: "And he shall send his angels with a great sound of a trumpet, and they shall gather together his elect from the four winds, from one end of heaven to the other."

And again, Mark says (13:27): "And then shall he send his angels, and shall gather together his elect from the four winds, from the uttermost part of the earth to the uttermost part of heaven."

God has elect people in every direction, from the uttermost part of the earth to the uttermost part of heaven, and he is going to bring them together, and be with them, and rule over them, for they are his people and he has promised to be their God. Now there were none of Adam's race among these elect If I don't establish that I will give up and quit.

I invite your attention to 1.Thess. 1:4: "Knowing, brethren beloved, your election of God." Now we see they were elected of God. Elected of God, how? On conditions? No, there is nothing said about conditions. They were elected, and they were elected of God too. Who has a right to put conditions where God has not put them? When was this election? Was it when they did something? or performed conditions? We will read again. 2 Thess. 2:13: "But we are bound to give thanks always to

God for you, brethren beloved of the Lord, because God hath from the beginning chosen you to salvation through sanctification of the Spirit and belief of the truth." This seems to have been an apostolic doctrine I am preaching. Chosen you from the beginning. I don't care when he makes the beginning if he puts the election before they believed.

I don't want to make the Bible contradict itself. I am not here to do that. It does not contradict itself. There are no contradictions in it

Now I turn to 2 John, and read the first verse, and you will see that there is a lady in it. I love to talk about the ladies. Now listen everybody, for you are all interested in the reading when we read about a lady. "The elder unto the elect lady and her children, whom I love in the truth; and not I only, but also all they that have known the truth; for the truth's sake, which dwelleth in us, and shall be with us forever." This elect lady represents the church, hence I have found an elect church. And what does this mean? A church of elect material—its members are all elect.

Now we read Psalm 65:4: "Blessed is the man whom thou choosest, and causest to approach unto thee, that he may dwell in thy courts: we shall all be satisfied with the goodness of thy house, even of thy holy temple." Here the church is represented by a man. First, we found it represented by a lady, now it is by a man, that takes in both women and men.

Now read Isaiah 65:9: "And I will bring forth a seed out of Jacob, and out of Judah an inheritor of my mountains: and mine elect shall inherit it, and my servants shall dwell there." Here we have a seed, and God's elect, and their inheritance. That talks like my proposition, does it not? Now you all see that I know you do. Your pleasant faces and sparkling eyes show that you are all interested in this great subject.

We will read Isaiah 53:4-8: "Surely he hath borne our griefs, and carried our sorrows: yet we did esteem him stricken, smitten of God, and afflicted. But he was wounded for our transgressions, he was bruised for our iniquities: the chastisement of our peace was upon him; and with his stripes we are healed. All we like sheep have gone astray; we have turned every one to his own way; and the Lord hath laid on him the iniquities of us all. He was oppressed, and he was afflicted, yet he opened not his mouth: he is brought as a lamb to the slaughter, and as a sheep before her shearers is dumb, so he opened not his mouth. He was taken from prison and from Judgment: and who shall declare his generation? for he was cut off out of the land of the living: for the transgression of my people was he stricken."

We are healed by his stripes, not by the sinner's stripes, or by our own stripes. Healed by his stripes when we do something; when we comply with conditions. God says for the transgression of my people. Jesus was stricken for God's people, and was he stricken for any others? The book says he was stricken for my people, that implies that he was not stricken for any others; and that is clear proof that the Lord had a people for whom Jesus was stricken. Does the book say that they should be the Lord's people if they would comply with a lot of conditions? It ought to read that way to suit my opponent.

Let us next invite your attention to Daniel 9:24: "Seventy weeks are determined upon thy people and upon thy holy city, to finish the transgression, and to make an end of sins, and to make reconciliation for iniquity, and to bring in everlasting righteousness, and to seal up the vision and prophecy, and to anoint the most holy."

Seventy weeks are specified to take the daily sacrifices out of the way. What for? To get a more perfect sacrifice. If Jesus undertook the salvation of sinners, and, after living thirty-three years, did not accomplish his work, I doubt the propriety of Dr. Herod or Dr. Brents undertaking the task. I think it a reflection on the Saviour to intimate that he did not accomplish the object for which he came. If he did accomplish his work, then transgression was finished; an end was made of sins, reconciliation for iniquity was made, and everlasting righteousness was brought in for his people.

Now we want to read Isaiah 72:5-9. Listen, everybody, to the rending, for it is in the word of the Lord: "And I looked, and there was none to help; and I wondered that there was none to uphold." Therefore, the sinner's arm brought salvation. Is that the way it reads? I must read again, for the brethren are shaking their heads all around. Surely it ought to read that way to suit the theory of my opponent. But I will read it as It is now: "Therefore mine own arm brought salvation unto me; and my fury, it upheld me, And I will tread down the people in mine anger, and make them drunk in my fury, and I will bring down their strength to the earth. I will mention the loving-kindness of the Lord, according to all that the Lord hath bestowed on us, and the great goodness toward the house of Israel, which he hath bestowed on them according to his mercies, and according to the multitude of his loving-kindnesses. For he said, Surely, they are my people, children that will not lie: so he was their Saviour. In all their affliction he was afflicted, and the Angel of his presence saved them: in his love and in his pity, he redeemed them; and he bare them, and carried them all the days of old."

None to help—none to uphold. Is that true? The Angel of his presence saved them—did they save themselves? If any thing they did, saved them, I ask if they did not save themselves, and not the Angel of his presence? He bestowed on them loving-kindnesses and tender mercies because they were people, and not to give them a chance to become his people if they would perform a lot of conditions.

My brother keeps giving his interpretation of Scripture. Why not read the book and let it speak for itself. Religious divisions come about by mere cunning and giving opinions. I prefer to read you the word of God and give no opinions. I agreed to be governed by the Bible in deciding this question, and I am not going to deal in opinions. One man's opinion is as good as another, for no man's opinion is worth anything in deciding what God has done, will do or ought to do concerning salvation.

I believe in Christian duties—I preach Christian duties—more than I can get the people to do; but Christian duties never saved a soul. I am discussing salvation; and Jesus is the Saviour, and the only Saviour, and nothing that we can do wilt save us, or in anyway induce God to save us. The salvation of every man who will ever be saved at all was secured through Jesus Christ, before the foundation of the world, and nothing that man can do will change the purposes of him that changes not. He is the same yesterday, to-day and forever.

Can man measure arms with God the Almighty, and thwart his purposes? Such an idea is degrading to the character of God. The ransomed of the Lord will give all the glory to God, and none to themselves. If any man glory let him glory in the Lord. The salvation is for the saints, but the glory belongeth to the Saviour.

(Time expired.)

DR. BRENTS' SECOND REPLY.

MR. PRESIDENT:—My opponent says the gifts and callings of God are without repentance, and applies that to the conversion of the sinner. A greater perversion could not be imagined. These gifts and callings were not for the benefit of the called, but were intended to benefit others through them. He introduced the cases of Jacob and Esau, and made Paul say that God loved Jacob and hated Esau before either of them was born or had done good or evil. The election of Jacob did not secure the salvation of him and his posterity, nor did the passing of Esau condemn him and his posterity. It is certain many thousands of Jacob's descendants were lost, nor can it be shown that none of Esau's posterity were saved—indeed, he cannot show that Esau himself was lost True, he was a profane person when he sold his birthright, but his conduct when he met Jacob indicated that he was a better man than Jacob had once been. Paul made two quotations, which Elder Herod throws together as if they were one; and he makes an individual and personal application of what was intended to be national. Gen. 25:23: The Lord said to Rebecca that "Two nations are in thy womb, and two manner of people shall be separated from thy bowels; and the one people shall be stronger than the other people; and the elder shall serve the younger." That is, the elder people shall serve the younger people —the people who shall descend from the elder son shall serve the people who shall descend from the younger son. This was said to Rebecca before the children were born; but the other quotation— "Jacob have I loved and Esau have I hated"—was said long after both men were dead, and referred to the nations, Israel and Edom, represented by them. See Malachi 1.1-4: "The burden of the word of the Lord to Israel by Malachi. I have loved you, saith the Lord. Yet ye say, Wherein hast them loved us." Notice the form of expression—the word of the Lord to Israel. Wherein hast thou loved us?— not one child. "Was not Esau Jacob's brother? saith the Lord; yet I loved Jacob, and I hated Esau, and laid big mountains and his heritage waste for the dragons of the wilderness." Esau had no mountains, or heritage either, before he was born. "Whereas Edom saith, We are impoverished," etc. Yes, Edom was the nation that descended from Esau, and of that nation this was true, but of Esau personally it was not said, nor would it have been true had it been said. This was said, "Jacob have I loved and Esau have I hated," nearly fifteen hundred years after they were both dead, and yet Elder Herod applies it to the children before they were born! And still he complains that I explain the scriptures and give my construction of them, in place of reading them, as he does. Yes, it would be right nice if I would let his perversions go unexposed. He run read, and "transpose," and misapply more scriptures in half an hour than Paul could straighten in a whole day, if he were here; but he takes good care not to attack my explanations when I have made them. If he does not want me to explain his proof texts, he must quit perverting and misapplying them. He will greatly abridge my labors, and I shall be greatly obliged to him for every improvement he will make in this direction.

But I showed that twenty-four thousand of his eternally elect have gone to hell, and he objects to this because the judgment is yet future. Well, this is pretty hard on him, I admit. When we ask where persons are, the answer is, they have gone to town, or somewhere else, when they have only started; so, when persons die in the condition these Jews were in, we say they have gone to hell; and it is certain they have made a start in that direction, to say the least of it. But I suppose Elder Herod never says any one has gone to a place until he has made the landing. But how about the judgment, on his theory? I insist that the judgment took place before the world began, when his eternal decree of election was fixed up. The only use he will have for a judgment is to separate the sheep from the goats according to that decree.

(Herod): "I will have good ground for a judgment."

(Brents): Yes, the decree of election will be the only condition of your judgment, and not the works or deeds of men, as the word of God says it shall be. What a ridiculous farce it will be to judge men according to their works, when their destiny was irrevocably fixed before the foundation of the world! We challenge him to show that this is not the ground of his judgment,

But let us look after those elect that fell in the wilderness, Paul says they "were all baptized unto Moses in the cloud and in the sea; and did all eat the same spiritual meat; and did all drink the same spiritual drink; for they drank of that spiritual Rock that followed them; and that rock was Christ." My friend says there was no such thing as preparation for heaven or hell under the Old Testament; and he talks about Adam's water and Christ's water. Look here, my friend, don't you think those persons got a sip of Christ's water when they drank of that spiritual rock that followed them, and that rock was Christ? But what became of those descendants of Abraham through the line of Isaac? "But with many of them God was not well pleased; for they were overthrown in the wilderness.' Now these things were our examples, to the intent we should not lust after evil things, as they also lusted. Neither be ye idolaters, as were some of them; as it is written, The people sat down to eat and drink, and rose up to play. Neither let us commit fornication, us some of them committed, and fell in one day three and twenty thousand." Twenty-four thousand died in this plague, twenty-three thousand in one day. See Numbers 25:9. "Neither let us tempt Christ, as some of them also tempted and were destroyed of serpents. Neither murmur ye, as some of them also murmured, and were destroyed of the destroyer. Now all these things happened unto them for examples, and they are written for our admonition upon whom the ends of the world are come. Wherefore let him that thinketh he standeth, take heed, lest he fall." Now, are these idolaters and whoremongers fit for heaven? "For some, when they had heard, did provoke; howbeit not all that came out of Egypt by Moses. But with whom was he grieved forty years? was it not with them that had sinned, whose carcasses fell in the wilderness? And to whom sware he that they should not enter into his rest, but to them that believed not" (Heb. 3:16-18), Now, God swore they should not go to heaven. Elder Herod says they have not gone to hell. I insist that he locate them. Will he say that they have gone, or will go to heaven, when God has sworn they shall not?

(Herod): "No, no."

(Brents): Then you give up your proposition. They were God's elect—had drank of Christ—were children of Abraham through the line of Isaac, yet you say they have not gone to heaven because they were wicked. That settles the question—knocks the bottom clear out of the proposition. Eternally and unconditionally elect, and will not get to heaven after all that. Well, where are they? I insist that he locate them. Has he a sort of purgatory fixed, in which he is keeping them until he gives them another chance for heaven? Will he tell us about them? I fear we will not hear from him at this point any more. Come, my friend, don't forsake these elect brethren; they need your help.

But he does not want the Bible to contradict itself. O, no; not he! Yet, when I showed yesterday that they who have done good shall be resurrected to life, he read, when he knew that I could not reply: "There is none that doeth good, no, not one." Then, if the Bible does not contradict itself, and only those who have done good will be resurrected to life—and "there is none that doeth good, no, not one "—then there will be none resurrected to life, and all are lost That is not universal salvation, but it is universal damnation, without remedy.

But he gives us his authority for preaching, and he refers us to where Paul is speaking of spiritual gifts (Eph. 4:11): "And he gave some apostles." Is he an apostle? I reckon not "And some prophets." Is he a prophet? I thought all the prophets were dead, but false ones. "And some evangelists." Is he an evangelist? Not such as Paul spoke of, I guess. "And some pastors and teachers." Is he a pastor? If so, he only feeds the chosen few. I did not know that they could starve, or even get very hungry. And I am not very favorably impressed with him as a teacher. I think the world would be as well off without his teaching as with it. But he is to comfort the Lord's people. While his preaching might comfort the few, it would be death to the many. It would not be very comforting to tell the people that God had made no provisions for them; that he never loved them; Christ never died for them, and eternal punishment only awaited them, let them do as they might. Even the elect would not be comforted much by such preaching as this; but I never knew any one who believed this that did not think himself one of the elect. Of course, my friend feels sure that he is a chosen vessel. But my friend failed to catch my question. I did not ask him for his authority to preach; but I am curious to know where the people are to be benefitted by his preaching. If he cannot be instrumental in saving any one, or causing him to turn from sin to holiness, what good does his preaching do any one? If he cannot cheat the devil out of a single man, or save a soul from death, or turn a sinner from the error of his way, why trouble himself to preach? This is my point; I hope he now understands me. Will he tell us what good his preaching does? That is what I want to know, and it is what he has failed to tell.

But he tells us God is going to gather the elect from the four winds. Yes, certainly; who doubts that? He goes through the Bible hunting every passage that has the word elect in it, without even stopping to see who the elect were, what they were elected for, how they were elected, and whether or not they were saved by the election. This is downright tripling with the subject. Does he not know that it is unconditional election, and that where salvation was the object of the election that he is here to prove? Is it possible that he is going through the debate without knowing the import of the proposition he is affirming? Who are the elect? I answer, the saved. He will not call this answer in question. Then who are the saved? Jesus said, "He that believeth, and is baptized, shall be saved." He is the author of eternal salvation to all who obey him. These will be the elect who will be gathered from the four winds? Will he deny it?

The angel of the Lord said to the shepherds in the plains of Bethlehem: "Behold, I bring you good tidings of great joy, which shall be to all people; for unto you is born this day, in the city of David, a Saviour, which is Christ the Lord" (Luke 1:10,11). If my friend's theory be true, this announcement was false. How could the birth of a Saviour be good tidings of great joy for those he came not to save? Yet it was to be good tidings of great joy to all people. Then all people may be saved by this Saviour if they will accept salvation as offered them.

But he cites us to 2 Thess. 2:13: "God hath from the beginning chosen you to salvation through sanctification of the spirit and belief of the truth." This is very far from unconditional salvation, for Paul plainly says that belief of the truth was a condition through which they were chosen to salvation. But it had the word chosen in it, hence he must read it any way.

But he refers us to Isaiah 53:5: "With his stripes we are healed." Yes, but healed conditionally or unconditionally? Not a word on that subject. Peter, when writing to Christians who had been saved, says: "By whose stripes ye were healed" (1 Pet. 2:24). That this healing means saved, all agree. Now, Peter, did you mean that we are healed or saved by the suffering of Christ without doing anything ourselves? O, no, for we purify our souls in obeying the truth (1 Peter 1:22). And baptism doth also now save us (1 Pet 3:21). Peter, did you tell those wanting to be saved on the day of Pentecost, to repent and be baptized for the remission of sins? Yes, I told them that Why did you tell them that? I was speaking as the Spirit gave me utterance, and those were the words put in my mouth. Peter, did you, in your next discourse at Solomon's porch, tell the people to repent and be converted, that their sins might be blotted out? Yes, I said that, too. Then you could not have meant that by Christ's stripes we were healed without doing these things.

If God saves without obedience, then he must be a respecter of persons, and nothing but personal favoritism controlled the salvation. But the word of God says, "There in no respect of persons with God" (Rom. 2:11). "Neither is there respect of persons with him" (Eph. 6:9). "And there is no respect of persons" (Col. 3:25). "Of a truth, I perceive that God is no respecter of persons; but in every nation he that feareth him and worketh righteousness is accepted with him" (Acts 10:34, 85). Elder Herod has not perceived this yet, for he thinks the elect will be accepted with him whether they work righteousness or not. And he thinks those not elect will not be accepted if they work all the righteousness required of any one.

He tells us that the elect lady mentioned in 2 John 1:1 represented the church, and the church is composed of all the elect; now will he tell us who her children were? The quotation reads: "The elder unto the elect lady and her children, whom I love in the truth." John seemed to love the children about as well as the lady.

Then, if the lady represented all the elect church, who were these, her children? I hope he will tell us.

(Time expired.)

ELDER HEROD'S THIRD SPEECH.

BROS. moderators, ladies and gentlemen: —We are again present before you to resume the labor of this discussion; and before I proceed to call your attention, and my opponent's, to additional proofs as to my affirmation, I desire to announce it myself. It has already been distinctly read, that I affirm that the scriptures teach the unconditional election (I want you to note that it is not selection) and salvation from sin by Jesus Christ of all his seed or generation. I want to make an additional remark, by way of an inquiry, as to whether this is not true, or will ever be true, that it is seed or generation that is not only saved, but that enjoys a place at God's right hand?

I believe that my worthy opponent admitted on yesterday that election was a Bible doctrine. As a matter of course, he has his own way of defining and explaining it; but in view of what is involved in the passage that he said had a semblance in that direction, I put a question to him. What was it? When be admitted that election was a Bible doctrine, I put the question as to whether the election takes place in Christ previous to the time that the thing elected knew it. He has not answered. I want him to give an answer; for the very moment (hat he gives it, as I presume he will give it, that it existed before the thing elected knew it, then the knowledge of the fact did not secure the election, no act performed could have constituted the election; nor could any such act have reached backward behind the act to exert any influence in producing it, or bringing it about.

He has also asked me a question, and I might just as well answer it now, as it would not be in place to answer it after a while. He wanted to know whether or not I say it is unconditional. I have said it in my proposition, and I repeat it.

[Brents (from his seat): "I never asked you any such a question as that; of course I did not."]

I am now ready to continue my affirmative argument, and I call your attention to where I stopped. I cannot devote us much time as is necessary to get in the amount of testimony I desire to introduce.

I have already called your attention to the sixty-third chapter of Isaiah I have read one passage and gave the verse, but I now proceed to read further. I will read verses eight and nine. Now everybody listen, in view of the choice before the world was. The prophet says: "Surely they are my people, children who will not lie. He was their Saviour. In all their affliction he was afflicted, and the angel of his presence saved them. In his love and his pity he redeemed them; and he bare them, and carried them all the days of old." That tells it all. Do you all appreciate the wording of this passage? I have agreed to decide this question by the Bible. I do not give my explanation; that would be my opinion, not the Bible.

I now call your attention to this passage from Isaiah for the last time I will read it during the discussion of this question. I repeat the language and ask the attention of the people to it, for it is very important in settling this controversy. "Surely they are my people, children who will not lie. He was their Saviour. In all their 'affliction he was afflicted, and the angel of his presence saved them. In his love and in his pity he redeemed them; and he bare them, and carried them all the days of old." That means he is going to offer them salvation, does it? I now call attention to it again, as I have just remarked, and I shall then dismiss it and turn to something else. "Surely they are my people." Now, us a shepherd would have a right to claim and recover his property that was astray, so he had a right to recover them that were his. Now "they are my people, children who will not lie." In his love and pity—not in their acts of obedience—he redeemed them. He carried them all the days of old.

I now want your attention to Isaiah 53:10. Every one of you, listen now, because the proof of my proposition lies in this passage: "When thou shalt make his soul an offering for sin, he shall see bin seed, he shall prolong his days, and the pleasure of the Lord shall prosper in his hands. He shall see of the travail of his soul and be satisfied: by his knowledge shall my righteous servant justify many; for he shall bear their iniquities."

I now call your attention to the fourth chapter and last verse of the letter to the Romans, where the inspired apostle in plain language supports what I have already uttered: "He was delivered for our offenses, and raised again for our justification." Raised again for what? Our justification. God never justifies guilty things. He said he would not justify the guilty. Then Christ was delivered for our offenses and raised again for our justification; hence we were justified before he was raised from the dead.

I next refer to the last verse of the fifth chapter of the second letter to the Corinthians. Every one listen to this question of justification and the cause of it; and those who have realized themselves as sinners will appreciate the wording. I want everybody to get the sentiment. The apostle says: "For he hath made him to be sin for us who knew no sin; that we might be made the righteousness of God in him." The argument of my friend is to show that your righteousness is the result of your own acts. If he contradicts this, then he denies what he said, and he will not do that. O, my friends, what vast interest is involved in this question! Our Lord was male sin for us. Our sins were laid on him. What did he do with them when he got them there? He bore them in his own body on the tree.

And still you tell me salvation is conditional! You bow before me and my worthy opponent! What have we done for you? He, the Son of God, has done all, to whom be glory forever.

How was this accomplished? He was made to be sin for us, who knew no sin, that we might become the righteousness of God in him, by faith, repentance, and baptism, or any other thing that we can do or have done. This requires me to prove Christ to be the salvation from sin. Is not this proof ample enough? I want these words to sink into your hearts so that they will stay there. That we might be made, not make ourselves, the righteousness of God in him. it is God's righteousness, and not the signer's righteousness.

Psalm 22:30. Every one listen now. I have established the proposition. I have called your attention to the twenty-second Psalm and tenth verse. I read in the following plain and forcible language: "A seed shall serve him." My brother says that God has offered it to you, and you may accept it or not, as you please. This is honoring him very much, in it not? I include the entire paragraph on the subject. The language is: "A seed shall serve him; it shall be counted for a generation." I have a seed, a generation, and a Saviour, or I would not have gone into the discussion of this question. It is no matter what I have said, you have got the passage. I presumed he could have turned to it in a moment.

I next call your attention to the testimony of John. Now we begin to talk about who it is that are his subjects. I don't believe the doctrine of reprobation. I have A higher and more exalted opinion of God than to believe that stuff. John 18:36. One inquired of the Lord respecting the nature of his kingdom. Listen to the response which he gives. He said (everybody listen): "My kingdom is not of this world." Will you let him tell you what it is? He says children of this world marry and are given in marriage. My opponent preached twenty-four thousand in hell yesterday. I want everybody to come right up to the scratch now, and look at the record in which the Bible has given it.

First part of the paragraph—what is it? "My kingdom is not of this world; if my kingdom were of this world, then would my servants fight." It would go back to duet, and then Daniel's prophecy that it should stand forever would not be true. I want the serious thought of everybody on this question; and after reading the language just quoted, I call your attention to John 17:16: "You are not of the world", even as I am not of the world." A kingdom not of this world—and Jesus uses language that cannot be mistaken— "you are not of the world, even as I am not of the world." Where did Jesus come from? Now, my friends, take all these things together, and think for a moment, and you cannot fail to understand the question.

I here call the attention of my friend to Gal. 3:27. I have no trouble in citing the language I want to quote. Twenty-seventh verse: "As many of you as have been baptized into Christ have put on Christ" I want my friend to tell who it was. Men and women has been the cry ever since this debate began. I want the application immediately to what I am discussing. When I go away from here I want it said that I stuck to the question I was discussing. "As many of you as have been baptized into Christ have put on Christ." Listen closely now. "There is neither Jew nor Greek, there is neither bond nor free, there is neither male nor female." Down goes the cob-house. What kind of baptism was that? Was it water baptism? Did the Bible tell you so? I have traversed that Bible from one end to the other, and it does not say it. He says, after saying there is neither Jew nor Greek, bond nor free, male nor female, "you are." Is it now or some other time? You are now. You are what?

You are all one in Christ Jesus, and "if ye be Christ's, then are ye Abraham's seed, and heirs according to the promise."

Now I invite your attention to the first verse of the next chapter of Galatians. I am going to talk about a family—a generation, not about Adam, or about the flesh; they are not the children of God. The apostle said, "Ye are all," addressing, not men and women, but the church—it was addressed to a lady—the bride, the Lamb's wife. This refers to the same passage that I started from in the introduction of this question.

"Now I say that the heir, as long as he is a child, differeth nothing from a servant, though he be Lord of all." He was in sin. How did he get out? By obedience? I must read on, for my time will expire and I will not have Introduced a fourth of the testimony I intended, "But is under tutors and governors until the time appointed of the father, even so we, when we were children, were in bondage under the elements of the world; but when the fullness of the time was come, God sent forth his Son made of a woman, made under the law, to redeem them that were under the law, that we might receive the adoption of sons. And because ye are sons, God hath sent forth the Spirit of his Son into our hearts, crying, Abba, Father. "This assures us that the Father has given his Spirit to our spirit to bear witness; and the apostle has given another evidence— you should know that you have passed from death unto life because you love the brethren.

Next in order I want to call your attention to John 19: I believe I have failed to note the verse—I see I did not note it. Look at the tenth verse in the nineteenth chapter, I think you will find it. There you will find the Saviour acknowledges the mission for which he came into the world; and the language in which it is made. Listen now: "The Son of man is come to seek and to save that which was lost." Did Christ accomplish his mission? Did he perform the work he came to do? If he did, not one he came to save will be lost—not one. If any he came to save will be lost, then his mission was a failure.

Matt. 1:21. I am putting these in as testimony. I want him to answer what is said in the first chapter of Matthew and the twenty-first verse. The angel said that Jesus should do something. Do you think that that something should or could fail to be done? "Thou shalt call his name Jesus, for he shall save his people from their sins."

Was Jesus the Saviour? Did he save anybody? If he saved anybody, whom did he save? And from what did he save them? We are hunting for salvation from sin for the elect, and the angel said Jesus should save his people from their sins. Is this plain enough?

(Time expired.)

Dr. Brents' Third Reply.

MR. PRESIDENT: —My opponent wants to know whether the sinner is elected to salvation before he knows it or after he knows it. This question lifts nothing to do with the many elections of persons to portions for the benefit of others, but to the election of persons to their own salvation. I reply that persons are elected to salvation when they obey the gospel, and are saved; and when they obey the gospel they know it then. His trouble seems to be that he thinks every one was individually and personally elected to salvation when the plan of salvation was conceived in the mind of God. This is his mistake. Provisions were then made for the salvation of all men who would accept salvation on the conditions stipulated, but no one was personally and unconditionally elected then or at any other time. He makes a personal application to a few without conditions, of that which was provided for all on conditions.

The Brents-Herod Debate

He again quotes Isaiah 72:8, 9: "For he said, Surely, they are my people, children that will not lie; SO he was their Saviour, In all their affliction he was afflicted, and the angel of his presence saved them; in his love and in his pity he redeemed them; and he bare them, and carried them all the days of old." Of this he makes an application to the elect of to-day, when it was said of the children of Israel redeemed from bondage; and the very next verse to what he read shows that they rebelled against God and he became their enemy. Why did he stop there? Was it accidental? Now I must read the succeeding verses to correct his perversion. "But they re-belle', and vexed his holy spirit; therefore he was turned to be their enemy, and he fought against them. Then he remembered the days of old, Moses, and his people, saying, Where is he that brought them up out of the sea with the shepherd of his flock? where is he that put his holy spirit within him? that led them by the right hand of Moses with his glorious arm, dividing the water before them, to make himself an everlasting name? that led them through the deep an a, horse in the wilderness, that they should not stumble."

Why did he not read this, to show whom the Lord was talking about? Because it would have spoiled his argument if he had. It did not suit his purpose to show that those who were his people, and led by him all the days of old, were the Jews, and that God turned against them and became their enemy, and destroyed thousands of them for their wickedness; though they were his elect people—descendants of Abraham through the line of Isaac. By the way, he has not located that twenty-four thousand of these very people, redeemed by him and led by Moses. He says they are not fit for heaven, and did not go to hell; hence I insist that he locate them some where. They were God's elect, and you have, this morning, claimed them as your brethren in the Lord; now I

The Brents-Herod Debate

insist that you tell us where they are? Don't fail to notice this, please.

He next goes to Isaiah 53:10, 11, and reads: "By his knowledge shall my righteous servant justify many, for he shall bear their iniquities." Then he "translates" this to Romans 4:25: "Who was delivered for our offences, and was raised again for our justification." Here again, had he read the connection, it would have spoiled his whole theory. Let me read the preceding verses in connection with the one he read. I begin with the twenty-third verse: "Now it was not written for his sake alone, that it was imputed to him; but for us also, to whom it shall be imputed, if we believe on him that raised up Jesus our Lord from the dead; who was delivered for our offences, and was raised again for our justification." Yes, it shall be imputed to us if we believe; but what if we don't believe? Well, my friend is trying to make you believe that if you are one of the elect it shall be imputed to you, whether you believe or not. Is it not astonishing that he failed to see the verse right above the one he read, and it part of the sentence only separated by a semicolon?

He next goes to 2 Cor. 5:21: "'For he hath made him to be sin for us, who knew no sin, that we might be made the righteousness of God in him." This is an elliptical sentence. For he hath made him to be a sin offering for us. That this is correct is shown by the passage he quotes in connection with it. "Who his own self bare our pins in his own body on the tree." How did he bear our sins in his own body on the tree? Shall Paul answer? "He died for our sins according to the scriptures." And for whose nine did he die? "And that he died for all, that they which live should not henceforth live unto themselves, but unto him which died for them, and rose again" (2 Cor. 5:15). "But we see Jesus, who was made a little lower than the angels for the stifle ring of death, crowned with glory and honor; that he by the grace of God should taste death for every man." "And he is the propitiation for our sins; and not for ours only, but also for the sins of the whole world" (1 John 2:2). Thus we see that he bore the sins of all men in the same sense that he bore the sins of any one. I defy him to show any provisions made for the salvation of a few men that were not made for all men. If he will show how he was saved himself, I will show that every man in this house may be saved in the same way. I have called his attention to this before, but he has not noticed it.

He next quoted Psalm 22:30: "A seed shall serve him; it shall be accounted to the Lord for a generation." He must have quoted this passage because it has the words seed and generation in it, for it says not a word about conditional or unconditional salvation. "In the beginning God created the heaven and the earth," would have been just as appropriate.

He says he don't believe the doctrine of reprobation. Why not? It is a Bible term. It occurs six times in the New Testament and once in the Old.

(Herod): "I believe it"

(Brents): You do? Converted so soon! You said just a while gone that you did not believe it. But I am glad he is improving. Who are reprobates? Those who refuse to believe and obey the gospel. Those who make themselves such. But he says: "My kingdom is not of this world; if it were, then would my servants fight I! ye were of the world, the world would love its own." The word world is here used to distinguish the wicked from the disciples of Jesus. You are not of the wicked. "My kingdom is not of the world;" that is, it is not a political, but a spiritual government, authorized of God. But he uses this expression to prove that the subjects of his kingdom were not of the earth, when he told his disciples that they were not of the world, yet it was to them he was talking, and they were right there with him then.

But he goes to Gal. 3:27-29: "For as many of you as have been baptized into Christ have put on Christ. There is neither Jew nor Greek, there is neither bond nor free, there is neither male cor female: for ye are all one in Christ Jesus. And if ye be Christ's, then are ye Abraham's seed, and heirs according to the promise." Now he quotes this to show that men and women are not baptized into Christ, for in him there is neither male nor female; and he exclaimed, when he read it, "Down goes the cob-house!" I think so! I have seen many a cob-house fall before its builder got it done.

Jesus said, "Except a men be burn again, he cannot see the kingdom of God." When the Samaritans believed Philip preaching the things concerning the kingdom of God, they were baptized, both men and women. Who were baptized? Men and women. Down goes the cob house! The gentleman deserves a patent on his interpretation of this passage, but he need not trouble himself to take it out, for no one will intrude on his discovery, I'm sure. All the children of God, how? By faith. For as many as have been baptized into Christ have put on Christ, and Jew, Gentile, bond, free, male and female, all sustain the same relation to him, and are Abraham's seed and heirs according to the promise. How plain, but how unfortunate for my friend! He ought to keep at far away from such passages an possible.

He seems to have a theory here that he has not developed yet I wish he would bring it out fully. I want to understand him. Now I want to tell the gentleman, and I hope thereby to induce him to develop his theory, that it requires all of a man to make a man, and God intends to employ the whole man in his service. Paul says: "I beseech you, brethren, by the mercies of God, that you present your bodies a living sacrifice, wholly acceptable to

God, which is your reasonable service." Had my brother been there he would have cried out: "O, no, Paul; not these bodies of ours!" Glorify God in your bodies and in your spirits which are his. "I pray God your whole spirit and soul and body be preserved blameless unto the coining of our Lord Jesus Christ" (1 Thess. 5:23). Now, I think God made man just such a creature an he is, composed of soul, body and spirit, and he intended to employ the whole man in his service; and that my friend's theory needs to be brought out where we can see it Why does he want to keep it in the background? I have tried to get him to come out and take position, but he moves cautiously. He is like a man walking in the dark when he knows there are pitfalls all around him. He steps lightly; he is exceedingly cautions. I have tried to prise him out; I have tried to twist him out; but I guess I will have to smoke him out There was a covenant made between God and his Son about the destiny of the human race. He agrees that his Son may have a select party by giving his life for them. But there are few who go the narrow way, while the many go the broad road. Who gets them? The devil gets them without even shedding a drop of sweat for them. Who represented him in the arrangement? The covenant was made between God and his Son, yet the devil gets the larger share, and yet he was not represented in the covenant at all. Did God act as the Devil's proxy and secure to him the larger share? I hope my friend will come out and explain the whole matter, so that we can understand him fully.

Paul speaks of the adoption of sons—children—into God's family. If men are adopted into God's family, there is a time * hen it is done; and before the adoption they are not sons. If men are adopted into the family of God when they obey the gospel, it follows that they were not sons before the foundation of the world. The whole theory is shown to be false by the fact that conversion is represented by the figure of adoption and by the figure of the new birth. Will my opponent tell us how men may be adopted or born again into God's family, if they have been in it since the foundation of the world. Gal. 4:4-6.

But he quotes John 19:10. He did not find it, because he was mistaken in the reference. It is Luke six. 10: "For the Son of mm is come to seek and to save that which was lost." Well, who were the lost? Was there ever a time when the eternally and unconditionally elect were lost? We read Rom. 3:9-12. "What then? Are we better than they? No, in no wise: for we have before proved both Jews and Gentiles, that they are all under sin; as it is written, There is none righteous, no, not one; there is none that understandeth, there is none that seeketh after God; they are all gone out of the way, they are together become unprofitable; there is none that doeth good, no, not one." And again, verse 23: "For all have sinned and come short of the glory of God." Then all are lost; hence, if my brother's theory is true that he came to save, and did save all the lost, then universalism is true. He has a very flexible theory, truly. Yesterday he proved universal damnation, to-day he proves universal salvation. Well, of the two positions, I like the one of to-day better; it is more liberal, to say the least of it—but neither one is true. The world WAS lost, and "God so loved the world that he gave his only begotten Son, that whosoever believeth on him should not perish, but have everlasting life" (John 3:16). He en mo to save the lost, "For God sent not his Son into the world to condemn the world; but that the world through him might be saved" (verse 17), Yes, might be saved if they would be saved on his terms; and these terms are as free to every man as to any man.

He has again introduced the language of the angel (Matt. 1:21): "Thou shall call his name Jesus; for he shall save his people from their sins." I exploded his argument on this once. There is not a word about whether he shall save his people conditionally or unconditionally. "He became the author of eternal salvation to all them that obey him" (Heb. v, 9). Here we find whom he saves and how he saves them. All that obey him; not another one, but all of these. But as he quoted the angel If/ore his birth, we will add the testimony of the angel after his birth: "Behold, X bring you good tidings of great joy, which shall be to all people" (Luke 2:10). And again, verses 30-32. Good old Simeon said: "For mine eyes have seen thy salvation, which I have prepared before the face of all people; a light to lighten the Gentiles, and the glory of thy people Israel" His birth was a source of great joy to all people and prepared before the face of all people.

(Time expired.)

ELDER HEROD'S FOURTH SPEECH.

BROS. moderators, ladies and gentlemen: —I again present myself before you, to renew my labors in the prosecution of the discussion of this question. I am sorry that I trouble my friend so much. I am A sympathizing kind of man. I have not heard him make a single speech in this discussion, but what he complains of the passages I have selected. He says that they are all against me; but I notice in his case just what I have noticed up till now— where he runs against a hard one he tries to get it out of the way. What are you going here for, now? I want everybody to note the complaint, because it has been repeated every time, especially so since I have been introducing proof-passage that interpret themselves; otherwise you had better employ him as a spiritual guide.

He says something about faith. He don't seem to have any use for it I am going to tell you what it is. He has not defined it yet. I quote Heb. 11:, for the purpose of getting a Bible definition of faith. Everybody listen to the first verse: "Now, faith is the substance of things hoped for, the evidence of things not seen." Is that his act, or mine? Answer for yourselves.

Now, for the purpose of getting it more closely defined, I ask attention to the tenth chapter of the same, epistle. The explanation of the passage is easy—we can't mistake it. Substance: Now I turn back to the tenth chapter, and read: "Laying aside every weight, and the sin that doth so easily beset us, let us run with patience the race set before us, looking unto Jesus, the author and finisher of our faith." He has all the time been intimating that you can roll up a bundle of faith for yourselves, and it will furnish you with a passport to heaven. It was our duty to define it. I am going to take a passage from the fourth chapter of Romany and I will step over into the fifth chapter, and he cannote that, if he wants to: "He was delivered for our offenses, and raised again for our justification."

Just before he sat down, he became liberal enough to believe that he was saved by grace. I want every one to notice the inconsistency of that admission, and especially when it came from such a worthy opponent as he is.

Fifth chapter of Romans: The word faith is there. I have use for it; he has none. Having said, in the close of the preceding chapter, that He was raised for our justification, He says: "Therefore, being justified by faith, we have peace with God." Now say it is your act! Tell me where the necessity was for Christ being delivered and raised for the justification of his people? I want thinking men to look at the question, and I am done with it: "Therefore, being justified by faith, we have peace with God, through our Lord Jesus Christ." Who is the author and finisher of your faith? And it is through Him that you will realize the joys of your salvation. Look at this passage—you have no use for it.

I want to read a little more. I call your attention to John 3:3: "Except a man be born again, he cannot see the kingdom of God." Now I want him to note that. I have a question for him to answer, from the standpoint I have now reached—and everything is to turn on this quest ion: "Except a man be born again, he cannot enter the kingdom of heaven." What agency, my brother, has man to employ, in order to his birth? You may just get him ready to push right into heaven—what agency has the thing to employ, in order to be born? Listen and reply, now. What kind of a modus operandi is it? Additional I want him to note, What next? The Saviour's exposition of this: "That which is born of flesh, is flesh." He says you are to go to heaven or hell. Born of the Spirit of God. I want to fee! you [looking down at the audience]. You don't look like spirits. Look at the point I have raised. You know where I stand now.

The question is, What agencies are employed by the child to be born, in order to its birth?

Second question: "That which is born of the Spirit is spirit." Now, what is the difference between a man after he is born of the Spirit and before?

I say to you that the outer man is not regenerated—not rom again. You might have regenerated him forty times, and if it was flesh it would still be flesh, and if spirit it would still be spirit.

Isa. 31:: My proposition involves the necessity of saving from two things. What are they? Sin and death. He advised, now. Isa., 26:19: I want to read it now, to show the recovery from death by Jesus Christ. You can't get him up out of death by any agencies of the outer man. Is the outer man the subject to be saved? These are never saved. I defy him to show me. Now listen to Isaiah, contemplating death. What does the prophet say? If I don't translate right out of this into the New Testament, I ought to be put to blush for talking about salvation; and

yet could not tell what they were saved from? Chop. 31::
"Thy dead men shall live, together with my dead body
shall they arise. Awake, ye that dwell in the dust." It
must be the men and women of Adam's race. I want to
put part in hell and the balance in heaven ! Deliver me
from such a conclusion—of such a God!

"Thy dead men shall live." How shall they come up?
"Together with my dead body shall they arise. Awake
and sing, ye that dwell in dust: for thy dew is as the dew
of herbs, and the earth shall cast out the dead."

When did that take place? I will tell you. I am a most
accommodating man. It was a prophecy. It looked to the
accomplishment of salvation—a recovery from death.
When? Everybody make a note of this; I don't want you
to mistake it. Hosea 13:14: "He will ransom them from
the power of the grave." Is it not a wonder it did not say
graves? Preachers have got into the habit of Looking at a
hole in the ground, and of praying about the morning of
the resurrection. Let me read it as it is: "Will ransom
them from the power of the grave; I will redeem them
from death: O death, I will be thy plagues; O grave, I
will be thy destruction." Can you think of God wreaking
his vengeance on a hole in the ground? I am not worshiping that kind of a God. "I will redeem them from death:
O death, I will be thy plagues." He says, away back yonder—

(Brents, from his seat: "I have said not a word about
it.")

(Herod): We have got just as far back that way as the
third day— the Bible gives no fourth day. I am advised
in the Scriptures, and I know what I am talking about;
This is in Hosea 6:2. Everybody listen, now, because I
have called your attention as to when it is to be done:
"After two days will he revive us." It will be in the
fourth, Herod. To the morning of the resurrection you've
got to go, if you get that. Just such blundering as that is

astonishing. What is the resurrection? Can you be mistaken as to the fact there presented—" I am the resurrection and the life"? In the morning of Christ! After two days wilt he revive us, and in the last day raise us up!

We are now going to translate to Eph. 2:1. No mistake about it Everybody listen, and see why he docs what he said he would do by Isaiah. Is it a failure, and nobody saved? "And you hath he quickened, who were dead in trespasses and sins; wherein in time past ye walked according to the course of this world, according to the prince of the power of the air, the spirit that now worketh in the children of disobedience; among whom also we all had our conversation in times past in the lusts of our flesh, fulfilling the desires of the flesh and of the mind; and were by nature the children of wrath, even as others But God, who is rich in mercy, for his great love wherewith he loved us, even when we were dead in sins, hath quickened us together with Christ (by grace ye are saved); and hath raised us up together, and made us sit together in heavenly places in Christ Jesus; that in the ages to come he might show the exceeding riches of his grace, in his kindness toward us, through Christ Jesus. For by grace are ye saved through faith; and that not of yourselves: it is the gift of God: not of works, lest any man should boast."

When was the physical organization created? In Adam. Christ is the head and source of spiritual blessings; and Adam's people have the natural blessings. I know you can see it What else? "Through faith; that not of yourselves, it is the gift of God." "We are his workmanship, created unto good works, which God before ordained that we should walk in them." What more? It is already noted in the first chapter. The apostle comes to the following point: We get the words predestinate and choice. I am not going to twist the language, and try to get the passage out of my way.

"Blessed with all spiritual blessings in heavenly places in Christ Jesus, according as he hath chosen us in hint before the foundation of the world. Having predestinated us unto the adoption of children by Jesus Christ to himself, according to the good pleasure of his will, in whom we have redemption through his blood, the forgiveness of sins"—according to our obedience I Now I am over on your side. You see how he tries to explain that away! I roust explain that right. "In whom we have redemption through his blood, the forgiveness of sins according to the riches of his grace." I submit that it is in the blood that we enjoy the blessings in that passage.

Zech. 9:11: "As for thee also, by the blood of thy covenant I have sent forth thy prisoners out of the pit wherein is no water." That is where salvation is obtained for his people. You need not be Reared about going to heaven. I reckon that in the dust where I go, there the inner man will be wafted to the haven of eternal rest. You can see something in that: "As for thee also, by the blood of thy covenant I have sent forth thy prisoners out of the pit wherein i* no water."

I call your attention to John 11:48. What are you going there for? For proof, "Blessed is the nation whose God is the Lord, and the people whom he hath chosen for his inheritance." Just after the resurrection of Lazarus from the dead! Any miracle about that? The Jews seem to have gone in and taken dinner, and gone out; and the report went out as to the magnitude of the miracle performed. They call the kings and rulers together, and the question comes up, If this man Jesus is left alone, the Romans will come and follow him. Caiaphas said, "You know nothing. It is expedient that one should die, and not the whole nation perish." He prophesied that Jesus should die, and not only die for that nation, but to gather the children of God together; and he will gather them from the four winds, He will bring them in, every one of them. Not one of them will be lost. He redeemed them with his blood; they are his inheritance; they belong to him; and no man can pluck them out of his hand. A glorious band they will be—the general assembly and church of the first-born—whose names are written in heaven! Their robes are all made white in the blood of the Lamb, and not in the waters of a pool or branch. Their song will be glory to Him who redeemed them, and not to themselves for anything they have done.

(Time expired).

DR. BRENTS' FOURTH REPLY.

MR. president: —My brother says I complain at the selection of passages made by him. He misunderstands me. When I show that his proofs do not sustain his proposition, he must not understand me as complaining at him. Oh, no; I do not blame him for not selecting more appropriate proofs—there are none. I would, indeed, be cruel to complain at him. The trouble is, that his position it wrong, and cannot be proved. I do not blame him; he is doing the best he can; there is no doubt of that.

He defines faith as the substance of things hoped for, and then emphasizes the word substance, as though it were a material thing, and asks, Is that your act? It is that which stands under our hope— the evidence of things unseen.

He quotes Heb. 2:2: "Looking unto Jesus, the author and finisher of our faith." Faith is here, as it is often elsewhere, used to indicate the system of faith. Take one example, of many that might be given: "But the scripture hath concluded all under sin, that the promise by faith of Jesus Christ might he given to them that believe. But before faith came, we were kept under the law, sbut up unto the faith which should afterwards be revealed. Wherefore the law was our schoolmaster to bring us unto Christ, that we might be justified by faith. But after that faith is come, we are no longer under a schoolmaster" (Gal. Hi. 22-25). Here faith is used to indicate the gospel, or system of faith, in contrast with the law of Moses; and of this system of faith Christ is the author and finisher. He has had this up before, but I did not think it needed explanation; but he brings it up to show that faith is something manufactured in the heart by Christ, independent of any agency of man. Why cannot we please God without faith, if faith is something made for, or given to us by God? Is God going to be displeased with us for not having that which he alone could give us? Are we responsible for not having it? Paul says "faith comes by hearing and hearing by the word of God" (Rom. 10:17). This manufactured faith spoken of by the gentleman, is not the faith that comes by hearing. This faith it the belief of testimony; and when a man believes all that God has said, and believes it because God has said it, he has all the faith that God requires of any one. When Jesus told the centurion that he would go and heal his servant, the centurion told him that he was not worthy that he should come under his roof, but to speak the word only, and his servant should live. Jesus said to those about him, "I have not found so great faith, no, not in Israel;" he then said to the centurion, "As thou hast believed, so be it unto thee," thus clearly using belief and faith as synonymous. Without faith it is impossible to please God, for "he that cometh to God must believe." Other examples might be given, but thews are enough to show that belief is faith, and faith is belief; and we have already seen that belief is a condition on which depends eternal life, and without which the sinner must be damned. Jesus said it, and it is so.

He says he has use for faith, but I have not. Well, I don't know what use he has for faith to save a man that has been saved since before the foundation of the world—he wants faith to save a man who never was lost.

He quotes John 6:29: "This is the work of God, that ye believe on him whom he hath sent," to prove that belief is something God does. Does he not see that the language is "that ye believe," not that God will do it for you. Had he read the preceding verse he would have found the question to which his text was an answer; "What shall we do that we might work the works of God?" They did not ask what God was to do, but, What shall we do? To believe on Christ is God's work, because he has commanded it, not because he does it.

In the same connection he quotes Rom. 5:1: "Therefore, being justified by faith, we have peace with God," and with an air of triumph says, "Now say it is your act!" That settles it; I give it up! But he continues, "Tell me where the necessity was for Christ being delivered and raised for the justification of his people." That settles it again!! Who could resist such arguments? He used and left both these sentences just that way, without a word of application, as though they settled the whole question. Now I want him to tell us what faith does for a man, and how it does it—where it finds him, and where it leaves him. I say a man must believe in Jesus Christ, and trust in his blood for salvation, or he cannot be saved. Every act of obedience to God must be done in faith, for without faith it is impossible to please God. Still he says he has use for faith, and I have not.

But he says just before I sat down I became liberal enough to admit that man is saved by grace. Certainly. Though I said nothing about it in my last speech that I remember, I have never been less liberal than to believe that; and I am more liberal than to restrict God's grace to a chosen few. Paul says: "The grace of God that bringeth salvation hath appeared to all men." The grace of God moved him to give his only Son, that all men might be saved.

But the gentleman has reached the new birth at last, and he has attempted to separate soul and body before time. He denies that the body is regenerated at all. I would like to know if he can regenerate the soul, and have it born again, without the exercise of the body in which it dwells? Jesus taught the necessity of a man being born again, in order to enter the kingdom; and I respectfully suggest that it takes soul, body and spirit to constitute a man While all the change is produced on the inner man, yet all the operations of the inner man are through the outer man. God has made a system of government that was intended to embrace the whole man. I would like to see him attempt to baptize the inner man without baptizing the outer man.

In the phrase, "see the kingdom" the word we is used in the sense of enjoy, just as it is used in verse 36: "He that believeth on the Son hath everlasting life [that is, my friend would say, if he is one of the elect], and he that believeth not on the Son, shall not see [or enjoy] life; but the wrath of God abideth on him."

And why does the wrath of God abide on him? Because he was not elected in Christ before the world was! And whose fault was it that he was not so elected? Elder Herod blames Adam with everything; but Adam was not in fault in this election, for he had not come into existence yet. Adam is his scapegoat to bear him out of all his troubles; he lays all our wickedness to the old Adam that is in us. Luke 3:38, says: "Which was the son of Enos, which was the son of Seth, which was the son of Adam, which was the Son of God." This is a pretty good pedigree; I think Adam had some pretty good stock in him. He was the first man, or parent, and in that sense was head of the human race, and Christ is head of the Church, or spiritual family; but that the children of God, through Christ, were not descendants of Adam, but a race separate and apart, and distinct from Adam's race, is a matter that the gentleman has not yet made sufficiently clear to be accepted. And this is not the question in debate here, even if he were to prove it clear as a sunbeam. Why not debate the proposition?

But my friend wants to know how much agency a child has in being born into the world? And because he has none, he reasons that he has none in being born again. By making figures go on all four, he will destroy all figures. When Jesus is said to be as a lamb, he will want to know how long the wood was on his back? When he is said to be a lion, he will want to know how long his mane grew? When a sinner is said to be dead in trespasses and in sins, he reasons as though he were physically dead, and could not believe and obey the Lord. Death simply means the absence of life, and the sinner has no spiritual life; but that does not imply that he cannot hear, believe and obey the Lord. Man is regenerated when he receives the incorruptible seed into a good and honest heart. He is then prepared to be born again of water and of the Spirit; and he cannot enter the kingdom of God unless he is so born. Every day that he lives out of it, he lives that day a rebel against God. Now I have a question for my friend. He has the children of God, children before the foundation of the world—will he tell us how they are to be born again; and if they could be born again, as they are children of God before born again, and were so from eternity, what are they after they are born again?

But he cites us to Isaiah xxvi 19: "The dead men shall live, with my dead body shall they arise. Awake and sing, ye that dwell in dust, for thy dew is as the dew of herbs, and the earth shall count out the dead." Now I would like to know what this has to do with unconditional salvation. The prophet is talking about the resurrection of the body; and he says that dead men shall live, and arise with his dead body, I believe this; but Elder

Herod does not believe there will be a resurrection of the body. But he cannot draw me away from the subject in debate to discuss a resurrection of the body, unless he can show that it bears upon salvation.

Oh, but he "translates" it over into Eph. 2:1: "Dead in trespasses and in sins." No, sir; this is a very different matter. Isaiah speaks of the dead body arising. Paul says plainly, "dead in trespasses and in sins"—simply the absence of spiritual life, as already explained. "You hath he quickened who were dead in trespasses and in sins." There is not a Christian here to whom this is not applicable. There was a time when you were destitute of spiritual life—simply dead in trespasses and in sins, wherein in time past ye walked according to the course of this world. Now I want to ask my friend when the eternally and unconditionally elect were dead? Will he tell us? And if they were dead, how did they come to life? Will he quicken them for us who never were dead? They walked according to the course of this world—according to the prince of the power of the air. Once they served the devil; once they obeyed him; and among his subjects these had their conversation in time past in the lust of the flesh and of the mind, and were by nature children of wrath, even as others. "But the Lord, who is rich in mercy, for his great love wherewith he loved us, even when we were dead in sins, hath quickened us together with Christ." (By grace are ye saved.) Yes; but saved by grace conditionally or unconditionally? This is the point. My friend cannot see how we are saved by grace if we have to do anything. He can't see how God gives us bread, if we have to do anything to make it. Man had violated God's law, but God loved him, and he devised a system of salvation by which man might be saved. The wisdom of man could not devise a system of salvation for himself—God did it for him. It was unmerited on the part of man; it was therefore purely of grace. "God so loved the world that he gave his only Son to die, that man, through him, might live." Hence the grace of God came by Jesus Christ. "The grace of God that bringeth salvation hath appeared unto all men"—not to a chosen few, but to all men. Man could not devise a plan of salvation for himself—God did that for him. Man could not die for his own sins—Christ tasted death for every man. The blood of animals could not take away sins—"the blood of Christ cleanseth from all sin." The name of man could not even give authority to cast out a devil—there is no other name under heaven, given among men, whereby we must or can be saved, than the name of Jesus Christ. But man can believe and obey the gospel, and we will be lost if we do not.

We could not give ourselves the soil, the rain, the sunshine, the atmosphere, the strength and intelligence to make bread, hence our kind Father in heaven has graciously provided these for us; but we can prepare the soil, plant the seed, and cultivate the crop; and we will starve if we fail to do these things—yet by God's grace we get bread.

We need no clearer proof that God fixed up no such partial theory of salvation as Elder Herod has been advocating, than that God willed the salvation of all men.

Paul says (1 Tim. 2:4-6): "Who will have all men to be saved, and to come unto the knowledge of the truth; for there is one God, and one mediator between God and men the man Christ Jesus, who gave himself a ransom for all, to be testified in due time.

Again (2 Pet 3:9): "The Lord is not slack concerning his promise, as some men count slackness; but is long-suffering to us-ward, not willing that any should perish, but that all should come to repentance."

Here we learn that God willed that all men should be saved, and he willed not that any should perish. Hence if any perish, it is because THEY will not be saved an God proposes to save them. His will was that all should be saved.

We insist that God would not mock man by inviting him to be saved when he did not intend to save him. God says (Isa. 45:22): "Look unto me, and be ye saved, all the ends of the earth; for I am God, and there is none else." Jesus said (Matt 12:28-30): "Come unto me, all ye that labor and are heavy-laden, and I will give you rest. Take my yoke upon you, and learn of me; for I am meek and lowly in heart, and ye shall find rest unto your souls; for my yoke is easy, and my burden is light."

Rev. xxii, 17: "The spirit and the bride say, Come. And let him that heareth say, Come. And let him that is athirst, Come. And whosoever will, let him take the water of life freely." Here is what my friend calls Christ's water, offered freely to whosoever will partake of it

(Time expired.)

ELDER HEROD'S CLOSING SPEECH.

BROS. MODERATORS, LADIES AND GENTLEMEN: —I am proud of the opportunity of presenting myself before so large, so intelligent and respectable an audience as I now appear before. I am before you for the last time during the present discussion; and it will be well understood, that by the rule by which my friend and myself have agreed to be governed, I will have no right to introduce, new matter that he has had no opportunity to reply to before this speech. I expect, therefore, to confine myself to this rule, that when I leave the people of Simpson County and the City of Franklin, I may take the report with me that I have demeaned myself as a gentleman.

(Brents): "I arise to make a suggestion for the benefit of my friend. I do not understand the rule to prevent him from introducing new matter, if he chooses to do no. It applies to the final negative—not to the affirmant. He can introduce anything he pleases. Being in the negative, I cannot, but he can. Of course, however, I am not in the least interested, myself, in what I have suggested."

(Herod): I am glad that my venerable brother has made the suggestion that he has. I want to call attention to a few points. I want the attention of my brother to one or two passages, after which I shall cease to offer any new matter.

Matt. 23:8: "Be ye not called Rabbi; for one is your Master, even Christ, and all ye are brethren. And call no man your father upon the earth; for one is your Father, which is in heaven."

I submit the passage that I have introduced for the purpose of showing just what has been admitted by my opponent in his last speech. He admitted that Adam represented his natural family, and was the head of that family; and in the same connection he admitted that Jesus Christ represents the spiritual family; and that presents Adam and his race as one family, and Jesus Christ as another race. "Call no man upon earth father, for the reason that one is your Father, and all ye are brethren. You have one Father, and that is God." I now submit, as a conclusion, as to whether the divine Saviour would have come into the world teaching that these ladies and gentlemen, and boys and girls were to be advised to disown their parents, and refuse to recognize their sires.

The very moment you say that it is an improper course, you admit that he is advising a heavenly family. I was glad of his admission. I regarded it as equivalent to any argument that I could have made. God is your Father. Listen to one of the grandest conclusions that we could refer to, for a moment: "Little children, ye are of God." The apostle goes further, and says, "If children, then heirs of God, and joint heirs with the Lord Jesus Christ." I submit to the intelligence of this audience as to what constitutes a joint heir? Having the same father and mother—joint heirs. They are the offspring and heirs. Are Adam's children to have the inheritance of God's children here? Why? I am willing to settle it by the acknowledgment of my brother. He says it is the inner man that is born of God; and that's the thing that I am presenting in this argument in this discussion.

I now want 1 Cor. 2: What good would spiritual blessings do a natural man? I go where the Bible talks about something that has reference to it: "For the natural man receiveth not the things of God; they are foolishness unto him; they are spiritually discerned."

I now turn my attention to another sublime idea that has been presented in the latter clause of I, Cor. 1:15, 2 Cor. 4:, and a verse or two that I will present I have been talking about two sets of children. "Call no man your Father." The apostle says: "Though your outer man perish." Look here, now—suppose that had been different; and suppose, in place of that, the apostle had said the outer part perish, and the inner part is renewed day by day; that would have brought this conclusion—the one-half would have been dead, and the other half would have died, too. I am representing the seed of Jesus Christ—the spiritual family that came from heaven. We see, in the ninth chapter of the letter to the Hebrews, that heavenly things had to be purified with bitter sacrifice. Notice, now, it is a man; "Though our outer man perish" —die. We see our bodies on beds of languishing; they sink lower and lower; their hearts cease to beat; that physical organism that we used to love is conveyed to the tomb, there to rest with its mother dust—is that all? Why would we stand here and wear out our lungs, after we have passed our threescore years and ten, if there was nothing that concerned us more than this? I would not do it for a single moment.

The outer man is dead; what about the other man? "But the inner man is renewed day by day." How pleasingly I look to the anticipation! One falls back, the other ascends, escorted by angels to the celestial city. There is the home of the seed of Jesus Christ, This is the last speech; I am willing that you take it, and I shall go to Indiana reconciled with your verdict.

Brother Herod, you have left me in a bad fix. My house is falling down; where am I? Where is the Christian now? I want everybody to be contented with the Bible, without telling you something else. I am now approaching the grand Rubicon I have been approaching for the last half-hour. God has always been beforehand with his word, and made everything necessary for our comfort and perfect happiness. Now, where do they go? Let us step right out of the fourth chapter, and into the fifth chapter of Second Corinthians. He gives us the solution of the question. There is not one in the house that cannot appreciate the sentiment that comes from the divine inspiration of God: "For we know that if our earthly house of this tabernacle were dissolved, we have a building of God"—the home of the Christian, where your brother is. God is your Father, Jesus your Elder Brother; there they meet; there they enjoy the fruition of grace given them in the Lord before the world began.

My opponent said I called upon him to answer me by what agencies they were born, and in a moment he was over into another chapter. He turned right round, saying it is the spiritual man that is regenerated and born of the Spirit of God. So, he stepped upon the broad plank of my platform, and I pull him up on my Baptist platform. Now, my brother never thought of the trouble he involved himself in. I am not taking advantage—I am going to argue it out from his stand-point; you can judge.

If it was the spiritual man that was born again—he said the fleshly man was not changed at all—when will that fleshly man ever see the kingdom of heaven? It is the most serious thing that a Baptist preach one to heaven and the other to hell—it is ridiculous.

Jesus Christ is representing the whole nation—the family.

I refer to Luke 20:, and if you have any trouble I have it noted here; I cannot turn to the verse. Now, what was the trouble there? It was the very question that is before us—what is it, now? One born of Adam's family going to heaven, and the other to hell. And then he says some go to heaven because they do something to go there for; a portion goes where his twenty-four thousand went—that's to hell. The Sadducees deny that there is any resurrection of the dead; and they asked him, saying, "Master, Moses wrote unto us, if any man's brother die, having a wife and he die without children, that his brother should take his wife and raise up seed unto his brother, There were, therefore, seven brethren; and the first took a wife, and died without children; and the second took her to wife, and he died childless; and the third took her; and in like manner the seven also; and left no children, and died; last of all the woman died also. Therefore, in the resurrection whose wife of them is she? for seven had her to wife. And Jesus answering said unto them: "The children of this world marry, and are given in marriage, but they which shall be accounted worthy to obtain that world, and the resurrection from the dead, neither marry, nor are given in marriage."

Who are given in marriage? You want to be in heaven—the Saviour taught it so plain. Heaven wouldn't be a place for us if this physical organism went to hell and the other part to heaven. "Neither marry nor are given in marriage. "You are, are you not? [pointing to an old man]. That's plain. "Neither can they die any more, but are like the angels. "I answer in the language of Christ—

they are the children of the resurrection. "I am the resurrection and the life." Oh, how plain that is!

Rom. 4: —a great passage of Scripture that is left a matter of record to us. I introduce this to settle the question that salvation is of the Lord Jesus Christ What is it there, now? "It is therefore of faith that it might be by grace, to the end that the promise might be sure to all the seed. Not a part of it! That settles the question as to the road on which they go.

Isa. 35:8: If my brother requires me to furnish the verse I will, without any trouble; I cannot afford time now. Listen at the description of the way that leads to heaven; and if we find anything else but Christ in that, I shall confess I fail to understand language: "A highway shall there be; it shall be for the way-faring man"— the man who lives by the way, who relies upon the way, the way which is described by the prophet. Listen, and see what a grand idea is presented there in chap. 35:: "A highway shall there be, and a way of holiness; the unclean shall not pass over it; but it shall be for those; the way-faring men, though fools, shall not err therein. No lion shall be there, nor any ravenous beast shall go up thereon, it shall not be found there; and the ransomed of the Lord shall return and come to Zion." How can they return to where they never have been? How? "With songs and everlasting joy upon their heads; they shall obtain joy and gladness, and sorrow and sighing shall flee away."

Look at what a grand idea is presented. After saying, "Neither can they die any more," "they are equal to the angels," "being children of the resurrection," that the dead are raised up, was showed to Moses in the burning bush when he said, "I am the God of Abraham, and the God of Isaac, and the God of Jacob;" "as I live you shall live also. He has abolished death, and brought light and immortality to light through the gospel." The Jew comes to my thoughts.

Second chapter of the Roman letter: I call attention to the following conclusion, and you will see its pertinence to the question on the subject. He says: "He is not a Jew who is one outwardly" —that the outward circumcision was the work of hands. Doest thou make a Christian or a Jew? I want every one to note, and see where it gets to be, "But he is a Jew who is one inwardly, whose circumcision is of the heart in the Spirit, whose praise is not of men, but of God."

There you have a heartfelt doctrine—circumcision without hands, and without the use of a knife.

(Time expired.)

DR. BRENTS' CLOSING REPLY.

MR. PRESIDENT: —My friend stretches what I said of Adam beyond legitimate bounds. I did not say that Adam represented the whole natural family, but that he was the original parent, or head, from which the whole family descended. He also represents me as admitting that Jesus Christ represents one family and Adam represent another. He puts into my mouth a word I did not use. I believe Adam's descendants become Christ's family by obedience, adoption, or the new birth. I did not admit that Adam and Christ represented different families. Not all of Adam's family become Christ's family; but it is their own fault if they do not.

But I must not complain, for he serves Jesus Christ and the Apostle John worse than he does me. He cannot see how a man— the same man—may be a child of an earthly parent and a child of God at the same time. I cannot afford to trifle away the time of my last speech in replying to the like of this. He must excuse me; I can well afford to leave it to the intelligence of the audience. His whole argument amounts to this: George Jones cannot be the son of John Jones, because he has become a child of God and a member of his family. The audience may reply. I am ashamed of this, but I am not responsible for it.

He represents me, again, as admitting that the spiritual, or inner man, is born again, and the outer man not. Oh, no; I said no such thing as this. God has a system of government that brings the whole man into his service. While the inner man is the seat of all change produced by the new birth, still the inner man can do nothing as service to God or man, except through the outer man. What is the inner man? Paul says (Rom, 7:22-25): "For I delight in the law of God after the inward man: but I see another law in my members, warring against the law of my mind, and bringing me into captivity to the law of sin which is in my members. O wretched man that I am! Who shall deliver me from the body of this death? I thank God, through Jesus Christ our Lord. So then, with the mind I myself serve the law of God, but with the flesh the law of sin." Here, we see clearly that the mind is the inner man. He thinks that in the future life they neither marry nor are given in marriage, hence only the inner man has anything to do with the service of God on the earth. When he married his wife, did he marry a woman without a mind? I suppose he married a woman with mind and body. I am sure I would not want one destitute of either. But what has this to do with the question in debate? Just nothing at all.

But he asks what good would spiritual blessings do a natural man? And he goes to 1 Cor. 2:14: "But the natural man receiveth not the things of the Spirit of God; for they are foolishness unto him; neither can he know them, because they are spiritually discerned." Here is another of his miserable perversions that I must consume time in correcting, that I wanted to appropriate otherwise. He wants to separate the outer and inner man, and make the outer man, or body, the natural man, a thought that was not in the mind of the apostle at all. There is not a man here to-day that is not a natural man in the sense that Paul used the term. He was talking about revelations made by the Spirit to spiritual men, and says: "Eye hath not seen, nor ear heard, neither have entered into the heart of man, the things which God hath prepared for them that love him; but God hath revealed them onto us by his Spirit." Us who? "Which in other ages was not made known unto the sons of men, as it is now revealed unto his holy apostles and prophets by the Spirit." Then these spiritual things were revealed or made known to the "holy apostles and prophets by his Spirit" "For the Spirit searcheth all things, yea, the deep things of God. For what man knoweth the things of a man, save the spirit of man which is in him? even so the things of God knoweth no man, but the Spirit of God." That is, the Spirit of God knows the things of God, but the spirit of man does not, except as the Spirit of God reveals them to him. "Now we have received, not the spirit of the world, but the Spirit which is of God; that we might know the things that are freely given to us of God; which things also we speak, not in the words which man's wisdom teacheth, but which the Holy Ghost teacheth; comparing spiritual things with spiritual. "Now we spiritual men, apostles and prophets, have been doing this. "But the natural man receiveth not the things of the Spirit of God, for they are foolish unto him; neither can he know them," until they are revealed by spiritual men, "because they are spiritually discerned." Thus, we see that the natural man was simply the uninspired man, and hence all men are now natural, or uninspired men. The wise men of Egypt could not interpret the king's dream—why? Because they were natural men; but Joseph could interpret it, because he was a spiritual man—a discerner of spiritual things. The wise men of Babylon could not interpret Nebuchadnezzar's dream, because they were also natural men; but Daniel could interpret it, because he was a spiritual man —a discerner of spiritual things. Now, what a perversion to make the natural man the body, or outer man! The body, without the mind, cannot discern anything, whether it be a spiritual thing or a natural thing.

He quotes Paul (II, Cor. 4:16, 17): "Though our outward man perish, yet the inward man is renewed day by day; for our light affliction, which is but for a moment, worketh for us a far more exceeding and eternal weight of glory," Now what has this to do with conditional salvation? It simply shows that when the hand of affliction is laid upon us, we contemplate the uncertainty of life and realize our dependence upon God, and become more devoted as we become weaker in body. But did my friend think of the fact that it was connection with an afflicted body that gave spiritual strength? Separate from mind, the body cannot suffer at all, nor can there be a single mental function without the exercise of body. Elder Herod cannot separate them.

His last speech had no more to do with the question in debate than if he had not made it. We are talking about how men are to be saved, not about what they are. Not one passage did he produce that bears upon the subject of conditional or unconditional salvation. Is there one in this audience that remembers such a passage? All know he did not produce one—not one!

He sneers at the idea of one of Adam's race going to hell; he despises such doctrine! I told you he was a Universalist; but I did not expect him to so boldly avow it. He has just backed his ears and swallowed the whole thing, horns and all. This book says "they that have done good shall be resurrected to life, and they that have done evil shall be resurrected to damnation. The wicked shall go away into everlasting punishment, but the righteous into life eternal." The same word in the original qualifies the duration of the punishment of the wicked that qualifies the duration of the life of the righteous. If the punishment of the wicked will end, the enjoyment of the righteous will have an end. The idolaters, whoremongers, thieves and murderers are just as sure of heaven as the purest saint on earth. He asks, When will these bodies got to heaven? I answer, When they are immortalized. But suppose they never get there at all—does it follow that unconditional election and salvation is true?

Now I want to call your attention to some things I have urged upon the attention of the affirmant, without being able to get a word from him in reply. I asked him to tell us when, where, and between whom the covenant of grace was made, I have asked him to show what provisions were made for one person, or class of persons, that did not embrace every person, or class of persons, who would accept it on the same terms. I have called his attention to this as a most important matter; but he failed to give it any attention. I have asked him time and again to tell us just how he was saved, with the promise that I would show that every one in this house could be saved in the same way; but he would not reply in any way. I have tried to get him to locate the beginning in eternity past, in the garden of Eden, in the days of Abraham, in the time of Christ, or at any other time; but not a word of reply have I been able to get I have affirmed that God proposes to save all men on the same terms; and he cannot denied this.

I showed that twenty-four thousand (and there were thousands more) of God's elect, who were descendants of Abraham through the line of Isaac, after having drank of Christ, the spiritual rock that followed them, fell in the wilderness for their wickedness. I showed that God swore they should never enter into his rest, and my opponent agrees that they were not fit for heaven; he sneers at the idea of their going to hell. I have tried in vain to get him to locate them; he will not answer. If these elect fell, who may not fall? Their fall is recorded as a warning to us.

I asked him, just before dinner, when it was that those elected to eternal life before the foundation of the world were dead in trespasses and in sins. He has since closed his argument, but did not answer my question.

When I was speaking yesterday, he said, from his seat, that there was an everlasting Father, and eternal children. I asked how these eternal children could be born again, or enter God's family by the new birth, or by adoption. He has not answered. He is dumb as an oyster; yet Jesus says, "Except a man be born again, he cannot enter the kingdom." His eternal children are out of the kingdom, and have to stay out He cannot get them in. When we consign our children to the grave, so small as never to have had an evil thought, we must be in interminable doubt as to whether they are elect or non-elect—saved or lost.

I called on him for an explanation of Heb. 5:9: "He became the author of eternal salvation unto all them that obey him;" but if he has ever thought of it, he has not revealed his thought. Was it unworthy his attention?

I showed that "God is no respecter of persons; but in every nation he that feareth him and worketh righteousness is accepted with him" (Acts 10:34, 85; Rom. 2:11; Eph. vi, 9; Col in. 25; 1 Pet 1. 17). If God is no respecter of persons, and men are elected to salvation before the world began, on what principle were they elected? You say, on the principle of grace and love; then what was there to love before the world was?

I showed that his chosen generation, royal priesthood, holy nation, peculiar people, in time past, were not a people of God, "which had not obtained mercy, but now have obtained mercy;" and I called upon him very earnestly to know when his eternal children were not a people of God, and had not obtained mercy; but he failed to tell us. Why did he not tell us? I think this was a matter of sufficient importance to be worthy of notice.

I called attention to Eph. 2:11-13: "Wherefore remember, that ye being in time past Gentiles in the flesh, who are called Uncircumcision by that which is called the Circumcision in the flesh made by hands; that at that time ye were without Christ, being aliens from the commonwealth of Israel, and strangers from the covenants of promise, having no hope, and without God in the world; but now, in Christ Jesus, ye who sometimes were far off are made nigh by the blood of Christ." I tried to get him to tell us when these eternally and unconditionally elect were without Christ, without God, and without hope; but he paid not the slightest attention to this request. I give him credit for shrewdness in one thing —when he sees danger, he is as careful to keep away from it as any man I ever met. I do not remember that he has attempted to answer a single question I have put to him, or answer a single argument I have made, or give a different construction to any passage I have introduced, since the debate began. In one or two instances, he called up passages that I had used—several speeches after I had introduced them—but did not attempt to construe them. If he did, I have forgotten his construction.

I called his attention to the doctrine of a future judgment—that we are all to be judged according to our works; that every one may receive the things done in his body, according to that he hath done, whether it be good or bad. See 2 Cor. 5:10; Rev. 20:12, 13; Rev. 22:12. That, if his doctrine be true, the personal destiny of every man was fixed before the foundation of the world by the immutable decree of election, and that the line of separation must be just where the election placed it; and hence no man could, or would, be judged according to his works. What a sublimely ridiculous farce to assemble a world to judge them according to their work, when their destiny had been unconditionally fixed before time began! Suppose there are five hundred persons in this house; one hundred of them were personally and unconditionally elected to eternal life before the world began; the other four hundred were not provided for, and cannot be saved—where will the line of separation be drawn? Will it be drawn according to their works? Certainly not—but according to the election that fixed their destiny. From this conclusion, there is no escape for him. He turns up his nose at the idea of a man doing anything, being required to do anything, or being able to do anything to affect his salvation or future destiny in any way. Hence man can have no works by which to be judged, if he is correct.

(Time expired.)

The Brents-Frogge Debate
on Infant Baptism and the Role of the Holy Spirit in Conversion

A Theological Debate
Between

T.W. Brents
of the Church of Christ

and

T.C. Frogge
of the Methodist Church, South

The Brents-Frogge debate will begin on the 9th day of May, 1876 and continue from day to day until it closes—to be held at Caney Fork Meeting house, 12 miles south of Glasgow, Ky.

PROPOSITIONS:

1. The Scriptures teach that infant children have a right to membership in the church of Christ, and that the apostles baptized such. Eld. Frogge affirms.

2. The Scriptures teach that faith, repentance and baptism are equally essential to the remission of sins. Eld. Brents affirms,

3. The Scriptures teach that affusion is baptism and the apostles practiced accordingly. Eld. F. affirms.

4. The Scriptures teach that, in conversion and sanctification the Holy Spirit operates on persons only through the Word of truth. Eld. B. affirms

First Proposition

I propose to give your readers a synopsis of the debate which was held in this neighborhood between Eld. T. C. Frogge of the Methodist church South, and T. W. Brents of the church of Christ. It began May the 9th at ten o'clock A. M.

The following proposition was read: "The Scriptures teach that infant children have a right to membership in the church of Christ and that the apostles baptized such. Eld. F. affirmed. Prayer being offered, Eld. F. opened the discussion.

Frogge's First Speech

I am before you this morning to prove the truth of the proposition which you have just heard read. My proposition is a compound one, first, infant children have a right to membership in the church of Christ; second, that the apostles baptized infants. I am glad to meet my worthy Bro. Brents, of Tennessee, for if it is false, he is the man to show it and dispose of my proof.

I take my first stand-point on Heb. 3:1-4. The term *house* in the Scriptures is used figuratively for *church,* which you may clearly see by referring to a few passages of Scripture: See Isa. 2:2-3. I suppose that my brother will not deny that in this passage it has reference to the church. Well Paul expressly says it, 1 Tim. 3:15. See also Heb. 3:6. This church was in existence before the days of John the Baptist; for Moses was in this church, see Num. 12:4-7. Moses was a servant in this house, then it was not Moses' house: for the Lord said, my servant Moses is not so, who is faithful in all *mine house.* This was God's house and not Moses'. This same house is the church of the New Testament. Acts 7:37-38. Second, Christ built this house. Heb. 3:3. For this man was counted worthy of more glory than Moses, inasmuch as he who hath builded the house hath more honor than the house.

Brethren Moderators, I am a man of one book, and I am going to read in the book of the law of God distinctly and give the sense that you may understand the reading, as they did in the days of old. See Heb. 8:8. Well, Christ built this a Spiritual house; my proof of this is, first, the covenant with Abraham had as its object the blessing of all nations. Gen. 12:2, also 22:18. The provisions of this covenant were Spiritual, Secondly, Abraham had the gospel preached to him; See Gal. 3:8. And his posterity also had it preached to them. See Heb. 4:2. Thirdly they had the regenerating influence of the Holy Ghost. See Deut. 30:6, comp. Rom. 2:28-29. Fourthly, And did all drink the same Spiritual drink; for they drank of that Spiritual Rock that followed them, and that Rock was Christ. Fifthly, the benediction pronounced upon Israel corresponds to our benediction; see Num. 6:24. "The Lord bless thee, and keep thee; the Lord make his face to shine upon thee and be gracious unto thee: the Lord lift up his countenance upon thee, and give thee peace," is equivalent to "The grace of our Lord Jesus Christ, the love of God and the communion of the Holy Spirit, be with you."

My third position is, that Christ placed infants in this church by positive law. My proof is, first, when the covenant was made with Abraham, infants were embraced in its rich provisions. Second, they with their fathers were entitled to the rite of circumcision, Third, Luke 1:67-70, has respect to that covenant which was confirmed by an oath.

Fourth, in Deut. 29:9-13, we have this covenant made with all Israel, their captains, officers, elders, little ones, their wives and the stranger that was in their camp, and it was confirmed by an oath. The same word *(ekklesia)* rendered congregation in the Old Testament is the one rendered church in the New Testament, comp. Joel 1:15-17, with Acts 7:38, Having now shown that Christ built this church, and that it existed before the days of John the Baptist, and that it was a Spiritual church, we will therefore assume and prove that this church was perpetuated under the gospel dispensation. Our first proof is, that the Savior's work as described by John the Baptist, Matt. 3:12, was to purge his floor. The word floor is here used figuratively for the church. Christ came as a purifier and not as a destroyer of the old church; he did not come to build a new church, see Mal. 3:3. "And he shall sit as a refiner and purifier of silver &c." This we find Christ did. He went into the temple of God, and cast out them that sold and bought in the temple of God, and overthrew the tables of the money changers, and the seats of them that sold doves, and said unto them, it is written, my house shall be called a house of prayer for all nations: but ye have made it a den of thieves." Mat. 21:12-13.

My second argument in proof of this is drawn from John 10:16, here it is plain to be seen that the same fold to which the Jews belonged, still exists; and that the Gentiles are to be brought into this fold or church, and there is to be one fold, and one shepherd, See Ezek. 34:24 - 31. God had promised that Israel should be his fold and flock. Our third argument is founded on Mat. 21:33-43, here our Lord tells the Jews he will take the kingdom from them and give it to others who will bring forth the fruits of it.

DR. T. W. BRENTS REPLY.

I agree with my brother that in settling all religious differences we ought to appeal to the one book. Why then has my brother introduced a foreign word into the discussion. Does he expect to appeal to the one book in this way? He says the word *ekklesia* in Joel 2:15-17 is the same rendered church in Acts 7:38. My brother ought to know that *ekklesia* is not the original of Joel. But he says it is translated church, Acts 7:31, docs that prove that the Jewish commonwealth and the church of Christ are the same. *Ekklesia* is sometimes used to designate a mob, Acts 19:32, sometimes a lawful assembly, Acts six: 39, The word simply means assembly, sometimes of one character, and sometimes of another. We would be glad if our brother would tell us when this church had a beginning? What was the law by which people entered it? or were they put there by some law after birth? If they were born into the church, then the door into the church is as wide as the natural birth. Will my brother accept this? If they were not born into the church, from what were they cut off at the age of eight days if they were not circumcised? They could not be cut off from that to which they did not belong. If they did not belong to the church, to what did they belong? We want a little light along here. Again, if they are born into the church, into what does he baptize them'. I wish now to give some attention to Heb. 3:1-1, was Moses in his own house or in the church of Christ? Let Paul tell us, see Heb. 3:5-6. And Moses verily was faithful in all *his house*, as a servant, for a testimony of those things which were to be spoken after: "But Christ as a son over *his own house:* whose house are we, if we hold fast the confidence and the rejoicing of the hope firm unto the end."

The apostle clearly says, that Moses as a servant was faithful in his house; while Christ as a son was faithful over his own. The two houses are contrasted, if not our brother will please show the appropriateness of the apostle's figure here. But he says Christ built it—well in one sense Christ built all things. See John 1:3, Col. 1:17.

But my brother says it was a Spiritual house. What Spiritual qualifications were required of those who entered it? Did they have to believe, or repent, or confess the Savior, or be baptized, in order to enter this house in which Moses lived? I affirm that there was not one Spiritual qualification required of any one in order to enter it. The only qualification known to me was to be a descendant of Abraham or bought with his money. Furthermore, this Spiritual church of my friend had some of the blackest hearted men in it, that were in the world, and that too, in all classes, from the king on his throne, the priest at the altar, to the pauper in the street. See Isa. 1:1-10, can a more terrible picture of wickedness be drawn than the pen of the prophet has given of my brother's Spiritual church. There were of course some good men in it, such as Isaiah, Daniel and Ezekiel; but as a commonwealth they were corrupt and corrupters.

I will now introduce an argument to show that the church of Christ did not exist before the days of John the Baptist. See Mat. 16:16-18. *Will* is the sign of the first future tense and is never used in speaking of the past—and when the Savior said "I *will* build," he did not mean I have *already* built, or that it was built in the days of Abraham, Moses, David or Daniel, but that it would be done sometime in the future.

But my brother says that Abraham had the gospel preached to him. The word gospel is derived from God (good) and sped (tidings, news), the letter *d* was dropped for euphony, and we have gospel, good news or glad tidings. It was good news to Abraham to learn that in him, and his seed "all the nations of the earth were to be blessed." Heb. 4:1-4. What was the glad tidings to Israel, See Exe. 2:8, 6:6. That God would deliver them from bondage and give them a land flowing with milk and honey. This was the gospel preached to them.

John the Baptist, the Savior, and the twelve apostles all preached the gospel of the kingdom. See Mat. 3:2, 4:23. Mark 1:14-15. Mat. 10:7. Will my brother pretend to say that they preached the gospel of Christ. The gospel of Christ is the death, burial and resurrection of Christ, see 1 Cor. 15:1-4. Will my worthy opponent say that these facts were ever preached to Abraham, was it not false if it was preached to him.

But the organic law of the church of Christ is new, and not old see Jer. 31:31-34. The Lord said he would make a new covenant, not that he had made a new one with Abraham. But that he would make a new one with the houses of Israel and of Judah—houses which had no existence in the days of Abraham—but became separate houses in the days of Rehoboam. The Lord excluded infants from the church by the provisions of this new covenant. He says, but this shall be the covenant that I *will* make—not that I *have* made with Abraham or anyone else; but *will* make with the house of Israel. After those days, saith the Lord, I will put my law in their inward parts, and write in their hearts, and I will be their God, and they shall be my people. Can the infants have the law of God written in their hearts? we know they cannot. The Holy Spirit writes upon the hearts of men and women through the words of the apostles. The three thousand on the day of Pentecost heard Peter, who being filled with the Holy Spirit spoke as the Spirit gave him utterance. The people heard and received the law in their hearts, so of every case upon record. Can infants have the law written in this way upon their hearts? We want our brother to enlighten us here. Again, 34th verse, "and they shall teach no more every man his neighbor, and every man his brother, saying, know the Lord; for they shall all know me, from the least of them to the greatest of them, saith the Lord: I will forgive their iniquity, and I will remember their sins no more."

Can infants know the Lord? Have infants sins to be forgiven? We want our brother to enlighten us here.

But if infants are embraced in the provisions of the new covenant, they must be damned, according to the terms of that law, if they do not comply with its requirements. I do not charge my brother with believing infant damnation; but I am showing him according to his logic what it leads to. Every one to whom the organic law of the church of Christ is addressed, if he obeys it, is not damned. The Savior said "he that believeth not shall be damned." Infants cannot believe, if they are under this law they must suffer the penalties of it, if not obeyed by them.

MR. FROGGE'S SECONDSPEECH.

I know of no Jewish church. The church of God existed in the days of Abraham. The great organic law was given in the garden of Eden to righteous Abel and his posterity. Matt. 16:18 the word *oikodomesoo* means to renovate as well as to erect. Now with this view of the subject we have the true character of the Savior's work, for he was a refiner, see Mal. 3:3. Yes, the same gospel was preached to Abraham that was preached by the apostles.

I maintain that infants need salvation, that they are sinners, Rom. 5:12. They are redeemed by the blood of Christ, and regenerated by the Holy Ghost, and then we apply the outward sign of baptism, which is an emblem of the regenerating influence of the Holy Ghost. But how do we cut off the infants, when they are cut off? Well when they grow up and sin they are cut off. I say the house in which Moses lived was God's house—for God says so, see Num. 12:7. "My servant is not so, who is faithful in all *mine house.*"

But Jer. 31:31-34, my brother says it is not the covenant made with Abraham; but a new covenant. Well the term *new* does not always mean new, or just created—it also means to renovate, and this is the way we understand it. But infants could not have the law written in their hearts. Well in Psalms 119:11, it is said that David had it in his heart. Can infants know the Lord? Yes, they have eternal life, and "this is life eternal, that they might know thee, the only true God, and Jesus Christ, whom thou hast sent." John 17:3. Will my brother deny that they have eternal life?

But my brother says there were no Spiritual qualifications required of any one to enter the church under the old dispensation. Why I am surprised at my brother Brents from Tennessee. I read distinctly from the book, and gave the sense, that you might understand the meaning. I will read again, Deut. 30:6. "And the Lord thy God will circumcise thine heart, and the heart of thy seed to love the Lord thy God with all thine heart, and with all thy soul, that thou mayest live," and Rom. 2:28, 30. If this is not the regenerating influence of the Holy Ghost will our brother Brents be so good as to tell us what it is? But my brother says that my position involves the damnation of infants—I say not. I said that infants were redeemed by the blood of Christ, and then were made holy by the regenerating operation of the Holy Ghost. It is very far from being a consequence of our doctrine, I will present you an argument from Rom. xi; 16-18. My brother Brents says in his book that the good olive tree is the church of Christ. (Eld, B. requested Mr. Frogge to read that language out of his book.)

Mr. F. Do you deny that it is there?

Mr. B. I do most emphatically.

F. It is on page 424.

B. The gentleman will please read it (offers him a book.)

F. Do you think I am going to waste my time reading such trash?

The Gentiles were grafted into the good olive tree which was the church under the old dispensation. So, we have the apostle Paul to teach us that the church is the same under the old and new dispensations.

I now call your attention to the testimony of the prophet Amos 9:11. "In that day I will raise up the tabernacle of David which is fallen, and will close up the breaches thereof and I will raise up his ruins, and will build it as in the days of old: that they may possess the remnant of Edom, and of all the heathen that are called by my name saith the Lord that doeth this." Here it will be discovered that it is the same tabernacle or church, to which David belonged that is to be raised up. We cannot err in this, for in the council at Jerusalem, James applies this passage to the establishment of the church again in the days of the apostles. See Acts 15:13-17. This explains the setting up of the kingdom, as mentioned by Daniel 2:44. And in the days of these kings, shall the God of heaven set up a kingdom which shall never be destroyed &c. &c.

DR. BRENTS' REPLY.

In the last speech the gentleman alleged that I had said in my book that the good olive tree was the church. I asked him to read it, but he could not find time to do it. I suppose he referred to what I had said about the church, and olive tree, you will find my remarks on page 423 and ending on the next page. Now in all I said, I have not said that it represented the church. On page 423, the third line from the top of the page, I begin my reasoning on the supposition that it does represent the church, in the language, *"And if this* good olive tree represent the church, it is certain that it cannot represent the Jewish church, because its branches stood by faith, and were rejected for unbelief."

Infants were in the Jewish church, hence the olive tree could not represent it. This is the last place my brother ought to go to prove infant baptism or the identity of the church. All the remarks made in the passage following, are made in view of the supposition above. But we have Amos 9:11-12, Acts 15:13-17, my brother assumes that the tabernacle of David means David's church. What can he not prove by assumption. Did David ever have a church? But it means that Christ would restore the old Jewish church. Let us see. Isa. 16:5, "And in mercy shall the throne be established; and he shall sit upon it in truth in the tabernacle of David, judging and seeking judgment, and hasting righteousness." The throne of David was for a long time unoccupied by a descendant of his, and it was predicted that that throne should be re-established in his family. Hence says Peter: "Therefore being a prophet, and knowing that God had sworn to him with an oath to him that of the fruit of his loins according to the flesh, he would raise up Christ to sit upon his throne." Acts 2:30. Mr. Robinson, a celebrated Pedo-baptist Lexicographer, in defining the Greek word from which we have the word tabernacle, in the above quotation, says "Metaphorically, for the family, or royal line of David, fallen into weakness and decay," Louisville debate, page 78. But Jno. 10:16, the sheepfold, and this proves the identity. In the 19th verse of this chapter, the Lord says "I am the door: by me if any man enter in, he shall be saved, and shall go in and out and find pasture." 1st they are to enter the fold, 2nd be saved, 3rd, go in and out and find pasture. We can see very well what they feed on in the fold; but what do they feed on out of it, and what does my brother feed the babies on. Peter writing to brethren tells them to desire the sincere milk of the word that ye may grow thereby. Do the infants desire the milk of the word? Can my brother feed them on it? But again, does my brother give them the elements of the supper? Jer. 31:31-34. New does not mean just made, just created, not old. Very well, let us hear Paul, Heb. 8:7, "This covenant was established upon better promises, for the first was faulty, the second not faulty, 8th verse Paul quotes Jer. 31:31. 1400 years after the promise to Abraham, 600 years before Christ, it was to be new, and it was to be future. 13th verse, "In that he saith new covenant, he hath made the first old. Now that which decayeth and waxeth old is ready to vanish away." This new covenant was not made with Abraham, but with the house of Judah and Israel. My brother has already admitted that the covenant made with Abraham, and renewed to Isaac and Jacob, was the same renewed to Moses and Israel when God brought them out of the land of Egypt. Deut. 29:10-11. And he claims, that this covenant is the one in which infants are found. But the Lord said that the new covenant should not be like this one. Then the old covenant had babies in it, but the new covenant has not. We leave him to settle the matter with Paul who says it was an old covenant and that God would make a new one —the old was ready to vanish away, but the new was established upon better promises. I have pressed my brother to tell us by what law he puts infants in the church, I have pressed him to tell us whether they were born in the church by natural birth of the flesh or not, but up to this time he has been as silent as the grave on that subject. But he says that the church was organized in the family of righteous Abel. Well how did he learn that Abel had a family? Where did he learn that Abel's family was large enough for a church. I suppose if there was a church in Abel's family that he would think it was a Methodist church. Well what is a church? A congregation of faithful men. Discipline, page 25. Then this family of Abel must have faithful men, Enough for Bishop, presiding Elders, circuit riders, deacons, class leaders, and laymen.

But where did he learn that Abel had such a numerous family? Not in the book of God certainly. But in the course of events Cain killed Abel. What became of my brother's church then? Cain killed his church, so ends the church of my worthy opponent. But I said his position involved the damnation of infants. If they are sinners, and are embraced in the law, and liable to its penalties, his position does involve this. But he says they are redeemed by the blood of Christ. They sinned in Adam, and then are made holy by the blood of Christ. Well, let its see: Rom. 5:12-14 he says teaches that they are sinners, if that be so that the sinner is made holy by blood alone, then it applies to everybody, see Rom. 5:18, so that everybody is saved, so we will hand our brother over to the Universalists at once, for as many as were lost in Adam, by the blood of Christ are made holy. Everybody sinned, therefore everybody is made holy.

Why will not my brother baptize the children of their parentage. We want him to tell us what will become of them. He says the infants were brought into the church in the faith of their parents. How are the infants of unbelieving parents brought in. On whose faith are they baptized?

Mr. Frogge's Third Speech.

My brother called in question my veracity yesterday evening. I said that he had told us in his book that the good olive tree was the church. I will read from the Gospel Plan of Salvation, page 423, beginning at the period in ninth line from the bottom of the page. "Jesus as the promised seed of Abraham in whom all nations were to be blessed, was the root of the good olive tree or church established on the day of Pentecost among the Jews or natural descendants of Abraham, who very soon went back into Judaism, and rejected the Messiah, and were thus broken off for their unbelief, and the Gentiles were brought in, and to-day stand by faith, but the Jews are not yet grafted in again, because they abide still in unbelief." Now I have read it out of *his book* and *he* said it was not there. I've got him on his iron bed stead, and I'm going to hold him there till I take off his ecclesiastical head. But my brother wants to know where the sheep go, when they go out? Why they go into other pastures. But why don't I give them the supper? How does he know but what I do? But he wants to know how infants get out of the church. He says we never turn any out who are baptized in infancy. They go out of their own volition. They sin and turn themselves out. But my brother says Cain killed my church when he killed Abel, and wishes to know what has become of it? Well Abel has joined the church triumphant, but Paul says: "He being dead yet speaketh." I will now make an argument on the state of children at birth, children are born in a state of moral death (I believe in infantile regeneration) Ps. 58:3-4. "The wicked are estranged from the womb. They go astray as soon as they are born, speaking lies. Their poison is like the poison of a serpent. They are like the deaf adder that stoppeth her ear." See also Rom. 5:6, "For when we were without strength in due time Christ died for the ungodly." He died for the infants, therefore they must be in a state of moral death. Will my brother deny that they are, and that Christ died for them? Could anything be plainer than that they inherited a depraved nature, when the Psalmist says that their poison is like the poison of a serpent—and that they go forth from the womb speaking lies. I want to know if the serpent inherited its poison from its progenitors, or received it by practice. Their nature is corrupt—Eph. 3:11—3. "Among whom also we all had our conversation in time past in the lust of our flesh, fulfilling the desires of the mind: and were by nature the children of wrath, even as others." The phrase "of flesh" means "inherent depravity," See Rom. 7:5, also Rom. 8:8-9. So that they that are in the flesh cannot please God. "But ye are not in the flesh; but in the Spirit if so be that the Spirit of God dwelleth in you" &c. &c. They that are unregenerated cannot please God. Infants are born in a state of moral death—

then being regenerated by the Spirit have a right to baptism.

Well we will follow the example of our blessed Savior, he took little children in his arms and blessed them: Mark 10:13-14. "And they brought young children to him that he should bless them." See Matt. 18:3, six: 13-14. Does my brother receive little children? How does he receive them? And there must be some place to receive them. The Pedobaptist can obey this command but my brother does not. He does not receive little children in a sacred sense. Our blessed Lord in training his disciples taught them they must receive little children.

Mr. Campbell is on my side in this depravity of our nature. See Christian Baptist page 432 Question 121, and the answer also, 122, and he gives my proof texts to sustain him in his position. Will my brother take issue with the founder of his sect?

Dr. Brents' Third Reply.

Why did not my worthy opponent read all that I said about the good olive tree? Why select such passages as suited him and read them alone. It does not matter if he could prove that I had without limitation said that it was the church, if it does represent the church that is the last place for him to go to prove the identity of the church, for the members stand by faith, infants cannot stand by faith, so there would be no infants in it.

He says the infants go out by their own volition? He has one door to let them in, and another to turn them out.

But Ps. 58. My friend has found some extraordinary babies. They go forth as soon as born—talk —they can stop their ears, and behold they have teeth, and have great teeth, and this proves they are depraved. But Christ died for the ungodly. Will he say the infant is exposed to damnation if not baptized? But they are corrupt, yet he tells us that the Savior says of such is the kingdom of heaven, of totally depraved subjects. But he wants to know how I receive little children. I receive them just as they are, just like the Savior received them without baptism. The church of Christ is a distinct organization from the Jewish commonwealth, and cannot have infants in it. See 1 Pet. 2:5 "Ye also as lively stones are built up a spiritual house, a holy priesthood, to offer up spiritual sacrifices." Eph. 4:12- 16. 12th verse, How does my friend "edify" the infant? 13th verse.—Will my brother say that infants have faith or knowledge? 14th verse, "That we henceforth be no more children." 15th verse, "Speaking the truth in love," can infants speak the truth? 16th verse "From whom the whole body, fitly joined together, and compacted, by that which every joint supplieth, "What part does the infant supply? "According to the effectual working in the measure of every part." How does the infant work? "Maketh increase of the body unto the edifying of itself in love." How can the infant increase the body? Only by counting *one*.

I will now show you that the church of Christ is new in every respect. It has a new foundation. Eph, 2:19-22. "They were built upon the foundation of apostles and prophets, Jesus Christ himself being the chief corner stone." 1 Cor. 3:11. "For other foundation can no man lay than that is laid which is Jesus Christ." Was this foundation laid in Abel's or Abraham's day? We have a new law. See Isa. 2:3. It was given in the last days. See Acts 2:17-35. For the going forth, of this law—it went forth in the last days from Mount Zion in the city of Jerusalem, and Dot from Sinai, or in Abel's or Abraham's day.

The now one is perfect, see James 1:25. The old one imperfect see Heb. 10:1-4. This church has a new priesthood. Rev. 1:6. We are all kings and priests unto God. Under Moses only the tribe of Levi could approach the altar. The priesthood has been changed, see Heb. 13:10.

7:10. The priesthood being changed, there is made of necessity a change also of the law. The worship is different; their worship consisted in carnal ordinance. Heb. ix; 10. Ours is spiritual. Rev. 1:6, 1 Pet. 2:5. There is a new head, see Eph. 1:22- 23, also Col. 1:17-18. If the church existed before the day of Pentecost, it was a church without a head. The apostle sustains this view of a new church in Eph. 2:13-17. He says "Christ hath broken down the middle wall of partition between us; having abolished in his flesh the enmity, even the law of commandments contained in ordinances; for to make in himself of twain one new man, so making peace; and that he might reconcile both unto God in one body by the cross, having slain the enmity thereby, And came and preached peace unto you which were afar off, and to them that were nigh." All commentators agree that the one new man has reference to the church. If so, Christ made of two one new church: that is out of Jews and Gentiles he formed a new church. Not renovated or patched up an old one, but made a new church; one in which both Jews and Gentiles are reconciled unto God, and have access unto the Father by one Spirit.

Mr. Frogge's Fourth Speech.

My brother says that our Lord was made the head of the church after his death, burial and resurrection; we want the chapter and verse.

But he says it is a new church, but where is the proof? I have shown you that Christ came as a refiner, and purifier and not to build a new church; see Mal. 3:3, and Matt. 3:12. "And he will thoroughly purge his floor," not destroy his floor, and Matt. 21:12-13, and the Savior said, "Other sheep I have, which are not of this fold, them also I must bring, and they shall hear my voice and they shall be one fold, and one shepherd." John 10:16. And now the prophets maintain the same; see Amos

9:11-12. "In that day will I raise up the tabernacle of David that is fallen, and close up the breaches thereof; and I will raise up his ruins, and I will build it as in the days of old; that they may possess the remnant of Eden, and of all the heathen that are called by my name saith the Lord that doeth this."

Well how was it built "in the days of old." See Deut. 29:10-12. "Ye stand this day all of you before the Lord your God; your captains of your tribes, your elders, and your officers, with all the men of Israel, your little ones, your wives, and the stranger that is in thy camp, from the hewer of thy wood unto the drawer of thy water: that thou should'st enter into covenant with the Lord thy God, and into his oath, which the Lord thy God maketh with thee this day." It was built in the days of old with the little ones in it, and it is to be continued under the new dispensation with them in it.

Isaiah, whose lips were touched with a live coal from off the altar, when looking forward to this dispensation said of Christ, "he shall feed his flocks like a shepherd; he shall gather the lambs with his arms and carry them in his bosom," see Isa. 40:11. Brother moderators, how can we understand this is in any other sense than that Christ should take the infants in his arms, and would he not teach his apostles to do so? But I read again distinctly from the book (oh how I love this book) and give the sense that you may understand the reading. Again it is written, "Thus saith the Lord God, behold, I will lift up mine hand to the Gentiles, and set up my standard to the people: and they shall bring thy sons in their arms, and thy daughters shall be carried upon their shoulders, and kings shall be thy nursing fathers and their queens thy nursing mothers." Isa. 49:22-23. Now what can be plainer? They shall bring their sons in their arms, and in the church they shall find nursing fathers and mothers, that shall train them up in the nurture and admonition of the Lord. Well now, brethren moderators, who acts more in accordance with this prediction? Pedo-baptist or anti-pedobaptist? Most certainly the Pedo-baptist.

But my brother says that the church under the new dispensation, has a new law, I deny that there is a new law of pardon. We have the same law of pardon that Abel had; I call for the proof that there is a new head. The church under the old dispensation had the same pass-over that we have.

Christ was the passover in that as he is in this; all that were saved under the old dispensation were saved by the intercession of our blessed Lord. Yes, Abel had the same gospel that we have.

I now come to the commission, Matt. 28:18-20, "Go ye therefore, and teach all nations, baptizing them in the name of the Father, and of the Son and of the Holy Ghost," the word *matheteusate* primarily means to disciple. Go disciple all nations by baptizing them, infants are a part of all nations, so we carry out the commission by baptizing them. Mr. Campbell is on my side in this question, he says it was to disciple, and that baptizing was the discipling act. I must say, brother moderators, that the Pedo-baptists are the only persons who carry out this commission of our blessed Lord.

Dr. Brents' Fourth Reply.

My worthy opponent tells us that we have the same law of pardon that Abel had, where did he learn that? did he ever read where Abel was commanded to believe, repent and be baptized for salvation? Let him give us chapter and verse for his assertion.

But he says Abel had the same gospel, we would like to have chapter and verse for that assertion, too. But Deut. xxix; 9-13—my brother has already admitted that the covenant made with Abraham, and renewed with Isaac and Jacob, and renewed with Moses was the same—this is the one which has circumcision in it, the one respecting Abraham's natural offspring, and the one which has infants in it.

But the Lord by the mouth of Jeremiah said, "I will make a new covenant with the house of Israel, and the house of Judah, not like the old one made with their fathers when I took them by the hand to lead them out of the land of Egypt." See Jer. 31:31-34, Amos 9:11-12, I have shown you from good Pedo-baptist authority that "tabernacle" is here used metaphorically for the royal line of David, which had fallen into weakness or decay.

Well my brother has at last got to the commission, he ought to have been here all the time as Mr. Ditzler says in the Louisville debate, that this is the only authority we have to baptize anybody, page 15. My brother says that the phrase "all nations" embraces infants, therefore he baptizes them. Are there not murderers and thieves in all nations? Will my brother baptize them, too? they are embraced in the phrase "all nations." But he says *matheteusate* means to disciple, and he baptizes in order to disciple. Does he disciple the adults in the same way? he says he baptized every negro baby he owned, did he baptize old ones, without faith or repentance? he ought to have baptized them in order to make them disciples if he wished to appear consistent with his theory.

But he says that John the Baptist was made a member of the church at eight days old? how was he made a member? I have pressed my brother hard in every speech to tell me how they were made members; but up to this time he has never given us the law for it. I will now resume my own line of argument against the practice of infant baptism.

It makes void the commission, Mark 16:15-17, "He that believeth and is baptized shall be saved." Infants were not included in this commission, they cannot believe, and if infant baptism was universally practiced it would make void believers' baptism. Acts 2:38. If all were baptized in infancy, no man could preach like Peter did on the day of Pentecost. There were no infants here that were commanded to be baptized. Peter commanded those present to repent and be baptized, every one of them, and as the infants cannot repent, Peter's instructions could not be obeyed by them. "They that gladly received his word were baptized," infants were not baptized for they could not gladly receive the word. In the 42nd verse, "And they continued steadfastly is the apostles' doctrine and fellowship." Can infants continue steadfastly in doctrine and fellowship? Can they break bread? Can infants pray as did those who were baptized on the day of Pentecost? in the 43rd verse Luke says, "And fear came upon every soul." Can infants fear? Acts 8:5-11. Those to whom the gospel was preached in this case could give heed, even from the least to the greatest, the same *they* were baptized "both men and women," therefore all the people from the least to the greatest did not include one infant, Rom. 6:3-6, how can it be possible that infants know anything about baptism? Can infants arise to walk in newness of life. 1 Cor. 1:13. Could an infant answer these questions intelligently? Gal. iii; 26-27. Are baptized infants the children of God by faith?

Col. 2:12, are infants buried in baptism and raised through faith? Such are the expressions used by the apostles to the early Christians in every epistle. Infants are not capable of being thus addressed. 1 Pet, 3:21. Baptism reaches the conscience, what response does the conscience of an infant make?

John's baptism excluded infants, see Matt. 3:5-10. Infants could not go out, those baptized did go out, they confessed their sins, they desired baptism of John. But infants could not do any of these things, therefore John did not baptize infants. Infants did not know anything about Abraham being their father. If there were infants among them they must all have been cut down, for they could not bring forth fruit. Will my brother accept this? I have tried to call him out on this matter for some time to know if they are not baptized will they be damned?

I have tried every way to get him out, but he will not tell us. I will read to you from the doctrinal tracts of the Methodist church, published by order of the General Conference. "As to the ground of it: (infant baptism); if infants are guilty of original sin, they are proper subjects of baptism; sinning in the ordinary way they cannot be saved unless this be washed away by baptism. It has already been proved that this original stain cleaves to every child of man; and that hereby they are children of wrath, and liable to eternal damnation. It is true, that second Adam has found a remedy for the disease which came upon all by the offence of the first. But the benefit of this is to be received through the means which he hath appointed. Through baptism in particular which is the ordinary means he hath appointed for that purpose; and to which God hath tied us, though he may not have tied himself. Indeed, when it cannot be had, the case is different; but extraordinary cases do not make void a standing rule. This therefore is our first ground. Infants need to be washed from original sin; therefore, they are proper subjects of baptism." Wesley's treatises on Baptism, Doctrinal Tracts, pages 151-152,

Here is the whole thing in a nutshell. I of course do not charge the consequences of his position on him but here his own brethren have put the matter fairly before us. He certainly will not repudiate the teaching of Mr. Wesley.

Mr. Frogge's Fifth Speech.

My brother read from Doctrinal Tracts. Well this is the doctrine of the English church. Mr. Wesley was a high churchman. He belonged to the English church at the time he wrote this.

But he wants to know why I baptize infants, We baptize them because they are in a justified state. My brother says if infant baptism was practiced universally it would exclude believer's baptism—well we would have a happy time then, when all belonged to the church of the Lord. But can infants fear? I think they can, every mother in this audience knows that they can.

But my brother says, that the church was builded upon the foundation of apostles and prophets, Jesus Christ being the chief corner stone. Well they were all builders on this foundation. It has been built upon since the days of old, Isaiah 28:16, "Therefore, thus saith the Lord God, Behold, I lay in Zion for a foundation a stone; a tried stone, a precious corner stone, a sure foundation: he that believeth shall not make haste." It was laid in the days of old—Moses and all the prophets and apostles built on this foundation.

But can infants be edified? Infants are edified: we baptize them and then teach them. Acts 2:38-39. I maintain that the promise here is the one which God made to Abraham, and it embraces the infant children in its rich provisions; for the promise is to you and your children. *Teknois* here means infants as well as posterity. In the 3rd chapter the apostle says, "Ye are the children of the prophets, and of the covenant which God made with our fathers, saying unto Abraham, And in thy seed shall all the kindreds of the earth be blessed." This covenant was renewed to Isaac and Jacob and then to Israel, see Deut. 29:6. This is the old ship of Zion; it took on board Abraham, Isaac, Jacob, Moses, and all Israel, with their wives, and their little ones. And on the day of Pentecost it took on men, women and children.

Household baptism,—Acts 16:33. The jailer and all his house were baptized. There must have been infants in his house as the original word for house indicates. Acts 16:13: "And on the Sabbath we went out of the city by a river side, where prayer was wont to be made; and we sat down, and spake unto the women which resorted thither. And a certain woman named Lydia, a seller of purple, of the city of Thyatira, which worshiped God, beard us: whose heart the Lord opened, that she attended unto the things which were spoken of Paul. And when she was baptized, and her household, she besought us, saying, If ye have judged me to be faithful to the Lord, come into my house, and abide there. And she constrained us." The Lord opened her heart to attend to the things spoken of Paul. 1 Cor. 7:

The children of Christian parents are holy, 1st on the atonement of Christ, 2nd, by the regenerating influence of the Holy Ghost and are made ceremonially holy by baptism.

Justin Martyr says, "Several persons among us, of both sexes, some sixty, and some seventy years old, who were made disciples of Christ from their childhood or infancy do continue disciples." Justin Martyr, Apol. I, Hendric on baptism. Justin wrote about forty years after the apostolic age. Irenaeus, who wrote some sixty-seven years after the apostolic age, says, "Christ came to save all persons by himself: all I mean, who are by him regenerated to God, infants, little ones, and children. Wall, Hist. Infant. Bap. vol. 1, chap. 3. The churches which came after the apostles were Pedobaptist churches for one thousand years. Let my brother show that there was any other.

DR. BRENTS' FIFTH REPLY.

My worthy opponent says that Mr. Wesley was a member of the English church, when he wrote his Tracts on Baptism. What if he was? I have shown that the Methodist church had it published, and it was done by the authority of the General Conference. They adopted his views of infant damnation by such publication.

But my brother says that the corner stone was laid in the days of old, Isaiah 28:16. But Peter says it was done after the Jews had rejected it. Luke tells us, that Jesus was rejected in his crucifixion, see Luke.

Acts 19:30-34, The jailer's household. There were no infants here for they all had the word of the Lord spoken to them; they all believed, and when they were baptized they rejoiced. Can infants believe and rejoice? This statement of the apostle destroys the theory of my brother.

But my brother has found infants in Lydia's household. He tells us that the apostles baptized them—this my brother has to assume, for the account says not one word about it. My brother has to assume that Lydia was a married woman, or had been. 2nd, that she had children, and that they were infants; 3rd, that she having come a distance of 250 miles, had brought them with her; 4th, that the apostles told her that her infants should be baptized, which is not in the account nor anywhere else in the Bible. On these assumptions his argument rests.

1 Cor. 7:14. Children are made holy by baptism. Are they unholy until baptized? Will he tell us? I have tried to get my brother to tell us, what will become of them? Are they saved or unsaved? He says the children of believing parents come on their parents' faith, but on what do the children of unbelievers come, or do they come at all?

But Justin Martyr says that there were many living in his day who were discipled in childhood. What if they were? Does that prove they were infants when they were discipled? Josephus says of himself, "And I made mighty proficiency in the improvement of my learning, and appeared to have both a great memory and understanding.

Moreover, when I was a child, and about 14 years of age, I was commended by all for the love I had to learning, &c." See Life of Josephus, page 1st, section 2nd. Josephus says he was a child, but he was fourteen years old, and while he was yet a child the principal men and priests came and consulted him, on points of the law. This is the way the word child was understood in the days of the early Christians. Will he defer baptism until the infant comes to this stage of life? If so we will help him baptize such on their faith and repentance. But he states that Irenaeus says that Christ came to save all, infants, little ones, &c. All I have to say of this is that it is a base forgery, and I will produce the evidence, if my statement is called in question.

I will now submit some syllogisms:

1st, Teaching was made by Christ and the apostles a necessary prerequisite to baptism. Infants cannot he taught; therefore, infants are not subjects of baptism.

2nd, Faith was required as a prerequisite to baptism. Infants cannot believe: therefore infants are not subjects of baptism.

3rd, Repentance was required as a pre-requisite to baptism. Infants have nothing of which to repent, and cannot repent. Therefore, infants are not subjects of baptism.

4th, Confession with the mouth was also required as a qualification for baptism. Infants cannot confess with the mouth; therefore, infants are not subjects of baptism.

5th, Baptism is for the remission of sins. Infants are not sinners: therefore, infants do not need baptism.

6th, Baptism is the answer of a good conscience. Infants' consciences are not affected by baptism: therefore, infants are not subjects of baptism.

7th, Baptism was a matter of choice, Acts 8:36. Infants cannot choose or desire baptism: therefore they are not subjects of baptism."

8th, Paul wrote to the churches, addressing all who had been baptized, 1 Cor. 12:13, Gal. 3:27. Infants are not capable of being addressed by letter: therefore, there were no infants among the baptized.

9th, All who were baptized arose to walk in newness of life. Rom. 6:3-4. Infants a few weeks old cannot walk at all: therefore, infants are not subjects of baptism.

10th, Peter says the church is composed of lively stones. Infants are not lively stones in that sense: therefore, there are no infants in the church.

11th, There is an effectual working in the measure of every part of the church, to the increase of the body. Infants cannot effectually work: therefore, there are no infants in the church.

12th, All the members of the church have a care for and sympathy with each other, Infants cannot sympathize with or care for any one: therefore there are no infants in the church.

13th, Whatever Peter bound on earth was to be bound in heaven. Peter never said anything about infant baptism: therefore, infant baptism is neither binding on earth nor in heaven.

14th, Paul did not shun to declare all the counsel of God. He did not declare infant baptism: therefore, infant baptism is no part of the counsel of God.

15th, All things are given to us that pertain to life and godliness. 2 Pet. 1:3. Infant baptism was not then given: therefore, infant baptism neither pertains to life nor godliness.

16th, All with whom the new covenant is made know the Lord, from the least to the greatest. Infants cannot know the Lord: therefore, infants are not subjects of the new covenant.

17th, All who were admitted into the new covenant, had sins which were to be remembered no more. Infants have no sins to be remembered or forgiven: therefore, there were no infants in the new covenant.

18th, That which neither reason nor revelation says anything about is useless. Neither reason nor revelation say anything about infant baptism: therefore, infant baptism is useless.

Second Proposition

Moderator arose and read:

The Scriptures teach that faith, repentance and baptism are equally essential to the remission of sins. Dr. B. affirms.

Dr. Brents' First Speech.

Gentlemen Moderators, Ladies and Gentlemen:

This is not the time or place for me to find fault of the terms of a proposition, however, I would have preferred to have had the substance of this proposition expressed in another form, but I accept it as it stands, with some explanation. The word *equally,* we think, gives room for quibbling.

We affirm that each item, Faith, Repentance, and Baptism have in their respective positions in the law of pardon, an office each peculiar to itself and they are all necessary in their respective positions to the remission of sins. Neither one can occupy the place of the other, they are in this respect all equally essential to the remission of sins.

My first argument is based upon Mark 1:4, John did baptize in the wilderness and preached baptism for the remission of sins. The baptism of repentance, or the baptism growing out of repentance is said to be for the remission of sins. See also Luke 8:3.

My second argument is based upon John 3:5. Those who are out of the kingdom are unsaved, and need to enter it in order to salvation, but the Savior tells Nicodemus that no man can eater the kingdom of heaven until he is born of water, that is unless he is baptized, therefore baptism is essential to remission.

Before I proceed to develop my third argument I will read a rule to which my worthy respondent will not object since it was accepted by Mr. Hughey, see Braden &

Hughey debate, page 200. "When anything is promised upon the performance of certain conditions, all the conditions must be complied with, before the thing promised can be obtained; and although in some places some of the conditions may not be specified, when the thing promised is spoken of, all the conditions must be understood, though not expressed."

The commission of our Lord before his ascension, places salvation after baptism. Mark 16:15-16. "Go preach the gospel to every creature, he that believeth and is baptized shall be saved." The order is go preach the gospel, faith, repentance, baptism salvation or redemption. This is to be done in the name of Christ beginning at Jerusalem. See commission given by Matthew, Mark, Luke. This does not teach us that he that believeth is saved, and may or should be baptized, but "he that believeth and is baptized shall be saved." Jesus put salvation after baptism and not before it. I want my worthy respondent to come out along here and let us see where he stands.

On the first proposition he told us that baptism was the disciplining act, go teach the nations meant go disciple the nations, baptizing was the manner in which it was done. I now wish our brother to tell us whether a man can be saved without being a disciple of Jesus.

My fourth argument is based upon Acts 2:38. The Pentecostians asked what they must do. Peter told them to repent and he baptized, every one of you, in the name of Christ for the remission of sins. In other words- Peter commanded them to repent and be baptized for the remission of sins. Whatever relation repentance may have to remission, baptism sustains the same, by the law of language. Is repentance in order to remission? so is baptism, the conjunction *and* connects them together for one and the same object. We call our brother's attention to this argument, we want him to dispose of the terms of

Peter's answer, and show that they were not given with a view to remission of the sins of the inquiring multitude.

I will call your attention to the next case of conversion to confirm the position we have taken, Acts 3:19. "Here Peter told them to repent and be converted, that your sins may be blotted out." What condition did the commission contain? 1st to preach, 2nd to believe, 3rd to repent, 4th to be baptized, the result is 5th, shall be saved. Peter preached, the people believed, repented, were baptized and were saved. By our rule all the conditions must be performed before the promise can be obtained, and if any are not expressed, they must be understood. The commission requires baptism, Peter required it of the Pentecostians in order to remission, and it must be understood in the case of those in Solomon's porch.

My fifth argument is based upon Acts 22:16. Paul heard, believed, repented, and the Savior told him to go into the city of Damascus, and it should be told him what he MUST DO; he went, and Ananias told him to arise and be baptized and wash away his sins, calling on the name of the Lord. Baptism is here declared essential to salvation. I have Mr. Wesley with me on this passage. He says baptism, administered to real penitents, is both a means and seal of pardon. Nor did God ordinarily in the primitive church bestow this away unless through this means.

My sixth argument is based upon Rom. 6:3-7, 16-18. We are made free when we obey from the heart that form of doctrine which is delivered unto us. The doctrine is a death burial and resurrection, see 1 Cor. 15:1-4. The form must be like it, we die to sin by faith and repentance, and are buried by baptism into the death of Christ from which we "arise to walk in newness of life," see

Rom. 6:3-4. Will our brother tell us what form of doctrine he requires men to obey to free them from sin?

MR. FROGGE'S REPLY.

Brother Moderators and the Audience:

I appear before you this morning in the negative on the proposition which you have heard read, and which my learned brother Brents has to maintain before you. If it can be done he is the man to do it, he is learned and talented, if he fails it will not be for the want of these qualifications, it will be because he is in error.

I read from Christian System pages 119, 193, 194, 197, 232.* I will lay down a rule to which I suppose my brother will take no exceptions.

Rule: An argument which contradicts plain passages of the Bible is false. This rule is admitted by all critics as a true canon of interpretation.

Brother Moderators, that we are justified by faith is a doctrine clearly taught in the Bible. 1st. There are degrees of faith, see Matt. 8:26, "And he said unto them, Why are ye fearful, O ye of little faith? Here we have some who have little faith In the tenth verse Matt. says, "when Jesus heard it he marveled, and said to them that followed, Verily I say unto you, I have not found so great faith, no, not in Israel." The first of these is the faith of assent, which does not bring salvation, see James 2:19. "Thou believest that there is one God; thou doest well: the devils also believe, and tremble." The 2nd degree is confidence or trust in God.

[I turned to the pages mentioned, but did not find Mr. F. reading—I must have got the wrong page, or the Edition of my copy is not the same as his.]

Acts 16:31. The first degree is the belief of the truth preceding repentance. See Acts 20:21. Romans 1:17. The apostle says that in the gospel the righteousness of God is revealed from faith to faith. See also Matt. 21:22. Heb.

11:6. I intend to follow my brother and stick close to the arguments which he makes.

His first argument is based on Mark 1:4. Repentance is for the remission of sins, see 2 Cor. 7:10. "For Godly sorrow worketh repentance to salvation not be repented of." Well we are baptized into this great doctrine of repentance.

His second argument is based on John 3:5, but now the mode is to sprinkle, and this is an emblem of that regenerating operation of the Holy Ghost. Pardon is something done for us, an act passed in the mind of God.

Well Mark 16:15-16. The salvation here spoken of is not a present salvation, but a future one, for we are saved by faith. Well Acts 2:38. Godly sorrow brings us to repentance which is unto salvation, and repentance brings you to trust in God. This then is the saving faith, so you see we are saved by faith. Acts 22:16. Paul was pardoned before he was baptized. Before his baptism the Lord said he was a chosen vessel unto him. Would the Lord have chosen him while he was a wicked man? I will say the Lord did not. Will my brother say he did? Will my brother say that the Lord ever did choose a bad man for a minister? But my brother says that Mr. Wesley is with him on this passage, and against me, but Mr. Wesley taught that whenever a man believed, he was pardoned, justified. Well we have Rom. 6:2-4. This is not water baptism. The Romans believed the facts of the Bible, and this faith brought them to repentance, and repentance is to salvation; this is not water baptism, because we are forbidden by Paul to go down into the deep to bring up Christ again from the dead, Rom. 10:5-7. And Paul was baptized in the house, and he was standing up at that. This is the baptism of the Holy Ghost by which we are regenerated, and made children of God. And water baptism is the emblem of the regenerating operation of the Holy Ghost. Baptism does not make us dead to sin, it is the Holy Ghost that does this. The form of doctrine is faith, repentance, and trust in God; so we are made free from sin by faith.

DR. BRENTS' SECOND SPEECH.

Gentlemen Moderators, Ladies and Gentlemen:

My friend has spent a great deal of his time in endeavoring to prove that we are saved by faith, he says that justification by faith is clearly taught in the Bible. What if he does prove it? He only helps me along in my proposition, for I affirm that Faith, Repentance and Baptism are equally essential to the remission of sins. But the point is, are we justified by faith alone? He has not proved this and we call for the chapter and verse which teaches it.

But he says there are degrees in faith: what if there are does that prove that baptism is not essential to the remission of sins?

But repentance is for the remission of sins. Well I have affirmed that. But he tells you that we are baptized into the great doctrine of repentance. Well, if we are, isn't baptism necessary to salvation? But he says John preached repentance, so do 1 But he preached the baptism of repentance, that baptism which grows out of or belongs to repentance for the remission of sins.

Mark 16:15-16. My brother says the salvation spoken of here is a future salvation. Well suppose it is, it is still necessary to salvation in Heaven, according to my friend's theory. Why contend about its being necessary for present salvation? On the first proposition my worthy respondent said that baptism was the discipling act, no teaching before baptism, but all teaching followed baptism. I want him to tell us now if a person can be saved without being a disciple of Jesus? But Acts 2:38. My brother makes a very weak effort on this. The copulative conjunction *and* connects repentance and baptism, the connection is so close that all effort to separate them according to the laws of language must prove abortive. Let my brother try his hand, whatever one is for, the other is. We call upon him to try his skill, as a critic here.

But he says, Paul was pardoned before his baptism, but where is the proof? Ananias told him to arise and be baptized and wash away his sins. Mr. Wesley says that it is both as a means and seal of pardon. But he says, if the Lord chose Paul before he was pardoned he chose a wicked man, and wants to know if the Lord ever done such a thing. Yes, Judas was a bad man, and he was among the apostles.

My seventh argument is based upon Col. 2:10-13. The Colossians are said to have put off the sins of the flesh. How is it done? Paul says by being buried and being raised again. "Buried in baptism, wherein ye are also risen with him, having forgiven you all your trespasses." Forgiveness is here through baptism.

My eighth argument is based upon the fact, that we do not realize any of the promises of the new covenant out of Christ. All Spiritual blessings are in Christ. Eph. 1:3. Redemption in him. Rom 3:24. Forgiveness of sins in him. Eph. 1:7, Col. 1:17. "We are new creatures in him." 2 Cor. 5:17. For other blessings enjoyed in Christ see, I Cor. 15:22, Phil, 2:1, 1st Thes. 4:16. How then do we get into Christ? Paul answers, Gal. 3:26-27. "For ye are all the children of God by faith in Christ Jesus. For as many of you as have been baptized into Christ have put on Christ." Then baptism must be in order to the realizing of the promises of the new covenant. If so, then it is for the remission of sins.

Our ninth argument is based upon figurative baptisms, see 1 Cor. 10:1-4. The Methodist discipline has quoted this passage in it, and says, it is a figure of Christian baptism. Discipline, page 160. "Almighty and everlasting God, who of thy great mercy did save Noah and his family in the ark from perishing by water; and did safely lead the children of Israel, thy people, through the Red Sea, figuring there thy holy baptism." Then if it is a figure of Christian baptism what is the lesson taught by it? 1st. Moses was the leader. 2nd. He went and preached, the people heard, believed, and were baptized unto Moses in the cloud and in the sea. But were they saved before they were baptized, let us see. Ex. 14:26-30. After their baptism it was said "the Lord saved Israel that day out of the hands of the Egyptians," not saved them when they heard Moses *preach*, not when they *believed* but when they were baptized unto Moses in the cloud and in the sea, that day the Lord saved them.

My tenth argument is based upon 1 Pet. 3:20-21. "When once the long suffering of God waited in the days of Noah, while the ark was preparing, wherein few, that is, eight souls were saved by water. The like figure whereunto baptism doth also now save us, (not the putting away the filth of the flesh, but the answer of a good conscience toward God,) by the resurrection of Jesus Christ." The words *"like figure,"* in the above quotation, are from the Greek *antitupou,* which should be rendered *antitype;* thus: "the antitype whereof baptism doth also now save us." Here Peter says in plain terms that baptism saves us, and that it is the antitype of Noah's salvation in the ark by water. Now, if baptism does not save us from sin, from what does it save us? I want my worthy respondent to tell us from what we are saved by baptism if it is not from sin? It does not save us from temporal punishment, such as persecution, insult, hunger, sickness, death, for the baptized man is as subject to these as the unbaptized. Nor can Peter allude to final salvation, for he says baptism now saves us. We want our friend to answer from what it saves us.

Our eleventh argument is based upon the laver of the tabernacle. See Ex. 40:30. The position of the laver was between the altar of burnt offerings and the door of the tabernacle. One, the altar of burnt offering, is a type of the offering of Jesus, for sins, and the tabernacle a type of the church which Jesus built. Now anyone entering into the tabernacle to worship, must wash at the laver before entering; the antitype of this is baptism, by which a person must be washed before he enters the church of God in which Spiritual sacrifices are offered to God. "He that violated Moses' law died without mercy, but he who violates the law of Jesus, there awaits for him a sorer punishment than death without mercy. Hence they are cut off from Spiritual worship if not baptized.

MR. FROGGE'S SECOND REPLY.

Brother Moderators and the Audience:

My brother lays down a rule to which I take no exceptions. My brother wishes to know whether a man can be saved without being a disciple of Jesus, I say that he certainly can. But Mark 16:15. This salvation is a future salvation and I want my brother to reconcile this passage with 1 Peter 3:21.

My brother did not read all from Mr. Wesley, if he had he would have found that he taught a different doctrine than that baptism is necessary to the remission of sins. The washing here spoken of is emblematical, baptism is the emblem of the operation of the Holy Ghost. Paul's sins were pardoned, he was then baptized, and washed his sins away emblematically. I want book, chapter and verse for Judas being a bad man.

Will my brother maintain that baptism is regeneration? But Col. 2:10-13. This is Holy Spirit baptism, and not water baptism. But 1 Cor. 10:1-4. I thought God delivered the children of Israel through Moses, my brother's salvation of the Israelites is not like ours. According to his theory when we are saved we ought to be carried away out into the desert where we would get snake bit,

But this will not suit my brother's theory for he will not baptize the children, and men, women and children were baptized unto Moses in the cloud and in the sea. I have got him on his iron bedstead again, and I intend to hold him there till I take off his ecclesiastical head.

Well, 1 Pet. 3:21. Baptism is a figure, the rain falling on the ark is a figure of our baptism, it is a figure of the work of the Holy Spirit. What is it that gives a good conscience? See Heb. 3:14. The blood of Christ gives a good conscience.

But the tabernacle—we bring no man into the church but by washing. I have now attended to all my brother's arguments. And now Mr. President, I propose to cut out some work for him.

God's law of pardon existed in the days of righteous Abel, and all along down to Abraham, David, and all the prophets. And we have the same under the new dispensation. See 2 Chron. 7:14. "If my people, which are called by my name, shall humble themselves, and pray, and seek my face, and turn from their wicked ways; then will I hear from heaven, and will heal their land." Here is God's law of pardon, men must humble themselves and pray, *and seek my face.* Now what is this, Mr. President but *getting religion?* Then God says he will forgive their sins. And in Ez. 18:30, we have the same law of pardon. And Isaiah, whose lips were touched with a live coal from off the altar said, "seek the Lord while he may be found, and call upon him while he is near." Now Mr. President, what can this be but *getting religion,* and we have the same law of pardon in Isaiah's day. Well David's experience is like ours. I will read it, by your permission, Mr. President: "I acknowledge my sin unto thee, and mine iniquity have I not hid, I said I will confess my transgressions unto the Lord; and thou forgavest the iniquity of my sin. Selah. For this shall every one that is godly pray unto thee. In a time when thou mayest be found: surely in the floods of great waters they shall come nigh unto him." Now this is like the confession of our sins, and it is like the experience of all who are pardoned, and it is the same old law of pardon which Abel had. When we seek the Lord, we are seeking religion. Mr. President, religion is the same in all ages, I love that law, and now what is that but religion. When men are brought to trust in God they obtain pardon. See Gen. 15:6. And he believed in the Lord and He counted it to him for righteousness.

DR. BRENTS' THIRD SPEECH.

Gentlemen Moderators, Ladies and Gentlemen:

My worthy respondent declares that persons can be saved without being disciples of Jesus, he places baptism first, and teaching afterward, if no teaching, then there is no faith, or any other condition of salvation. I will turn my worthy respondent over to the Calvinists. If there be any other condition of salvation, in his theory what is it? He cannot have one interpretation of the commission for the infant, and a different one for the adult, he baptizes both classes under this commission and into the formula laid down in it. We want him to remove these difficulties and let us see where he stands.

Well he wants me to reconcile Mark 16:15, with 1 Peter 8:21, they need no reconciling. Jesus said "he that believeth and is baptized shall be saved." And Peter declares that "baptism doth also now save us," they both teach salvation by baptism, the very thing I affirm the Scriptures teach. But he wants book, chapter, and verse for Judas being a bad man. Well he is by this passage like he was in the case of the "cup of cold water," he denied that it was in the Scriptures. When I produced it, that was the last we have heard of it. Well I will accommodate my brother once more, see John 6:61-71.

But Col. 2:10-13. He says this is Holy Spirit baptism, but where is the proof, has he given any?

But 1 Cor. 10:1-4. He says the Israelites went *way* out into the desert, and got snake bit. Yes, and men get snake bit now. But he says that men, women, and children were baptized. Yes, and pots, and cups, and all their cattle, sheep, and beasts of burden. I see my friend is very sore, yes, literally *blistered all over,* on the first proposition. If my brother can find authority for baptizing the infant without faith he has the same authority to baptize the cattle, sheep, and beasts of burden, and it is equally binding on him to do so. Well 1 Peter 3:21. Mr. Wesley I suppose is good authority with my worthy respondent, he renders the word *antitupon,* anytitype so does Mr. Watson, whose work is put into the hands of every Methodist preacher, and he is required to study it; Watson says "it is thus that we see how St. Peter preserves the correspondence between the act of Noah

in preparing the ark as an act of submitting to Christian baptism, which is also obviously an act of faith, in order to the remission of sins, or the obtaining of a good conscience before God." Institutes, Vol. II, pp. 624, 625. Mr. Wesley says: "The antitype whereof the thing typified by the ark, even baptism, now saveth us. That is through the water of baptism we are saved from the sin which overwhelmed the world as a flood; not indeed the bare outward sign, but the inward grace—a divine consciousness that both our persons and our actions are accepted through him who died and arose again for us." See Wesley's Notes. Will my brother repudiate the teaching of his own church.

My twelfth argument is based on Eph. v 26. The church is sanctified and cleansed by the washing of water by the word; how is water used in any other way than in baptism, in order to sanctify and cleanse a person? Baptism is the only way in which we are authorized to use water in the name of Christ. Alford renders the word wash, laver; Watson, Wesley, Clark, McKnight, Whitley, Scott, Bloomfield, Conybare & Howson, and Burket say that baptism is here referred to. Will my brother take issue with these distinguished Pedobaptists.

My thirteenth argument is based on Eph. 4:4-6. The one baptism: The apostle shows there is one body for all—one sealing, and that by the Spirit—one hope to animate that body, one Lord of that body, one faith common to all, one baptism, and one God and father of all. What is baptism for in this connection? We have one body, and are reconciled in it. Eph. 2:16. And all drink in of the one Spirit. 1 Cor. 12:13. Rom. 8:9, We are saved by hope. Rom. 8:24. One Lord of salvation. Acts 4:31. We are saved by faith. Acts 16:31. It is impossible to please God without faith. Heb. 2:6. Now when all these declarations are made—the church, Spirit, hope of the one Lord—faith, that they are necessary to save a man, what position does baptism occupy? The Scriptures have declared them to be necessary to salvation. What does it say of baptism? Peter says it saves us. 1 Pet. 3:21, for remission. Acts 2:38, shall be saved Mark 16:16.

I now call upon my brother to tell us what baptism is for in this connection. The great fundamental principles of Christianity are here brought together.

My fourteenth argument is based on the interpretation of *critics'* John Calvin understood baptism to be in order to the remission of sins. "Whenever we have fallen, therefore we must recur to the remembrance of baptism, and arm our minds with the conditions of it; that we may be always certified, and assured of the remission of sins." Campbell on baptism, page 262, 263. Wesley says that baptism is both a means and seal of pardon. Nor did God ordinarily, in the primitive church, bestow this on any unless through this means.

Luther also speaks of baptism as necessary to salvation, Campbell and Rice debate page, 460. Smith's Bible Dictionary pp. 18, 95, 96. And my brother's church maintains, or has maintained the same. See Doctrinal Tracts, pages 249, 250, "For as many as are baptized into Christ in his name have thereby put on Christ." (Gal. 3:27.) That is, are mystically united to Christ and made one with him. For by one Spirit are we all baptized into one body (1 Cor. 12:13) namely, the church, the body of Christ (Eph. 4:12.) From which Spiritual, vital union with him proceeds the influence of his grace on those that are baptized, as from our union with the church, we share in all its privileges, and in all the promises Christ has made. See also Methodist Discipline, (old edition,) pp. 111, 112, 113.

Our fifteenth argument is based on the fact that all the writings of the apostolic fathers, which have come down to us, show that in the age of the apostles and that immediately succeeding, they so understood the Scriptures. Barnabas, "Consider how he hath joined together both the cross and the water. For this saith he, blessed are they, who putting their trust in the cross, descend into the water; for they shall have their reward in due time. The significance of which is this; that we go down, into the water, full of sin and pollution, but come up again bringing, forth fruit: having in our hearts the fear and hope which are in Jesus by the Spirit. Apost. Fathers chapter 2

Barnabas who traveled with Paul, ate, drank and slept with him, is an important witness, and must in these things reflect the mind of the great apostle to the Gentiles. If so we have the clearest evidence, that Paul taught baptism in order to the remission of sins. So of Hermas, and all the apostolic fathers for the first four hundred years.

Mr. Frogge's Third Reply.

Gentlemen Moderators, and the Audience:

We receive pardon in the name of Christ. Peter says, "To him give all the prophets witness, that through his name whosoever believeth in him shall receive remission of sins". Acts 10:43. It is in the name of Christ, and this law has been the same through all ages, for the prophets taught it. Acts 4:12. Peter says it is in the name of Christ, and in no other; this law was taught by Paul, see Rom. 3:29-30. "Seeing it is one God that shall justify the circumcision by faith, and the uncircumcision through faith, &c. &c." Also Rom. 4:3-9, So you see that Paul tells us that we are saved by faith.

Well, Cornelius was saved by this law, he was saved before he was baptized; Peter preached to him salvation in the name of Christ through faith. See Acts x; 43, also Acts 15:7-9. Cornelius believed Peter's preaching and his heart was purified by this faith, so we see he did not have to be baptized in water, in order to the remission of his sins, and the Lord gave the household of Cornelius the Holy Ghost. We are not debating about the cleansing of the sinner, but about the law of pardon.

I have now shown that God's law of pardon is the same in all ages, from Abel down to the apostles. That we are justified by faith is clearly taught in the Bible. "He that believeth is not condemned," my brother's proposition is false, for it contradicts the Bible. But 1 Pet. 1:22-23, Is there anything here that tells us that baptism is essential to the remission of sins,

Titus 3:5, Is it here said that baptism is essential to pardon. We wait for the renewing and then we do the washing. Eph. 5:26. This is a ceremonial cleansing. Where is it found that baptism is essential to the remission of sins?

Eph. 4,: I do not intend to say this teaches the baptism of the Holy Ghost, it is water baptism, and all the units are essential. Well my brother quotes Barnabas, I will answer him like he did my quotation: "The mystery of iniquity doth already work."

Well Hermas, I quoted facts, but he their theological notions. He says that our discipline did teach baptism in order to remission, but we removed the language from our discipline on account of its being misunderstood. I have given him a passage which positively forbids that a person should go down into the deep. Rom. 10:5-9. The Spirit has never taught any man to put another into the water. My brother's proposition comes in conflict with the teaching of Paul, Acts 16:31. "Believe on the Lord Jesus Christ and thou shalt be saved and thy house." Rom. 5:2, Justified by faith, and not by faith and baptism. My brother's proposition comes in conflict with John 3:15-16. "And as Moses lifted up the serpent in the wilderness, even so must the Son of man be lifted up, that whosoever believeth in him should not perish, but have eternal life." "For God so loved the world, that he gave his only begot- ten Son, that whosoever believeth in him should not perish, but have everlasting life." Also, the 18th verse "he that believeth on Him is not condemned." My great fear is that they will take the faith of assent, and will go on, and will never be regenerated.

Brother Moderators, I have shown that the same law of pardon existed from Abel to the apostles, and that God has never changed this law. I have read to you from the book, and given the sense that the people might understand the reading. And I have shown that my brother's proposition contradicts the plain teachings of the Bible.

Third Proposition.

The Scriptures teach that affusion is baptism and the apostles practiced accordingly.—Eld. Frogge affirms.

Frogge's First Speech

My proposition is a compound one. 1. "Affusion is baptism." 2. "The apostles practiced affusion in baptizing." My brother says in his book that baptism is administered to show the death of Christ—also A, Campbell, Pendleton and Graves. Our rule is, that any theory which contradicts a plain passage of the Bible is not true. Well the Savior says "there shall be no other sign but Jonas the prophet." Matt. 12:39, 40. According to my Bro. Brents we have two signs given by our blessed Lord, that of Jonas the prophet and baptism.

I will now present the design of baptism as an argument. Baptism is a sign of the regenerating influence of the Holy Ghost. Under the old dispensation we have two things, one representing Christ's death, and another to represent the operation of the Holy Ghost—the passover and circumcision. See Deut. 31: Rom. 4:11. Rom. 2:28, 29. Does it look reasonable that under the former dispensation we should have two things representing the same under the new dispensation. Circumcision answers the same under the former that baptism does under the latter. See "Carson on Baptism" page 229, a learned Baptist writer maintains this position, Paul was baptized in the house standing, see Acts 22:16. The Holy Spirit was the agent—the blood of Christ was the means by which the heart was purified. Carson says: "The baptism of Paul shows that baptism is a figure applicable only to those who are washed from their sins." "Be baptized and wash away thy sins," Paul's sins were already washed away by faith in the blood of Christ. Yet he commanded him to wash them away in baptism. This shows that baptism is a figure of washing away sins, with respect to those who are already washed." (p. 180.) 1 Pet. 3:21. This is a figure of a figure; it is the baptism of the Holy Ghost that saves us. The falling of the rain upon the ark represents the falling of the Holy Ghost, his being shed forth; it is the blood of Christ that cleanses us from sin which was found out. See Heb. 9:13, 14.

Titus 3:5. This is baptism, shed forth in the mode of the Holy Ghost baptism; which is represented by baptism, pouring is the proper word. 1 Jno. 5:8, water, like the Holy Ghost is poured. We pour out the wine in supper—and the blood is sprinkled, two of the three agree; so we would have pouring for baptism. Heb. 10:21. The heart being sprinkled is the internal work of the Holy Ghost. See Rev. 1:5. Baptism is a sign of this. Ezekiel the prophet predicted this when he said, "Then will I sprinkle clean water upon you, and ye shall be clean." See Ezek. 36:26. Baptism then is by affusion.

We reason from the import of the word *baptizo*—that it is by affusion. The Rev. Spencer H. Cone in his address to his brethren at the second anniversary of the American Bible Union, says, "Since the English word *baptize* according to our standard, lexicographers, means to sprinkle, pour, asperse, christen, the American Bible Union must come up to the help of the Lord against the mighty, take off the Papish cover from his pure word, disabuse the public mind led astray by Doctors and Dictionaries, and among all other revealed truths show to all who understand our language, that baptism is immersion only." See *Western Recorder*, extract Nov. 12, 1851. The Rev. J. L. Waller says, "The effect of all the missionary efforts, together with the present commercial arrangements of the nations will certainly be the introduction of the English language into all nations of the earth if not ultimately to make it the classic language of the world—and as fast as this event takes place, the demand will be made for the great Law Book of the Christian; and then if the Baptists have not a supply of English Bibles to circulate among the readers the inquiry may be made, why do these Baptists in their own land use a word to express the ordinance that their lexicons tell us means to sprinkle, pour or immerse, just as these Presbyterians, and Episcopalians, and Methodists tell us, and thus a vast amount of odium may be thrown around the Baptist translation." *Western Recorder* for Jan. 28, 1852. Our Baptist friends fully concede the fact that the import of the word baptize is against them, and in our favor. They are afraid that the heathen will find out that they are using a word in their own land which means to pour, sprinkle or immerse.

The lexicons maintain my proposition. Pickering says *baptizo* means to wash. Greenfield N. T., "to wash perform ablutions, to cleanse." Schrevillius renders by *murgo,* to put under water, dip, plunge, sink, immerse, overwhelm; to immerse one's self to be drowned.—*Abluo,* to wash, to wash off, to make clean, to purify. —*Sooo,* to wash, to bathe, moisten, be sprinkled, bedew. Alexander Carson concedes that all the lexicons are against him. He says in reference to *baptizo*: "My position is that it always signifies to dip; never expressing anything but mode. Now AS I HAVE ALL THE LEXICOGRAPHERS AND COMMENTATORS AGAINST ME IN THIS OPINION, IT WILL BE NECESSARY TO SAY A WORD OR TWO WITH RESPECT to the lexicons. Many may be startled at the idea of refusing to submit to the unanimous authority of lexicons as an instance of the boldest skepticism. Are, lexicons it may be said, of no authority!" Carson on Baptism pp. 55, 56. The lexicons all agree that *baptizo* means to wash. This is especially the New Testament meaning.

The word *bapto* from which the word *baptizo* is derived means to sprinkle. Groves gives it as one of the meanings and it is sustained by the translators of the common version. See Dan. 4:33. I want my brother to show where the dip is in this passage. Nebuchadnezzar was wet with the dew of heaven, and no *dip* in the case.

The difference between us is that the Baptists claim that it is a word of mode. See Carson p. 55. Campbell on B. p. 120. We claim that it is a generic term. Baptism by affusion was practiced before the days of the apostles as we have shown. The King James translation translated this word *pour*—so we have the lexicons with us and the common version.

Dr. Brents' reply.

My worthy opponent has wandered over a large field without coming to the point at all until his time had almost expired. He tells that baptism came in the room of circumcision. Does that prove that affusion is baptism? Was circumcision performed by pouring or sprinkling? But my worthy opponent says that: it is the sign of the regenerating; operation of the Holy Ghost. There fore, affusion is baptism. We want better authority than simply by his assertion. We are not discussing the operation of the Holy Ghost now. We will give him plenty of work to do when we get on that subject. What we want now is the proof that affusion is baptism.

But he says Paul was baptized in the house and standing up at that. My brother is the man to baptize people in any other position than that of standing, if affusion is right. We want men to stand up to immerse them, but if affusion be baptism then it could be performed without standing up. But he was in the house when he was baptized. This is like a great many other of my friend's assertions it is without foundation. And if he was in the house, could he not have been baptized there, (immersed) Paul tells us that he was "buried by baptism into death." Rom, 6:3, 4.

1 Pet. 3:31. My friend tells us that this is a figure of the baptism of the Holy Ghost and of the sprinkling of the blood. There is no word in the passage to be rendered "a figure of a figure," the word *antitupon*— according to Mr. Wesley and Watson should be rendered antitype; but the salvation by baptism is the type and our salvation is the antitype. So, baptism is not here said to be a type of anything. The salvation by water, is the figure or type of the antitype. Whereof baptism doth now also now save us, so that baptism is not a type of anything. But "the rain falling on the ark is the baptism of Noah." Did the rain fall upon Noah? But Mr. Wesley says, the thing typified by the ark, even baptism. Noah was shut up or buried by the flood of waters in the ark. This is the last place my worthy friend ought to prove affusion.

"There can be but one type under the old dispensation answering to an antitype under the new dispensation." My brother will not deny that we have many types foreshadowing the death of Christ.

Heb. 10:22, "Having our hearts sprinkled from an evil conscience," sprinkled with blood. He won't tell you that it is *baptizo* rendered sprinkle in this verse. We are not debating about sprinkling blood. No one denies that blood was sprinkled; but was water sprinkled in baptism? This is the question. Why don't my friend tell us the place where *baptizo* was rendered sprinkle or pour. Titus 3:5. The washing or regeneration and the renewing of the Holy Ghost which he shed on us. Mr. Wesley renders the "washing of regeneration" "the laver of regeneration," so of many eminent critics, a manifest allusion to the laver in the tabernacle and temple service. The priests were required to wash in the laver. See 2 Chron. 4:7. My worthy opponent will find no comfort here. The phrase "shed forth" does Dot describe the manner of washing. The water in the laver was neither poured nor sprinkled upon the priest, but they washed *in it*. But 1 John 5:7, 8. My friend says the blood was sprinkled and the blood was poured out or shed forth and the water must be poured to agree; therefore pouring is baptism. What if the blood is sprinkled and the Holy Spirit poured, does that prove that *baptizo* means to pour or sprinkle—the word *baptizo* is not in the passage.

Ezek. 36:26. The water here called clean water is an admixture of ashes, blood and water, called the water of separation, see Num. 19; and in this instance was used to cleanse the people from idolatry, and has no reference to baptism at all.

But our English lexicons define baptism to pour, sprinkle as well as immerse: Our English Lexicographers were bound to define the word as used by the people at the time they wrote. The word had acquired these meanings since the Greek language ceased to be a living language. But Mr. Webster defines *baptisma, baptismos* from *baptidzein,* to baptize, from *baptien,* to dip in water. Then he defines baptism as from these: the act of baptizing, the application of water to a person as a sacrament or religious ceremony, by which he is initiated into the visible church of Christ. This is usually performed by sprinkling or immersion. When defining the Greek it means to dip, but in these days it is usually performed by sprinkling or immersion. Can dipping be done by sprinkling?

Dan. 4:33. We would inform our friends that *bapto* the word used here is not the one the Savior used when he commanded the apostles to go and baptize. Daniel did not write his prophecy in the Greek language. But Carson says that he has all the lexicons against him in the meaning of *baptizo*. Mr. Carson contended that it was a word of mode never expressing anything but mode, and in that opinion he had all the lexicons against him. See

Com. p. 56, on p. 57 he says: (as to the meaning) on this point I have no quarrel with the lexicons. There is the most complete harmony among them respecting dip as the primary meaning of *bapto* and *baptizo.*

I now invite your attention to a few lexicons. Liddell and Scott, *baptizo,* (from *bapto* to dip repeatedly; of ships to sink them; to bathe. This lexicon is a text book in the University at Nashville, Tennessee, which is under the control of the Methodist Church.

Robertson: *Baptizo*—To immerse, to wash. Donnegan: *Baptizo*—To immerse repeatedly in a liquid, to submerge, to soak thoroughly to saturate hence to drench with water, metaphorically, to confound totally; as Schrevillius, whose definitions are given in Latin, defines *baptidzo, baptizo murgo, abluo, lavo,* which we translate I baptize, I immerse, I cleanse, I wash. Parkhurst: Baptidzo—To immerse in or wash with water, in token of purification. Figuratively, to be immersed or plunged into a flood or sea, as it were of grievous afflictions and suffering. Wahl: *Baptidzo* (from bapto—to immerse;) more frequently to immerse in N. T.) To immerse always in Josephus, Ant. 9:10, 2, etc. Polyb., etc.) properly and truly concerning sacred immersion. Hedricus: *Baptidzo*—I plunge, immerse, overwhelm in water, I cleanse, wash, I baptize, in a sacred sense. Baptism—immersion, dipping, baptism. *Baptistes:* one who immerses who washes; one who baptizes; a baptizer.

I have presented you the testimony of several learned men with respect to *baptizo* and *baptisma,* their unanimous testimony is that immerse, dip, plunge &c. are the proper and primary meanings of the word. All secondary are such that they retain the sense or radical idea or the primary meaning. We have other lexicons at our room which we will present if necessary.

We also have seventy learned critics and commentators, who are with us in this instance, and they are all from my brother's side of the house, they are Pedobaptists. I will present a few of them. The learned Beza says, "Christ commanded us to be baptized, by which word it is certain immersion is signified. To be baptized in water signifies no other than to be immersed in water, which is the external ceremony of baptism." Dr. Geo. Campbell; "The word baptizein, both in sacred authors and classical, signifies to dip, to plunge, to immerse, and was rendered by Tertullian, the oldest of the Latin fathers, tingere, the term used for dyeing cloth, which was by immersion. It is always construed suitably to this meaning." Martin Luther: "The term 'baptism' is a Greek word; it may be rendered into Latin by *mersio*—when we immerse anything in water, that it may be entirely covered with water. And though this custom be quite abolished among the generality (for neither do they entirely dip children, but only sprinkle them with a little water,) nevertheless they ought to be wholly immersed, and immediately drawn out again, for the etymology of the word seems to require it." Prof. Moses Stuart: "Bapto and baptizo mean to dip, plunge, or immerse into anything liquid. All lexicographers and critics of ANY note *are agreed in this.*" Smith's Dictionary of the Bible: "Baptisma, baptism, (the word *baptismos* occurs only four times, viz: Mark 7:4, 8. Heb. 6:2, 9:10.) The word baptidzein (from baptien,) to dip, is the rendering of the Hebrew by the LXX, in 2 Kings 5:14. The Latin fathers render *baptidzein* by *tingere, murgere,* and *murgitare.* By the Greek fathers the word *baptidzein* is often used figuratively, for to immerse or overwhelm, as with sleep, sorrow, sin, etc. Hence baptisms properly and literally means *immersion."* This is a specimen of Pedo-baptist critics and commentators of undoubted learning and piety. And while they practiced sprinkling and pouring, they did so from different reasons than that which my brother offers to you; but when called upon for the meaning and use of the word *baptizo* they always give immerse, plunge, dip or a kindred word, never to sprinkle or pour. The word has never been translated by any man of note or learning "pour or sprinkle." But my brother says that the king's translators have rendered it pour, we call upon him for the chapter and verse, they only transferred the word but did not translate it when it referred to the ordinance of baptism.

I will now lay down a rule or two, to which I suppose no exceptions will be taken. The sense of a word cannot be diverse or multifarious, at the same time and in the same passage, or expression. In no language can a word have more than one literal meaning in the same place. Again: There can be no certainty at all in respect to the interpretation of any passage unless a kind of necessity compels us to affix a particular sense to a word, which sense must be one; and unless there are special reasons for a typical meaning it must be literal. In our investigations we must of necessity fix but one meaning to a word. Can it be possible that the word in question is an exception to our rules; if not it certainly cannot mean sprinkle and pour in the same passage.

ELD. FROGGE'S SECOND SPEECH.

My Brother tells us that he has seventy critics and commentators who practice affusion, and they are on his side and against me, and he quotes them to prove his positions!!

Yes Paul standing up was baptized and that by pouring; for we do not read about his going out to hunt water in which to be immersed. We propose to show that English translators were not trammeled in their labor. Rule third says, "That the old ecclesiastical words be kept," as church not to be translated congregation &c. Is *baptizo* an old ecclesiastical word? They did translate this word. See Deut. 4:33. *Bapto* is here translated *wet*. But where is the dip? See also Carson, page 37. Mark 7:4. "And when they come from the market, except they wash, they eat not." See also 8th verse; see Carson on baptism, page 68. See also Campbell, McKnight and Doddridge on Mark 7:4: 8. Heb. 9:10. "Which stood only in meats and drinks, and divers washings, (baptisms,) and carnal ordinances, imposed on them until the time of reformation." Here the apostle refers to the different washings under the law of Moses, all the various ablutions of the Jewish ceremonial law are called baptisms. Sprinkling was enjoined by the law; but when was immersion! See 'Carson on Baptism' p. 76. New version renders it "divers immersions." The word *diaphoris* as defined by Groves—*Diaphoris,* unlike, dissimilar; the washings were dissimilar or unlike. Now what could it refer to but the various pourings and sprinklings of the Jewish ceremonial law? But my brother says they were Episcopalians and practiced sprinkling. "The translators of the common version were all, or nearly all genuine Episcopalians, and at the very time they made the version, were accustomed to use a liturgy which made it the minister's duty, in the sacrament of baptism, to take the child and dip it in the water contained in the fount." Campbell on Baptism p. 140. We show that the translators were not restricted, for they were all required by their liturgy to dip, but their honesty required them to give the truth.

Well Groves defines *bapto* to sprinkle, and *baptizo* is derived from *bapto* and retains its meaning.

But my brother says that the word has not been translated sprinkle. It is so rendered in Peshito, and Ethiopics versions. See Rev. 19:13: *bapto* is here rendered sprinkle, "And he was clothed with a garment sprinkled with blood."

My brother wants to know when the word is rendered pour, in common version. See Matt. 3:11, it is rendered pour. Origin makes baptize and wash synonymous terms. See Wall's Hist. Infant Baptism, Vol. 2 p. 332. "How come you to think that Elias, when he should come, would baptize; who did not in Ahab's time baptize the wood upon the altar, which was to be washed before it was burnt by the Lord's appearing in fire?" 1 Kings 18:33. This Origen calls baptizing the wood. The pouring of the water was called baptism. *Ebapto Dou* 4:33, is rendered *wet*—but where is the *dip*. All lexicographers give to *baptidzo* more than one meaning. They give wash as a meaning; and we have shown that the translators of the common version were immersionists, and they rendered the word wash.

We now invite your attention to the baptism of the Israelites, 1 Cor. 10:1-3. We want to know if *baptizo* means to dip. Our immersionist friends make it a state of being, and not action. See Pendleton's "Three Reasons why I am a Baptist" p. 103. See also "Gospel Plan of Salvation." p. 350. My brother's own exegesis makes it a slate of being. What is the true exegesis? "The cloud went from before their face, and stood behind them: and it came between the camp of the Egyptians and the camp of Israel; and it was a cloud and darkness to them, but it gave light by night to them; so that the one came not near the other all the night." Ex. 14:19, 20. Moses says, "They went in upon dry ground and walked upon dry ground in the midst of the sea." David says, "The waters saw thee, O God, the waters saw thee: they were afraid: the depths also were troubled; the clouds poured out water," Ps. 77:16, 17. Here we find the Israelites were baptized by pouring. The Egyptians were immersed, but Israel was baptized.

Baptism for the dead, 1 Cor. 15:29, In Num, 9:11-13, the man has the water sprinkled upon him— "And that Saul shall be cut off from Israel because the water of separation was not sprinkled upon him, be shall be unclean, his uncleanness is yet upon him." We have a baptism by sprinkling, Paul says they are baptized for the dead. But how? By sprinkling water upon them. I maintain that the lexicons give wash as the primary meaning of *baptizo*. We read Pickering, N. T. "Wash to wash one's self." Groves gives "to wash, cleanse, purify &c." Andrews' Dictionary gives wet, moisten.

Christ's baptism Luke 12:50. "But I have a baptism to be baptized with and now am I straitened till it be accomplished" I maintain that this baptism was by affusion. Where is the dip in this case? I will call your attention to the predictions of Isaiah the prophet.; Isa. 53:4-6, in speaking of this baptism says, "He was stricken, smitten of God, wounded for our transgression, he was bruised for our iniquity; the chastisement of our peace was upon him; and with his stripes we are healed." Now brother moderators, can anything be any plainer? Every word used to describe it indicates that it was a coming down upon, and not a dipping. He was *"stricken" "Smitten."* Can anything be plainer; every word shows the mode.

Baptism of the Holy Spirit. Matt. 2:11: "I indeed baptize you with water unto repentance: but he that cometh after me is mightier than I, whose shoes I am not worthy to bear; he shall baptize you with the Holy Ghost and with fire." Acts 1:5. Acts 2:1-4. Dr. Carson says, on the baptism of the Spirit: "But though the baptism of the Holy Spirit is a figurative baptism; yet as respects the transaction. On the day of Pentecost there was a real baptism in the emblems of the Spirit, p. 107. The Dr. frankly admits that there can be no likeness in literal baptism. "No dipping" says the Doctor. By what mode was it done? Let us come to the one book to learn the mode. We are informed in Acts 2:19, that the Spirit was poured out; in 33rd verse we have the phrase "shed forth"—terms which indicate sprinkling or pouring, a coming down upon. "But no dip in the case." We now invite your attention to another case of the baptism of the Holy Ghost. See Acts 10:44, "While Peter yet spake these words, the Holy Ghost *fell on* all them which heard the word: And they of the circumcision which believed were astonished, as many as came with Peter, because that on the Gentiles also was poured out the gift of the Holy Ghost." What is the mode? it is indicated by the words "fell on," and poured out." I maintain brother moderator that we have sustained our proposition here.

DR. BRENTS' REPLY.

My friend still says that Paul was baptized in the house; but Paul tells us that he was "buried by baptism." My friend has to assume that he was baptized in the house. If sprinkling or pouring was baptism, there was no necessity for Saul to get up at all.

My friend tells us that the English translators were immersionists. We will see. Mr. Wall says, "From the time of King Edward, Mr. Walker (who has taken the most pains in tracing this matter) derives the beginning of the alteration of the general custom. He says that 'dipping was at this time the more usual, but sprinkling was sometimes used which within the time of half a century" (meaning from 1550 to 1600) "prevailed to be the more general (as it is now almost the only) way of baptizing." Wall Hist. Inf. Baptism, Vol. 2 p. 398. Again, he says, "And when there was added to all this the resolution of such a man as Dr. Whitaker, Regius Professor at Cambridge—though in case of persons that are in health, I think dipping to be better; yet in the case of infants, and of sickly people, I think sprinkling sufficient—the inclination of the people, backed with these authorities, carried the practice against the rubric; which still required dipping, except in case of weakness. So that in the latter times of Queen Elizabeth, and during the reigns of King James and of King Charles I., very few children were dipped in the font. I have heard of one or two persons now living, who must have been born in those reigns, that they were baptized by dipping in the font; and of one clergyman now living, that has baptized some infants so, but am not certain." Wall's Hist. Vol. 2 p. 401.

Here we have Mr. Wall testifying that the clergy and people were changing the custom of the English church, the rubric of which required the minister to dip the child. "Dipping was at this time the more usual, but sprinkling was *sometimes* used: which within the time of half a century (meaning from 1550 to 1600) prevailed to be more general (as it is now almost *the only*) way of baptism." The change began fifty years before our present version was made, and at the time he says it was the *more general*. Again he says upon the authority of Dr. Whitaker and others with the "inclination of the people they carried the practice against the rubric; which still required dipping, except in case of weakness. So that in the latter time of Queen Elizabeth, and during the reigns of King James and of King Charles I., very few children were dipped in the font." Here, we see the practice was changed from dipping to sprinkling, and sprinkling became the "more general" just at the time of making our version. But upon the authority of the clergy with the "inclination of people" the practice of dipping was changed; the authorized Version was made from 1604 to 1611. That they were Pedobaptist is evident from their translation.

But Mark 7:4-8. And they translate *wash,* but did they translate pour or sprinkle? Is washing performed by pouring or sprinkling? We will see how the seventy used the term wash. "And Elisha sent a messenger unto him, saying, Go wash in Jordan seven times, and thy flesh shall come again to thee, and thou shalt be clean." 2nd Kings 5:10. Did he go and sprinkle into the Jordan, or pour himself into the Jordan? See 14 5: "Then went he down, and dipped himself seven times in Jordan, according to the saying of the man of God." Wash, according to the prophet, means to dip. Will my worthy friend accept this?

Heb. 9:10, Divers baptisms. And these are sprinkling and pouring! We will see. Of the unclean man. Lev. 15:5, "And whosoever toucheth his bed shall wash his clothes, and shall *bathe* himself *in water.*" See also verses 6 and 7; verse 12, "And every vessel of wood shall be *rinsed in water.* The washing was to be performed in water. Stuart says, respecting a vessel of wood, and respecting the hand of a person.—Lev. 15:11-12. "In these cases, our English version renders by the word rinsed, which implies immersion." See Stuart on Baptism, p. 120. So, the washings were immersions. We called for the passage where baptizo was rendered pour or sprinkle, our worthy friend tells that it is in Matt. 3:11. I will turn and read the passage. "I indeed baptize you with water, unto repentance."

"But Origen as quoted by Wall makes baptize and wash synonymous terms. What if he does, does that prove that affusion is baptism? If the pouring is the thing called baptism in this passage, then it was the water that was baptized upon the altar, and the altar was not baptized at all; but if pouring is baptism then there were twelve baptisms instead of one, and we ought to have baptisms in the passage instead of baptism. But the idea in the passage is that the wood was overwhelmed or thoroughly saturated.

My friend tells us that the lexicons give wash as the primary meaning of the word baptizo, and that it is especially the New Testament meaning of the word. We say that this is not the case with the lexicons. They give first the primary meanings of the word, then the topical, and in citing authority when they come to the New Testament they find the word wash and cite the passage, not as a New Testament meaning especially, but because they find the word so rendered there. We have shown how the word wash was understood by the translator in the case of Elisha, 2nd Kings 5:10-14. When told to go and wash, Naaman went and dipped himself in Jordan.

1 Cor. 10:1-2. The Methodist discipline says that this typifies baptism, p. 160. Ex. 14:22-29, shows that the sea stood as a wall on each side and the Israelites passed through the sea on dry land, while Paul tells us that they were all under the cloud. But this cloud sent out a mist or poured out water. Let us see. Ex. 14:*28*. "And it came to pass, that in the morning watch the Lord looked unto the host of the Egyptians through the pillar of fire and of the cloud, and troubled the host of the Egyptians." It was a cloud of fire. "The cloud poured out the rain, since the baptism of Israelites in the sea."

Ex. 14:22. It was in the wilderness. Ps. 68:8-9. Stuart says of this transaction, "It is, therefore, a kind of figurative mode of expression, derived from the idea that baptizing is surrounding with a fluid. But whether this be by immersion, affusion, suffusion or washing, would not seem to be decided, The suggestion has sometimes been made, that the Israelites were sprinkled by the cloud and by the sea, and this was the baptism which Paul meant to designate. But the cloud on this occasion was not a cloud of rain, nor do we find any intimation that the waters of the Red Sea sprinkled the children of Israel at this time. So much is true, viz: that they were not *immersed*. Yet, as the language must evidently be figurative in some good degree, and not literal, I do not see how, on the whole, we can make less of it, than to suppose that it has a tacit reference to the idea of surrounding in some way or other," Stuart on Baptism, page 113. Prof. Stuart is a Pedobaptist of great learning and research, but he tells us that this cloud was not a rain cloud, neither were the Israelites sprinkled by the waters of the Red Sea, but that this example was a tacit reference to *surrounding* in some way or other.

Baptism of suffering, Luke 12:5. Jesus alludes to his overwhelming sufferings in death. Did he suffer a little sprinkling or pouring of suffering? Follow him to the garden, and hear, and see his agony. See him when he rolls in his own sweat and gore in the garden of Gethsemane. Go with him to the cross and see the nails sent hissing through his quivering flesh. See him languish and faint upon the cross with no one to give him a sip of cool water to moisten his parched lips, or cool his throbbing temples. Then say if such suffering could be designated by sprinkling or pouring. No, sir.

I now invite your attention to the baptism of Jesus. See Mark 1:5-1. John was baptizing the multitudes in the river Jordan when Jesus went to him and demanded baptism. Jesus was baptized in Jordan, and came up out of the water. Why did he go into the river to be baptized by sprinkling or pouring? this could have been done out of the river. His going in is in harmony with immersion; but not with affusion. I am posted as to the objection that may he offered here, but I will not anticipate my brother in what he may offer upon this argument.

Eld. Frogge's third speech.

My brother says that Paul was baptized by immersion. But Paul says, 'Say not in thine heart, Who shall ascend into heaven? (that is, to bring Christ down from above), or Who shall descend into the deep? (that is, to bring up Christ again from the dead)." Our immersionist friends go down into the deep, and bring up Christ every time they immerse a person. But we are positively forbidden by Paul to do it. I said that Paul was baptized by affusion, and he has told us so. See Titus 3:5, "Which he shed on us." So, Paul was baptized by pouring, and standing up in the house at that. I maintain that Isaiah's description of the Savior's sufferings, which Jesus calls a baptism, every word in it defines the mode to be affusion: "Stricken," "smitten," and the "chastisement of our peace was upon him." Brother Moderator, what else could it be but affusion?

But "Christ was baptized in Jordan," A man may be in Jordan and be on dry ground. See Josh, 3:17, "And the priests that bore the ark of the covenant of the Lord stood on dry ground in the midst of the Jordan, and all the Israelites passed over on dry ground until all the people were passed clean over Jordan." Carson, speaking of Ulysses' escape from shipwreck, says, "He might be in the river, yet not in the water: all within the banks is the river." Carson on Baptism, p. 339. Carson, the learned Baptist tells us that a man may be in the river and be on dry land. "All within the banks is the river." We see that the baptism could be performed without going down into the water. But we maintain that Jesus was baptized by affusion. Christ was baptized to fulfill the law. What law did he fulfill, that of the priesthood? "He was a minister of the circumcision." See Christian System, p. 166. The law required him to wash, see Num. 8:7, "And thus shalt thou do unto them, to cleanse them: Sprinkle water of purifying upon them, and let them shave all their flesh, and let them wash their clothes, and so make themselves clean." Christ was baptized to induct him into the office of a priest. No man entered the priesthood until his baptism. See Heb. 5:4-5. And the law required that the priest should be washed with water. Ex. 40:12. By what mode? see Numb, 8:7; by "sprinkling," Mr. Jones maintains the same position, that Jesus entered upon the duties of his sacred office by means of the ordinance of baptism administered by the hands of his forerunner, p. 36. (My Ed. of Jones' Hist. p. 38. A. A.) Now what was the mode? if by immersion, we want a thus saith the Lord. We maintain that it was by affusion. What is the use of the word baptize in the mouth of Jesus, John and Peter? It is to pour; John baptized the Jews by pouring. See Isa. 44:3-4. "For I will pour water upon him that is thirsty, and flood upon the dry ground: I will pour my Spirit upon thy seed, and my blessing upon thine offspring." What does he mean when he says: "I will pour my Spirit upon thy seed?" It is baptism. The mode of Holy Ghost baptism and water baptism is the same. The Spirit was poured out; then we must pour the water. The lexicons give wash as the primary New Testament meaning. The learned world testifies that baptizo is a generic word.

The prophets taught that affusion was baptism; Isa. 1:16. Mr. Campbell says this is baptism. "Wash you, make you clean; put away the evil of your doings before mine eyes; cease to do evil." How were they to wash? See Isa. 44:3, "I will pour water upon him that is thirsty." Now what else can be the mode, but to pour, and John baptized by pouring. And Ezekiel says, "Then will I sprinkle clean water upon you, and you shall be clean; from all your filthiness and from all your idols will I cleanse you." Ezek. 36:25. Old Ezekiel testifies that sprinkling is the mode.

We now call your attention to the places where baptism was performed, as being favorable to affusion, as the mode. John 1:28, "These things were done in Bethabara beyond Jordan, where John was baptizing." Robinson says the word Bethabara signifies passage house and it is built on both sides of the river. Robinson's Hist. of Baptism, p. 25. But John baptized beyond Jordan, John 10:39-40. It is said that Jesus escaped from the Jews and dwelt in the place where John baptized. Did Jesus dwell in the river? If John baptized there, he must for be dwelt where that was performed. Bethabara was where he baptized, but that is a passage house. The place certainly shows that it is more favorable to affusion than to immersion.

DR. BRENTS' REPLY.

My worthy friend tells us that *the* mode of the Savior's baptism of sufferings, was pouring. We will see how Mr. Wesley disposes of the case. "Our Lord was *filled* with sufferings within and *covered* with them without." Wesley's Notes, p. 123. He understood that the Savior was overwhelmed with suffering. Prof. Stuart whose partiality for affusion cannot be questioned, says, "I have a baptism to be baptized with—that is, I am about to be *overwhelmed* with sufferings, and I am greatly distressed with the prospect of them. Can ye indeed take upon you to undergo patiently and submissively, sufferings like mine—sufferings of an overwhelming and dreadful nature?" Stuart on Baptism, p. 72. This is the view of many eminent critics. A little sprinkle or pouring of sufferings was inadequate to express the idea conveyed by the dreadful sufferings he was to endure.

But he tells us that "a man may be in Jordan and be on dry land," and that Jesus might have gone down into the Jordan, and then been baptized by affusion, Yes, but was he? Mark says Jesus was baptized by John (*eis*) in (or into) the Jordan. Was he poured in the Jordan, or sprinkled into the Jordan? or was the Jordan poured or sprinkled upon him? Now we respectfully invite our worthy friend's attention to these difficulties in his way. But a man may be in the Jordan and be on dry land, Josh, 3:17. Will my friend say, there was such a miracle as this wrought in the baptism of the Jews by John? Where is the proof? My brother has a sleight at laying more labor upon an opponent by bald assertions than any man with whom it has been my lot to hold a discussion.

He tells us that "Jesus was baptized to fulfill the law, and that he was inducted into his sacred office of high priest by baptism." We will hear the apostle Paul on this subject. Speaking of Jesus as high priest he says, "For if he were on earth, he *should not be a priest*, seeing that there are priests that offer gifts according to the law." Heb. 8:4. We leave our brother to settle this matter with Paul. Paul tells us that if he were on earth he should not be a priest. Num. 8:7. This is the water of "pur-ification," a mixture of ashes, blood and water, which was to be sprinkled upon the unclean person. See Num. 19: The baptism for the dead—my brother says that the mode was sprinkle. We will read, Num. 19:17-20, "And for an unclean person they shall take of the ashes of the burnt heifer of purification for sin, and running water shall be put thereto in a vessel: And a clean person shall take hyssop and dip it in the water, and sprinkle it upon the tent, and upon all the vessels, and upon the persons that were there, and upon him that touched a bone, or one slain, or one dead, or a grave; and the clean person shall sprinkle upon the unclean on the third day, and on the seventh day; and on the seventh day he shall purify himself, and wash his clothes, and bathe himself in water, and shall be clean at even. But the man that shall be unclean, and shall not purify himself, that soul shall be out off from among the congregation, because he hath defiled the sanctuary of the Lord; the water of separation hath not been sprinkled upon him; he is unclean." It is not the administrator that is to bathe himself as my brother affirms, but the unclean person; the law says, he, the unclean, shall purify himself and wash his clothes and bathe *himself in water,* and shall be unclean at even. The clean person is to sprinkle the unclean, and the unclean is to bathe in water and at even he is to be clean. This is the water spoken of in Ezekiel 36:25. The water that was used to cleanse from idolatry—and water which no man now uses to baptize in or sprinkle upon any one.

We now invite your attention to the birth of water and of the Spirit, John 3:5. This is figurative language, but the figure is based upon and must resemble the fact from which it is taken—natural birth. What resemblance is there between sprinkling or pouring a few drops of water on any one and a natural birth? Birth contemplates delivery, hence if water it must be a deliverance from it, and to emerge from it they must be placed in it. Can anyone be delivered from or born of a less substance than themselves? A few drops of water! I suppose my brother will not deny that this is water baptism here alluded to. I now wish to lay down a rule to which I suppose there will be no exceptions taken. The sense of a word cannot be diverse or multifarious, at the same time and in the same passage, or expression. In no language can a word have more than one literal meaning in the same place. We now call your attention to the commission, Matt. 28:19- 20. The command takes effect upon the people and not on the water. The people are to be baptized, not the water baptized upon the people. If sprinkling or pouring be the act then the thing sprinkled or poured is baptized and not the people. Mr. Ditzler says this furnishes "all the authority he has for baptizing any one." W. & D. Debate, p. 15. Then when a man sprinkles or pours water upon another or immerses in water they must get their authority from this verse. The word baptizontes then in this passage means pour, sprinkle and immerse. How shall we reconcile this with our rule of exegesis? But when we have men performing the different acts, and each called baptism we would have three baptisms. Paul says, "There is one Lord, one faith, one baptism." Eph. 4:4. My brother says he is not going to deny that it is water baptism. Then says the apostle there is one baptism. Sprinkle and pour often occur but never as a translation of baptizo.

We now invite your attention to Rom. 6:3-5. We have shown that the lexicons give immerse as the primary meaning of baptizo, it follows that Paul has spoken of the burial effected by immersion. He says, "Therefore we are buried with him by baptism into death." Are we buried with him by sprinkling or pouring? There are three things in every burial expressed or implied. 1st, the thing buried may be a seed or a man. 2nd, the thing in which we bury. We may bury in water or in earth. 3rd, the act of burying must be a covering up or a concealment. Will a little water poured or sprinkled upon a person bury him? Will my brother tell us how he buries? The apostle tells the Colossians that they were buried with him in baptism. Prof. Stuart says, "Even in those controverted passages in Rom. 6:4-5, Col. 2:12, baptism is connected with the work of the Spirit, and is significant of his influence. It is a dying to sin and being raised to a new spiritual life, which is prefigured by it." Mr. Wesley is with us here. He says, *We are buried with him,* alluding to the ancient manner of baptizing by immersion. Wesley's Notes on Rom. 6:4.

We base another argument on the eunuch's baptism. See Acts 8:30- 39. Philip and the eunuch as they *came to a certain water.* "And he commanded the chariot to stand still, and they went down both into the water, both Philip and the eunuch; and he baptized him. They then came up (*ek*) out of the water." They came to—then went down into, (*eis*) carried them beyond the margin of the water or into it. *Ek* means out of, where *eis* carried them—as far into the water as *ek* brought them out. I now ask my brother to form a sentence in Greek or English which will express the idea of going into and coming out of the water clearer than we have it in this account. Why did they go down into the water? No man has ever yet gone into water to accomplish that which he could do out on the dry ground as well. Evidently, he went down into the water to immerse, not to sprinkle or pour a little water upon the subject.

We will now call your attention to Paul's baptism. My brother says, that "pouring was the mode." It was not said "arise and go to water." No. nor "arise and have a little brought." Go to the water was well understood. It is a certainty since Paul tells us that he was buried with Christ by baptism, Rom. 6:4. He not only says he was buried but the primary meaning is immerse. The rules of exegesis require the primary meaning used unless it involves an absurdity.

ELD. FROGGE'S FOURTH SPEECH.

My brother says the eunuch was immersed. Let us come to the one book. What was the eunuch reading when Philip came to him? Isa. liii, and he learned the mode from Isaiah. Isaiah says, "Wash you, make you clean." But what is the mode? "For I will *pour* water upon him that is thirsty." * * "I will *pour* my Spirit upon thy seed." Isa. 44:4. And again he says, Behold, my servant shall deal prudently, he shall be exalted and extolled, and be very high. As many were astonished at thee; (his visage was so marred more than any man, and his form more than the sons of men:) So shall be sprinkle *many nations;* the kings shall sbut their mouths at him; for that which had not been told them shall they see; and that which they had not heard shall they consider." Isaiah 52:13-15. Now brother Moderator, the eunuch learned the mode of baptism from Isaiah the prophet, and he learned that it was affusion. John 3:5. This is water baptism. But water baptism is the sign of the regenerating operation of the Holy Ghost, and the Holy Ghost baptism is by pouring. See Acts 2:17-33, "I will *pour* out of my Spirit." "He hath shed forth that which you see and hear," and Isaiah, "I will *pour* my Spirit upon thy seed." Isa. 44:4. So it is by pouring. Could the church have learned immersion from Isaiah? I grant that they went down into the water. I find that the word baptizo means sprinkle and pour as well as to immerse. The most learned men of earth say so.

Rom. 6:3-4. This is Holy Ghost baptism, and not water baptism. For the Spirit regenerates, and thus people rise to walk in newness of life. But Paul positively forbids us to go down into the deep to bring up Christ from the dead. See Rom. 10: Now our immersionist friends do this every time they immerse a person. But my brother wants to know how we bury? Why, we put the person in and pour the dirt upon him. Rom. 6:4. This baptism is the agent by which the burial is effected, while the man is *buried into death,* and not into water. "The water in baptism must be an emblem, not a means," says Carson. It has no share in the effect, either as an efficient, or as an instrument! Col. 1:10-11. We object to this baptism referred to in this place being called water baptism, from the fact that the circumcision and baptism here spoken of, are both performed without hands; but immersion must be with hands. When my brother buries a man in water does he wait for him to rise through the faith of the operation of God? or does he go to work and raise him by physical strength? It is evident that the baptism here spoken of, is not literal. Both in this and Romans vi, it is spiritual. But my brother says that Mr. Wesley agrees with him that the baptism of suffering is an overwhelming. Well if my brother wants uninspired men, let him quote them; but we will take the one book—it describes it as a coming down upon. But my brother tells us that Paul was immersed; we call for chapter and verse. Paul tells us he was baptized by affusion. See Titus 3:5 - 6.

We learn from the lexicons that the New Testament primary meaning is wash. We maintain that baptizo is a generic word. And the common version has rendered it wash, Mark 7:4 - 8, Heb. ix; 10. I maintain that it was by sprinkling and pouring. The law says the priest shall wash with water. Ex. xl, and Heb. 10:22. "Let us draw near with a true heart, in full assurance of faith, having our hearts sprinkled from an evil conscience, and our bodies washed with pure water." Our hearts were sprinkled with blood, and baptism is a sign of the operation of the Holy Ghost, so that we must have baptism with water just like the baptism of the Spirit. The diver's baptisms could not be anything else but the different sprinklings and pourings of the law. John baptized in Jordan. *Eis* is always compounded with a verb of motion when the writer intends an entrance into, and is never used singly. *Eis* is frequently rendered "to, at, into." How did John baptize? If John could stand in the river on dry land may not the people have done the same? I maintain that he baptized by pouring, for it was *with water*.

We now invite your attention to the places where baptism was performed. Bethabara beyond Jordan, and Jesus went and dwelt where he baptized. There could have been no immersion here, see Acts ix, The jailer was baptized in the outer prison, see Acts 16: Now could immersion have been accomplished in these places?

We invite your attention to the practice of the apostles; they always baptized at the time and in the place where the people were converted, see Acts 2:38. "And Peter said unto them, Repent, and be baptized every one of you in the name of Jesus Christ for the remission of sins," (verse 41). "And they that gladly received his word were baptized." We do not have anything said about the apostles going in search of water in which to immerse on this occasion. Acts 10:47, "Can any man forbid water, that these should be baptized, who have received the Holy Ghost as well as we?" The apostle did not have to hunt water—there is nothing in the passage which teaches that it was by immersion; but on the contrary, who can forbid water? not who can forbid their going to the water; but forbid it being brought, for they baptized with water. Acts 22:16, "And now why tarriest thou? arise, and be baptized, and wash away thy sins, calling on the name of the Lord. Paul was not commanded to arise and go to the water. But he must evidently have been baptized in the house and standing up at that; for he tells us that it was shed forth on him, Titus 3:5-6, Acts 16:33, "And he took them the same hour of the night, and washed their stripes, and was baptized, he and all his, straightway. When the earthquake shook the foundation of the prison and the doors flew open, the jailer called for a light, and sprang in, and came trembling, and fell down before Paul and Silas. Paul and Silas had been thrust in the inner prison when they were brought to prison. Verse 30 says, "And brought them out"—out of where? The inner prison—and into the outer prison, and said, Sirs, what must I do to be saved? "And he took them the same hour of the night and washed their stripes and was baptized, he and all his, straightway." Where were they baptized? In the outer prison; for we have no account of their leaving the outer prison to seek water. And after he was baptized he brought them into his house, brought them from the outer prison which was near, or adjoining his house. "And when it was day, the magistrates sent the serjeants, saying, Let these men go. But Paul would not depart privily." This he would have done, had he gone at the hour of midnight to be baptized. I maintain that he was baptized in the prison, and by affusion at that.

Dr. Brents' Reply.

My brother thinks that the eunuch learned that sprinkling was baptism from Isaiah 52:53, "So shall he sprinkle many nations"; it means so shall he baptize many nations. But Jesus did not baptize many nations, only the Jews. Gessenius translates that passage from Hebrew, "So shall he cause many nations to rejoice," p. 667. Davidson refers to this verse as the exaltation of Messiah. And Albert Barnes says that it does not refer to the ordinance of baptism at all. See Barnes' Notes on Isa. 52:15. The word Nazah does not mean to sprinkle. It means to sprinkle only when applied to liquids—here it is applied to nations, not to liquids, as learned critics and lexicographers testify. Why is it that my brother will not come to the Lawgiver, who instituted baptism, to find out what it is? In this passage Nazah should be rendered astonish to correspond to the preceding verse in sense.

Romans 6:3-1, and Col. 2:11- 12, "Is spiritual baptism." Acts 1:4-5. Jesus commanded his disciples to wait for the promise of the Father, that is the Holy Ghost baptism. But Paul told the Romans that they had obeyed from the heart that form of doctrine delivered them. Rom. 6:17-18. The disciples did obey a form of doctrine; but could they obey a promise? To be baptized in water was a command. Paul says there is a resurrection in baptism; then if it is spiritual baptism we are not only baptized into the Spirit, but must be raised out of it. Col. 2:12. Paul tells us that there is one Lord, one faith and one baptism. It seems that my brother has two here. But if this is spiritual baptism, how does my worthy friend reconcile this *burial* with the pouring or sprinkling a few drops of water as an *emblem* of it? Will a few drops of water sprinkled upon a person represent a burial? Buried by sprinkling or pouring! Does my brother bury by this mode? When three distinct and different acts arc called baptism are there not three baptisms? Yet Paul tells us there is one baptism, Eph. 4:5, and my brother tells us that this is water baptism. But he says that Paul positively forbids our going down into the water. Yes, and he says you shall not ascend up into heaven, to bring Christ down from above—but my brother and all his preachers call upon Christ to come down—to "come right now—do, O, Lord, come down and convert these sinners." They ascend up into heaven to bring Christ down by their prayers. My brother says the lexicons give the primary New Testament meaning of baptizo, to wash. I will attribute this error to his not knowing the plan upon which the lexicons are written. I will introduce Stokius as good authority against my brother in this case. Stokius defines in Latin, and is supposed to give some comfort to those who practice affusion and aspersion. The plan of his work is somewhat different from other lexicographers, as indicated in the title-page, which we give, as follows: "Cloris of Christian Stokius, Professor in Public Academy at Jena; opening the way to the sacred tongue of the New Testament; exhibiting, in convenient order, first, the *general* and then the special meanings of words; assisting especially the studies (or efforts) as well of tyros as of the cultivators of homiletics and exegesis; and then supplying the place of concordances with an index of words. Fourth edition, enlarged and improved." Stokius gives first the *general* and then the *specific* meanings, hence he defines baptizo, to wash, to baptize and then proceeds to define the word specifically as follows: "Generally, and by force of the word, it obtains the notion of *dipping* and an immersion. Second: Specifically and properly it is to immerse or to dip into water. Figuratively, by metalepsis, to wash, to cleanse, because a thing is accustomed to be dipped in water that it may be washed or cleansed; although washing or cleansing can and is accustomed to be done by sprinkling water," Thus Stokius in opening the way to the sacred tongue of the New Testament tells us that baptizo comes to mean wash, because things are accustomed to be dipped that they may be washed. He defines baptisms, 1. Generally, and by force of its origin, it denotes immersion or dipping. 2. Specifically, properly it denotes the immersion or dipping of a thing into water that it may be cleansed or washed; hence, it is transferred to designating the first sacrament of the New Testament, which they call [the sacrament] initiation. —namely, baptism, in which those to be baptized were *formerly immersed into water:* though at this day the water is only sprinkled upon them. Thus, we see the primary meaning is to immerse or dip—and that it means to wash only because things are accustomed to be dipped that they may be washed. Nor is this all; he most clearly shows that the custom of the present day is a departure from the original practice.

Schleusner's testimony is the same; he says: Properly, I immerse and I dip, I sink into water. And to my friend's boasted passage, Mark vii,: 4: Now because a thing is accustomed to be immersed, or dipped in water, that it may be washed, hence it marks (or denotes) I cleanse, I wash, I purge with water; thus it is used in Mark 7:4. Jesus did not wash himself before dinner, Luke 11:38. On baptisma, he says, 1, properly, immersion, dipping into water, a washing. Thus, you see that the lexicons are with us on the word wash. But why don't my brother bring us a passage in which the word is translated sprinkle or pour—or give us a reason that wash means to pour or sprinkle. But I will now show you that these washings were always *in water.* See Lev. 15:12, "shall be rinsed in water," also 11:32, any article here named which is unclean must be *put into water,* not to sprinkle the water upon them; but they must be put into water, or rinsed in water.

I will now call your attention to Heb. 10:22, Paul speaking of the consecration of the Jewish priests makes it adumbrate the consecration of Christians, who are called priests by Peter. See 1 Pet. 2:9. The law of Jewish consecration is given Ex. 29:4-9, "You shall bring them to the door of the tabernacle of the congregation, and shall wash them with water." See also Isa. 8:5, 6. But how are they washed? See Lev. 16:4, "Therefore shall he wash his flesh in water and so put them on (that is the garments.) In our consecration, our hearts are sprinkled from an evil conscience with the blood of Jesus and then we wash the body with pure water. What is the meaning of wash in a scriptural use. See 2 Kings 5:9-14, Naaman went and dipped himself. The N. T. lexicons maintain this position, and as the Jewish priest had to wash with water so must we—they washed in water, see Lev. 16:4.

Titus 3:5. And shed forth is the mode by which Paul was baptized —but it was the Spirit which was shed forth and not the washing of regeneration.

Divers baptisms. Heb. 9:10. That is baptism of different articles, as cups and pots &c, which we have shown in order to be washed they must be put in water, rinsed in water —not sprinkled or poured.

My brother tells us that the jailer was baptized in the prison; we will see, Acts 16:24—34. Paul and Silas were thrust into the inner prison, after the earthquake the jailer about to kill himself was arrested by the apostle, called for a light, and sprang in, and came trembling and fell down before Paul and Silas; and brought them out, and said, sirs, what must I do to be saved? And they spake unto him the word of the Lord and to all that were in his house. He brought them out of prison into his house where Paul preached to them. And he took them the same hour of the night and washed their stripes and was baptized, he and all his, straightway. And when he had brought them *into* his house, he set meat before them, and rejoiced, believing in God with all his house. Why did they leave the house in the night to be baptized; Surely if pouring or sprinkling had been baptism they could have brought enough water for that without taking them from the house. The facts in this instance all plainly indicate immersion and not affusion.

My brother tells us that they baptized *with* water, and *with* the Holy Ghost. Matt. 3:11, the word *with* is from *en* it should be rendered *in* Matt. 3:4-6. "And were baptized of him in Jordan." If *En* was rendered *with* here it would be a wondrous affair.

I wish now to invite your attention to controvertible terms. When the correct meaning of a word in a given place, is substituted for the word it must convey the sense of the word for which it is substituted and harmonize the other words in construction with it.

Another rule says "not any and every meaning which word may have any and everywhere, but the correct meaning for a given place." Without this rule there can be no such thing as a translation at all. Mark 1:5. "And there went out unto him all the land of Judea, and they of Jerusalem, and were all baptized of him in the river of Jordan, confessing their sins." Were all poured of him in Jordan, confessing &c. Were all sprinkled of him in the river of Jordan &o. Well let us try immerse. And were all immersed of him in the river of Jordan, confessing their sins. Pour means to turn out in a stream. But did John turn the people out in a stream in the river of Jordan? Sprinkle means to scatter in drops. Did John scatter the people in drops in the river of Jordan? Well you may say—the above on Acts 8:38, Rom. 6:4, Col. 2:12. It makes good sense with the primary and true meaning but nonsense with sprinkle or pour.

MR. FROGGE'S FIFTH SPEECH.

My brother tells us that Nazah, Isa. 52:15, should be translated "astonish." Dr. Clark says it means to sprinkle. Well I maintain that the eunuch learned that sprinkling was the mode from Isaiah.

I do maintain that the lexicons give wash as the N. T. meaning. See Mark 7:4-8, Heb. 9:10. Also see Pickering, Donnegan and Groves. I have read their lexicons to you. My brother read Schleusner that *inting* means to immerse, *tingo* means with or in a liquid—so he finds no shelter here.

My brother says that Naaman dipped himself in Jordan. I doubt it— The law required him to wash and the washing was performed by affusion. See Num. 8: here they were required to be sprinkled—and this was nineteen years before the law for the water of separation. I maintain that the jailer was baptized in the prison. Luke says that they were cast into the inner prison—the jailer brought them out into the outer-prison and they preached to them and then took them to a bowl or some vessel which was convenient and baptized them, and it was by affusion. Paul was baptized in the house and standing up at that. Well we have the prophets to maintain affusion as the mode. See Isa. 1:16, 44:3-4. Isa. 52:15, Isa. 53: Ezek. 36:26.

My brother denies that the learned world maintain that baptizo is a genuine word and is properly translated by affusion. Dr. Miller of Princeton, Mr. Wesley, Dr. A. Clark and others are opposed to him.

My brother says that the oriental church baptized by immersion. Dr. J. Newton Brown, one of the most learned and gifted Baptists, says in his Encyclopedia that the Greek church did practice immersion—after they practice affusion, p. 369. I maintain that Christ was made a member of the church at eight days old, and was inducted into the office of a priest at thirty, and it was done by his baptism. See also Mr. Jones Hist. p. 36. Num. 8 says he must have the water of purification sprinkled upon him, thus he was to wash.

I maintain that, in the baptism for the dead it is the administrator who is to bathe himself and not the unclean person. See Num. 19: So, the mode is sprinkle.

My brother tells us that the Methodist discipline teaches immersion, and wants to know why we practice immersion. My brethren get out of error very slowly.

Well, all Scripture was given to thoroughly furnish to every good work; we must go to the whole book to find the mode of baptism. No prophecy is of any private interpretation. Immersion has always been vacillating. My brother appeals to history. Gregory says that the rite was performed by three dips and that affusion was permitted to the sick. My brother may talk as much as he pleases, read the opinions and notions of men, but we must come to the one book. What is the mode of the book? The prophets teach that it is sprinkle. What is the meaning of *baptizo* in the mouth of Peter, John and Jesus? It is to pour. Then the place where Scriptural baptism was performed, forbids the idea of immersion, then the types teach us that affusion is the mode. So, brother moderator, we have maintained our proposition and baptism is Scripturally performed by affusion, and the apostles practiced accordingly.

Dr. Brents' Fifth Reply.

My brother tells us again that he maintains that the lexicons give wash as the primary meaning of baptizo We have asked him time and again to show his authority and to reconcile the lexicons and make their testimony harmonize, but he has never even attempted such a thing. What can a man not prove if assertions are to be taken as evidence? But I read from Stokius that it obtained the meaning of wash because things are accustomed to be dipped or immersed in order that they may be washed. So, of Schleusner, both of their N. T. lexicons. He tells that the word is rendered sprinkle in the Ethiopic and Peshito Syriac. Rev. 19:13. Tischendorf discovered a manuscript in the convent at Mount Sinai, from which no doubt the translation was made. The Sinaitic codex has the word perirer ammenon in Rev. 19:13, instead of bebamenon, from which the translation was thought to have been made. So, my brother will find no comfort from this quarter. But he doubts whether Naaman dipped himself in Jordan. Well he wanted to come to the one book but he doubts that it means what it says. It says wash means to dip and he can't see it.

But he goes to the prophets to prove that affusion is baptism. Why doesn't he come to the writer of the New Testament to settle its meaning instead of hunting up passages in the prophets that have no reference to Christian baptism.

But he tells us that Miller, Wesley, and Clark say that baptizo means to sprinkle and pour as well as immerse, but I have shown you that all those men have said that baptizo was properly rendered immerse. See Wesley's notes. But my brother has to resort to his own side of the house for evidence and to men who while they practiced affusion tell us that in the days of the apostles it was performed by immersion, and they practiced affusion on different grounds from my brother, as we will show. But Gregory says that baptism was performed by three dips. What of that? Does my brother think that three dips will make one sprinkle?

We now invite your attention to an argument based upon the history of baptism.

Mosheim says: "The sacrament of baptism was administered in this century (the first century,) without the public assemblies, in places appointed and prepared for that purpose, and performed by an immersion of the whole body in the baptismal font. Mosheim's Ecclesiastical History p. 28, Coots' Edition. So, of the second century, "The candidates for it were immersed wholly in water." See W. & D. debate p. 539. Neander says: "In respect to the form of baptism, it was in conformity with the original institution and the original import of the symbol performed by immersion, as a sign of entire baptism into the Holy Spirit, of being entirely penetrated by the same. It was only with the sick, when the exigency required it; that any exception was made; and in this case baptism was administered by sprinkling." Neander, Vol. 1 p. 310.

Moses Stuart: "Thirteen hundred years was baptism generally and ordinarily performed by the immersion of a man under water; and only in extraordinary cases was sprinkling or affusion permitted. These latter methods of baptism were called in question, and even prohibited," Bunner adds: "For sixteen hundred years was the person to be baptized, either by immersion or affusion, entirely divested of his garments." Stuart on Baptism p. 152, Again he says, "We have collected facts enough to authorize us now to come to the following general conclusion, respecting the practice of the Christian Church in general, with regard to the mode of baptism, viz.: that from the earliest ages of which we have any account, subsequent to the apostolic age, and downward for several centuries, the churches did generally practice baptism by immersion; perhaps by immersion of the whole person, and that the only exceptions to this mode which were usually allowed were in cases of urgent sickness or other cases of immediate or imminent danger, when immersion could not be practiced." Stuart on Baptism, p. 153. These utterances speak for the cause of truth too loud to be misunderstood or to need any comment.

We now invite your attention to the change from immersion to affusion. Calvin as quoted by Stuart: "It is of no consequence at all (minimum effort) whether the person is baptized, totally immersed, or whether he is merely sprinkled by an affusion of water, This should be a matter of choice to the churches in different regions; although the word baptize signifies to immerse, and the rite of immersion was practiced by the ancient church." Stuart on Baptism, p, 156, 157. Professor Stuart argues that the church had the right to change, and approves Calvin as a leader. His first reason is that the rite in question (baptism) is merely external, leaving it to the enlightened Christian to make his own choice. 2. That no injunction is anywhere given in the New Testament respecting the manner in which this rite shall be performed, he immediately concedes that the word itself means to immerse, but thinks it would prove too much if we stick too close to the letter, p. 158. Again, he says, "Must I show that we are not at liberty without being justly exposed to the accusation of gross departure from Christianity, to depart from the *modes* and *forms* of the apostolic church in any respect? I have shown that all the churches on earth do depart from these, in their celebration of the Lord's Supper, and yet without any apprehension of being guilty of an impropriety, much less of being justly chargeable with the spirit of disobedience and revolt." p. 169. He concedes that the modes and forms of the apostolic church have been changed—but tries to justify it on other grounds than that alleged by my brother. Again, he says: "But what is the case in respect to baptism? Well nothing but the *letter* is here? So, you may think and reason; but are you not entirely inconsistent with yourself?" p. 169-170. The letter required immersion—this he admits but thinks he has a right to change the form. "Accordingly, long before the light of the Reformation began to dawn upon the churches, the Roman Catholics themselves were gradually adopting the method of baptism by sprinkling or affusion, notwithstanding their superstitious and excessive devotedness to the usage of the ancient churches." So, testifies one of the most intelligent and useful ecclesiastical writers of the earlier part of the dark ages: I mean Walafried Strabo (ob. 84, 9,), abbot of the convent of St. Gall. His words run thus: "It should be noted, that many have been, not only by immersion, but by affusion .... and they may yet be baptized in this manner, if there be any necessity for it ... It is safer to baptize by the mode of immersion, because it has common usage in its favor." But those very words show that a different usage was coming in, and that Aquinas did not look upon it with any strong disapprobation. Stuart on Bap, p. 171. We will close the concessions by one more quotation from Stuart: "It will be seen from all this, that Christians began somewhat early to deflect from the ancient practice of immersing." p. 175. You can see at once the difference between my worthy friend in defending affusion and Stuart's defense of it. We have a number of Pedobaptists telling us how and when the change. All the fathers for centuries after the apostolic day practiced immersion and not affusion and it was two hundred and fifty years before the first one had water poured on him for baptism. We then see no reason in our friend's asserting that immersion had always been vacillating. But what may we not prove by assertion?

Fourth Proposition

Fourth Proposition.—The Scriptures teach, that in conversion and sanctification the Holy Spirit operates on persons only through the Word of truth.

Dr. Brents' First Speech.

We have the operation of the Holy Spirit before us for discussion to-day. The proposition which you have heard read does not express the subject as clearly as we wish to have it. We object to the word *only* because it gives room to squirm and quibble and our accepting of the proposition is not any reason why it should be debated in the future. We invite your attention to our first argument which we base upon the constitution of the human mind. All impressions must be made upon it through the five senses. 1st, We cannot taste the Spirit or any communication from it. 2nd, We cannot smell the Spirit or any communication from it. 3rd, We cannot feel the Spirit or any communication from the Spirit so as to recognize it as such. 4th, We can see no communication from the Spirit not embodied in words. 5th, We can hear no communication from the Spirit so as to gain a spiritual idea from it unless embodied in words. Hence God has spoken to man when he would convey any idea to him. See Heb. 3:7-10, "Wherefore as the Holy Ghost saith." How does the Spirit talk? See 2nd Sam.'l 23:1-3, "The Spirit of the Lord spake by me, and his word was in my tongue." Acts 1:16. The Spirit in addressing man on his spiritual good used the tongues of men. Therefore, all such communications on such subjects must be through words understood by man.

Our second argument is based on the fact that the heathen know not God, where the light of the gospel has not gone or some tradition from it, and with them spiritual darkness prevails. Two thirds of the human race are in spiritual darkness. Now if the Holy Spirit operates here where the Bible is, without the word, why not there?

We want our brother to tell us of one single instance in which one man has been converted by the Spirit without the word. This was the case under the law of Moses as it is now under the law of Jesus. See Luke 16:27-31. We do not hear of any operation of the Holy Spirit without the word in this case. We are told that if they would not hear Moses and the prophets they would not be persuaded, though one rose from the dead.

Our third argument is drawn from the fact that faith comes by hearing, see John 20:30-31, Romans 10:14-17, "These things were written, that ye might believe that Jesus is the Christ, the Son of God, and believing ye might have life through his name. How shall they call on him in whom they have not believed, and how shall they believe in him of whom they have not heard? and how shall they hear without a preacher? So, then faith cometh by hearing, and hearing by the word of God." How are spiritual ideas imparted? By the preacher—preaching—hearing and the word of God.

Our fourth argument is based on the course pursued by the first preachers. When John came to prepare a people he came preaching the word, see Matt. 3:1. So of Jesus, Matt. 4:17. So did the twelve, Matt. 10:5-9. And this was the course pursued by the seventy, see Luke 10:9. When Jesus prepared his apostles to preach after his departure he gave them the Spirit to bring to mind what he had said and guide them into all truth and enable them to speak in all languages, then charged them to go and preach the word. What for? Because faith comes by hearing—Matt. 28:19, Mark 16:16. This then was God's system in the days of the apostles, for "It pleased God by the foolishness of preaching to save them that believe." 1 Cor. 1:21. This system was to be perpetuated, see 2 Tim. 4:1-2. It did not please God to save men by the direct operation of the Spirit. But under the commission of Jesus they were to preach so that every creature might hear and by hearing might believe.

Our fifth argument is drawn from the fact that we are said to be born (begotten) by the word; see 1 Pet. 2:23, "Being born again not of corruptible seed but of incorruptible, by the word of God which liveth and abideth forever." Paul speaking of the same thing says, "In Christ Jesus I have begotten you through the gospel," 1 Cor. 4:15. James says, "Of his own will begat he us by the word of truth that we should be a kind of first-fruits of his creatures," James 1:18. This is clear that those to whom Peter, Paul and James wrote and who at that time composed the great majority if not all the Christian world were begotten by the word of truth. Now we call upon our brother to show one single case where a man was begotten any other way than through the truth; one case will do, and will settle the matter and end the discussion. But Paul tells the Corinthians that they were saved by the gospel—not by a direct operation of the Holy Spirit; Jesus prayed that his disciples might be sanctified through the truth; "thy word is truth." Again, Jesus says, "Now ye are clean through the word which I have spoken unto you."

We base our sixth argument on the parable of the sower, Matt. 13:18- 23.1,Without seed there can be no crop. 2, The sower soweth the *word*. 3, Then if there is no word sown there can be no crop. You might as well look for a crop of wheat without seed wheat as to look for a spiritual crop without the word of God. The word is sown and falls into the heart and produces faith and brings forth fruit.

Our seventh argument is based on the commission which Paul received Acts 26:15-18. Why did the Lord have to explain this in words if men could receive spiritual ideas without words or could receive them by the direct operation of the Spirit. Will our brother explain? And if the Gentiles could be turned from darkness to light without the gospel, why send Paul to preach to them? But the word of God was able to turn them from darkness to light and from the power of Satan unto God. 2 Tim. 4:1. Paul charged Timothy to preach the word. Why preach the word, if the work could be done without it? Why send for the best revivalist—a good exhorter—to come and hold a protracted meeting in order to success? Will my brother tell us? Paul tells us that "The world by wisdom knew not God, it pleased God by the foolishness of preaching to save them that believe." Not by direct contact or impress of the Holy Spirit with or upon our hearts or spirits.

Our eighth argument is based on the fact that the word of God is called the power of God, see Rom. 1:15-17. The gospel is not *a* power, but *the* power of God unto salvation. Suppose the word of God fails. Then the power of God fails, not man's power, nor *a* power of God, but *the power of God unto salvation.* Then God has made an unwise selection of means, provided they have had a fair chance and failed. See also Heb. 4:12, "For the word of God is quick and powerful, and sharper than any two-edged sword, piercing even to the dividing asunder of soul and spirit, and of the joints and marrow, and is a discerner of the thoughts and intents of the heart. Not a dead letter killing the dead sinner." The prophet that hath a dream, let him tell a dream; and he that hath my word, let him speak my word faithfully. What is the chaff to the wheat? saith the Lord. Is not my word like as a fire? saith the Lord; and like a hammer that breaketh the rock in pieces? Therefore behold, I am against the prophets, saith the Lord, that steal my word everyone from his neighbor," see Jer. 23:28-30.

Our ninth argument is based upon the fact that all the conversions recorded in the Bible were by preaching the word. 1, Peter preached to the Pentecostians, Acts ii, and three thousand were converted. 2, Peter preached at Solomon's portico, Acts iii, and many asked what to do. 3, Philip preached to the Samaritans, Acts viii, and a whole city turned to the Lord. 4, Philip preached to the eunuch and he was converted. Here was a fair chance in which we could have had a conversion without the word of the Lord had it been the law of God. Why send Philip to this man to preach, if it could be done without preaching? Why not send the Spirit directly and convert him? 5, Ananias preached to Saul, Acts 9. 6, Peter preached to Cornelius and family, Acts 10: Another case in which a good opportunity was offered for the conversion of persons without the word. 7, Paul preached to the jailer and all his house, see Acts 16. 8, Paul preached to the Thessalonians and many believed, Acts 17:1-4. 9, Paul preached at Berea and many believed, Acts 17:10-12. 10, Paul preached at Mars' Hill, and Dionysius, Damaris and others believed, Acts 17:34. 11, Crispus and all his house believed, Paul preached and many of the Corinthians also believed, Acts 18:8.

We have presented the course pursued by the apostles and evangelists as recorded in the Acts of the Apostles. The apostles in addressing letters to these people after they had left them, always call their attention to the fact that they had been converted by the word of God. Paul to the Romans said to them that the "gospel of Christ is the power of God to salvation," Rom. 1:16. "So then faith cometh by hearing and hearing by the word of God," Rom. 10:17. To the Corinthians that he came not with enticing words of man's wisdom, "that your faith should not stand in the wisdom of men, but in the power of God" (the gospel) 1 Cor. 2:4-5. Again, "Though ye have ten thousand instructors in Christ Jesus, yet have ye not many fathers; for in Christ Jesus have I begotten you through the gospel." 1 Cor. 4:15.

MR. FROGGE'S FIRST REPLY.

I am in the negative of the proposition which you have heard read this morning. I deny that the Holy Ghost in conversion and sanctification operates *only* through the word. Webster defines sanctification, 1, The act of consecrating, or of setting apart for a sacred purpose; consecration. There are several measures of the Spirit, but the Spirit was not given to Christ by measure, I agree. The Holy Spirit was imparted in the baptism of the Spirit, and by the imposition of hands.

My brother makes an argument on the constitution of man, and wants to know if a man can smell or taste a spiritual idea. David said, "O taste and see that the Lord is good," Ps. 38:8. David thought that men could taste of the Lord. Matt. 13: Does this teach that there is no mystery in the operation of the Holy Spirit in conversion and sanctification? What portion of it teaches that the Spirit operates only through the word of truth? Luke 16:27— the rich man and Lazarus. What does this teach? That the Spirit operates through the word. Well I believe that but does it teach the doctrine my brother contends for? we say most assuredly not. I admit that Christ prepared men to preach, John, the twelve and the seventy did go and preach, but does that prove that the Spirit operates only through the truth? I say it does not.

The Spirit told Peter to go down to the house of Cornelius, but that does not prove that the Spirit operates *only* through the word. Acts ii, where is the proof that the Holy Ghost operates only through the truth? Acts vii, they were cut to the heart, but not converted. Will my brother say Nehemiah maintains the same? 9:30. But does that prove that the Spirit operates only through the truth? But my brother tells us that there is more darkness where the word of God is not. This is not true. He says no man can give a spiritual idea not in the book of God. Well the Bible is a complete book. Rom. 10:14-17. Read the 18th verse, "But I say, have they not all heard? Yes, verily their sound went into all the earth, and their words unto the ends of the world." So, my brother is mistaken when this word went into all the world. David says, "The heavens declare the glory of God, and the firmament showeth his handiwork. Day unto day uttereth speech, and night unto night showeth knowledge. There is no speech nor language where their voice is not heard." Ps. 19:1-3. The sun, moon and stars preached to the heathen.

I will now cut out a little work for my brother. Evangelical sanctification, the act of God's grace by which the affections are purified or separated from things of the world. 1, The Scriptures teach that the honest heathen living up to the light which they have will be saved in heaven. 2, Without holiness no man shall see the Lord. 3, The heathen have a degree of light, John 1:9. That was the true light that lighteth every man that cometh into the world. *Every man*—the whole human family— preached to them all, see Ps. xix, John 16:8-11, "he will reprove the world of sin." Honest heathens will be saved, Rom. 2:16. in the day when God shall judge the secrets of men, by Jesus Christ according to my gospel. They are to be judged by Jesus Christ. The apostle says, "For when the Gentiles which have not the law, do by nature the things contained in the law, these, having not the law, are a law unto themselves; which show the work of the law written in their hearts, their conscience also bearing them witness, and their thoughts the mean while accusing, or else excusing, one another." Rom. 2:14-15. Here the apostle tells us they have not the law—but they have the work of the law written *in their hearts*. Who wrote it there? The Holy Ghost who is to reprove the world of sin. John saw in his vision in the Isle of Patmos many of these; see Rev. 14:1, "And I looked, and lo, a lamb stood on Mount Sion, and with him a hundred forty and four thousand, having his Father's name written in their foreheads." Now who could these be but the honest heathens who had the work of the law written in their hearts? Here we have a definite for an indefinite number. "A great multitude which no man could number."

We base our second argument on the baptism of infant children. They are sinners and the Holy Spirit must operate on them to sanctify and cleanse them, otherwise they would be lost. Mr. Campbell says that infant children are sinners, see Christian System, pp. 27-29, "Thus by one man sin entered into the world, and death by that one sin; and so death, the wages of sin, has fallen upon all the offspring of Adam; because in him *they have all* sinned, or been made mortal, and consequently all born under condemnation to that death which fell upon our common progenitor because of his transgression. Again: "Condemned to natural death and greatly fallen and depraved in our whole moral constitution though we certainly are, in consequence of the sin of Adam, still, because of the interposition of the second Adam," &c. Here Mr. Campbell teaches that we were morally corrupted by the fall of Adam; see also Christian Baptism, p. 32, Quest. 121 and 122 with their answers. We are saved by the whole Deity. Through the atonement of Christ, we are forgiven by the Father, and sanctified by the Spirit.

My third argument is based upon the fact that the Holy Spirit in the land of Bibles is not confined to the word: see Luke 11:13, "If ye then being evil, know how to give good gifts unto your children, how much more shall your heavenly Father give the Holy Spirit to them that ask him?" We are taught by our blessed Savior that the Holy Spirit is given in answer to prayer. 1 Thes. 5:23,

"And the very God of peace sanctify you wholly; and I pray God your whole spirit and soul and body be preserved blameless unto the coming of our Lord Jesus Christ." 1 Thes. 1:5, "For our gospel came not unto you in word *only,* but also in power; and in the Holy Ghost, and in much assurance; as ye know what manner of men we were among you for your sake." Paul said that the gospel did not come in *word only.* How did it come then? he says "in the Holy Ghost." Here we have the apostle teaching the direct operation of the Holy Ghost. We want our brother to tell us where we will find that the Spirit operates only through the word.

DR. BRENTS' SECOND SPEECH.

We were showing when we closed our first speech that the apostles, in their letters addressed to the churches, used such expressions as evince that those to whom they wrote were converted by the Spirit through the truth. Paul let us know that the Corinthians were converted by the word. To the Galatians he said: "This only would I learn of you, Received ye the Spirit by the works of the law, or by the hearing of faith?" "Are ye so foolish? having begun in the Spirit, are ye now made perfect by the flesh?" Gal. 3:2-3, They had begun in the Spirit. How? By the "hearing of faith," the hearing of the gospel. See Acts 15:7. To the Ephesians he said: "In whom also ye trusted after that ye heard the word of truth, the gospel of your salvation; in whom also, after that ye believed, ye were sealed with the Holy Spirit of promise." Eph. 1:13. We now call our brother's attention to the fact, that the word was present in every case of conversion, and that in the apostolic epistles, the apostles used such expressions, as conveyed the idea that those to whom they wrote were converted by the word. I will now call upon my brother to bring one well authenticated instance of any person ever having been converted without the word: If he can, then we will yield the point. We will illustrate. It never rains upon us unless there is a cloud over us; so, the Spirit always operates where the word is; but never, in conversion unless the word is there. As soon would we expect the rain to fall where there is no cloud, as for the Spirit to operate where the word is not.

Well, my brother tells us that "honest heathens, living up to the light which they have, will be saved." What if they are? Does that prove that the Holy Spirit operates without the word? Ps. 19: The sun, moon, and stars preached to the heathen, and preached the gospel at that!! What did they say to the heathen? Will our brother tell us? Preaching must be done by words which are the signs of ideas? But if they preached the gospel—then I cannot see how my brother will find relief here; for the word was sent to them. So, the word is present at last. But Rom. 2:15- 16, "They have the works of the law written in their hearts." What if they have, does it prove that the Spirit wrote it there by a direct operation? We have the infants again: will my brother say that they are in a lost condition? Jesus took them in his arms and blessed them, and said, "Of such is the kingdom of heaven," but my brother and the Savior do not agree very well. We pressed our brother, when on infant baptism, to know if the depravity of which he spoke as having been transmitted to infants would be sufficient ground of damnation; but we could not get him out, and he made much ado about Mr. Wesley's sentiments, which I introduced from Doct. Tracts pp. 251, 252. But my brother, I see, is not satisfied with his effort on infant baptism, or he would not work at it so faithfully in every proposition.

But he tells us, that the Holy Spirit is given in answer to prayer, Luke 11:13, and that proves that the Spirit operates without the word. But they must hear before they can call on the Lord. See Rom. 10:14- 17,

"How shall they call upon him in whom they have not believed?" is the language of Paul; But Paul wanted his brethren to pray for him, and he prayed for them. What if he did? Is there any possible interpretation of this that will give my brother any comfort? If there is we want him to show it. 1 Thess. 1:5, "Our gospel came not unto you in word only." What if it did not? That is only another proof that it came to them *in the word* and not *without the word*. Certainly, there is no comfort here for my worthy brother.

We now present our tenth argument, based upon the perfection of the word of God. 2 Tim. 3:16, 17, "All Scripture is given by inspiration of God, and is profitable for doctrine, for reproof, for correction, for instruction in righteousness; that the man of God may be perfect, thoroughly furnished unto good works." What need then has the man of God for the direct operation of the Spirit? If the word of God thoroughly furnishes him for every good work, he certainly does not need anything more. The word of the Lord "quickens" Ps. 119:50, "For thy word hath quickened me." 3rd verse, "I will never forget thy precepts, for with them thou hast quickened me." 104: "Through thy precepts I get understanding; therefore, I hate every false way." Not quickened by a direct operation of the Holy Spirit; but "by thy word," "by thy precept." He got understanding through the precepts of the Lord, and not without them. "The word of the Lord is a lamp." See 105th verse. "The law of the Lord is perfect converting the soul." See Ps. 19:7, and "enlightens." See 8th verse. The word of the Lord gives an "inheritance and builds up." See Acts 20:32.

Our eleventh argument is based upon the fact that we are "washed and cleansed by the word," "sanctified through the truth" &c. See Eph. 5:25-27. Of the church, Paul says: "That he (Christ) might sanctify and cleanse it with the washing of water by the word." Here we have

Paul telling the Ephesians that they were sanctified by the word. Jno. 17:17-21. The Savior prays, "Sanctify them through thy truth, thy word is truth." He sent his disciples into the world to pray the same prayer; to pray God to sanctify them through the truth. He sanctified himself "that his apostles also might be sanctified through the truth," not *without truth*. Jesus prayed for those who "believed on him through the apostles' word." And finally, Jesus tells us that, "Now ye (the disciples) are clean through the word which I have spoken unto you." Jno. 15:3. These are the views advanced by Jesus and his apostles and preachers whom he sent to instruct the world. They cannot be wrong.

Our twelfth argument is drawn from Eph. 6:10-17. Here we have the armor of the Christian soldier spoken of. We are commanded to put on the whole armor of God, that we may be able to stand against the wiles of the devil. Every part is named in the word of God. The "girdle of truth" "the breastplate of righteousness"— shoes of "the preparation of the gospel of peace," "the shield of faith," "the helmet of salvation"—"the sword of the Spirit, which is the word of God." Every part is protected, and the soldier is not only able to shield himself, but furnished with weapons of an offensive character.

Among this armor where is there a piece that will correspond to my brother's doctrine of the direct operation of the Spirit? But we will call in vain on him.

Our thirteenth argument is based upon the fact that every false doctrine shelters under the doctrine of the direct operation of the Spirit. Every doctrine under the sun may be proved the same way you proved this. If we may be under the influence of the Spirit of God, why may we not be under evil spirits, especially when they transform themselves into angels of light. We want our brother to tell us by what rule of recognition and interpretation he knows the evil from the good spirits? The

Catholics, the Mormons and the Mohamedans feel like they are right. They claim to have direct communications from the Spirit of God. We want our brother to tell us how we may know the right from the wrong.

ELD. FROGGE'S SECOND REPLY.

My brother has produced a good many passages of Scripture, but they do not prove his position. 1 Pet. 1:23. "Only through the word" is not in this passage. Neither is it in 1 Cor. 4:15. There is only one word in his proposition that I object to; the word *only*. We both agree that the Holy Ghost operates through the word, but my worthy brother Brents says that it operates *only* through the word of truth. I object.

James 1:18, the word only is not here. 1 Cor. 15:1-3. This don't say that the Spirit operates only through the word. Heb. iii; 8, as quoted from Ps. 95, I deny that it says only through the truth. The doctrine of only through the word is not in 2 Sam. 23:2, 3. Acts 1:15: There is no proof here. What has my brother proved by referring to the history of the churches of Asia? He is only establishing what we both believe. Well my brother tells us that the word of God is perfect. I believe that, Yes, the same moon and stars preached the gospel one thousand years before the apostles, Rom. 1:15 teaches the reverse of my brother's proposition. Baptism does make us ceremonially holy. John 17:21, that is truth: but this truth teaches us the direct operation of the Holy Spirit, I want my brother to tell me how the heathen and infants are saved. I will conclude my third argument, that the Holy Spirit, in this land, is not confined to the Book. Paul tells his brethren to continue in prayer, and watching, the same with thanksgiving, "Withal praying for us, that God would open unto us a door of utterance, to speak the mystery of Christ for which I am also in bonds." Col. 4:2, 3. See also Eph. 6:18, 19, 20. Paul wants the Ephesians to "pray always" "and with all prayer and supplication in the Spirit," pray that he might have "utterance" that he might "open his mouth boldly to make known the mystery of the gospel." Again, Paul says, "Now the Lord is that Spirit; and where the Spirit of the Lord is there is liberty." Well we see that the apostle teaches the direct operation of the Spirit in answer to prayer.

Our fourth argument is, that the Scriptures teach that the Holy Ghost operates through the word of truth; but not the word alone. See 1 Cor. 3:6, "I have planted; Apollos watered; but God gave the increase." All the power which Paul had was exhausted in preaching the word; and God then gave increase. How did he do it? Eph. 3:16,20: "That he would grant you, according to the riches of his glory, to be strengthened with might by his Spirit in the inner man. That Christ may dwell in your hearts by faith; that ye being rooted and grounded in love, may be able to comprehend with all saints what is the length and depth and breadth and height; and to know the love of Christ, which passeth knowledge, that ye might be filled with all the fullness of God. Now unto him that is able to do exceeding abundantly above all that we ask or think, according to the power that worketh in us."

Then there is a power in us that worketh above all that we can think or ask. What power can this be, brother moderator, but the direct operation of the Holy Ghost? It can be no other, so we maintain that the Holy Ghost operates without the word sometimes, and our beloved brother Paul is with us and against our beloved brother Brents. I would like to come here and hold a protracted meeting for my brethren, the Reformers, and would like to see this altar full of mourners—I think we could have a good time. I want them to see the good effects of the mourners' bench. But who are we to invite to the mourners' bench? All for whom Christ died. But my brother wants to know my authority for the mourners' bench. See 1 Cor. 14:23, "If therefore the whole church be come together into one place, and all speak with tongues, and there come in those that are unlearned or unbelievers, will they not say ye are mad? But if all prophesy, and there come in one that believeth not, or one unlearned, he is convinced of all, he is judged of all: and thus, are the secrets of his heart made manifest, and so falling down on his face he will worship God, and report that God is in you of a truth." What could this be, but that he would fall down and get religion. Paul tells his brethren, "Let us come boldly unto the throne of grace, that we may obtain mercy and find grace to help in time of need." Heb. 4:16. This is coming to the mourners' bench to get religion. But when does my brother and his brethren come to the throne of grace? One of his brethren said in Burksville "that he did not see any use in praying." Now we have shown our authority for the mourners' bench and for calling men to it.

DR. BRENTS' THIRD SPEECH.

My worthy friend admits that the word of God is perfect, and thoroughly furnishes the man of God unto every good work; but it needs help in his estimation to convert the sinner, supernatural help. But Rom. 1:16 teaches the reverse of my proposition? It teaches that the gospel is *"the* power of God unto salvation, not *a* power, or *some* power; but *the* power. Then where does my brother find the necessity for another power in order to conversion? We have shown that it is perfect and that all who were converted in the days of the apostles were converted by the word. 1. By an appeal to the Acts of the apostles, which show, that in every ease of conversion, the word was always present. 2. By an appeal to the Epistles, which the apostles wrote to the churches. Peter addressed two general epistles to all the Christians in the world, in which he reminded them of the fact that they were born again, not of "corruptible seed: but of incorruptible, by the word of God which liveth and abideth forever." This Epistle was addressed to the whole Christian world. Then they must have all been "born again" of the word of God. James, who wrote an epistle to the Jewish Christians, says: "Of his own will begat he us, with the word of truth, that we should be a kind of first fruits of his creatures." James 1:18. Here then we have the two races, Jews and Gentiles, and the manner of their conversion presented. How does the apostle tell us it was accomplished? "By the word of truth." But I now call in vain upon my friend to bring us one clear and well-defined case of conversion, from the Bible or anywhere else, which took place without the word.

1 Cor. 3:5, 6. "God gave the increase." How? By direct operation of the Spirit? If so, we could never learn it from this passage. But how? We must admit that it is through his power. Paul tells us, that "the gospel is his power." Rom. 1:16. Heb. 4:12; again, this accords with the Savior's theory of conversion. See Luke 8: "The seed is the word of God." Again, Paul says: "And now brethren, I commend you to God, and to the word of his grace, which is able to build you up and to give you an inheritance among all them which are sanctified." Acts 20:32. God gave the "increase" through Paul planting the seed (the word), Apollos watering, the increase was made through the power in the "seed" the "word of God."

Well he wants to come here and hold a protracted meeting. He wants to have an "altar full of mourners"!!! and have a "good time"!!! He wants the people to "get religion"! And 1 Cor. 14:23, teaches "the mode of getting religion"!! Does the apostle say the man would fall down on the mourner's bench, and pray for God to send the Holy Spirit down and convert him, and help him to get religion? No sir; the passage teaches that he is convinced by the teaching or prophesying of those who ministered the word to the church. He is convinced by the word. The apostle condemns these mourner's bench scenes. If the church be in confusion, one singing, another shouting and another praying, and another preaching, and another exhorting as our modern revivalists do, Paul says, that "the unbeliever or unlearned would say, ye are mad." But he shows them a more excellent way, "one talk at a time." Does my brother and his brethren in these excited scenes take the apostle's advice?

Well he says "coming unto a throne of grace is coming to the mourner's bench." Where did my worthy friend learn that "throne of grace" is a mourner's bench? Certainly not from this passage, nor from the Bible. It must rest entirely upon his assertion for proof.

We have presented arguments from the word of God, showing how the Spirit operated upon men and women in the days of the apostles. We have shown the power and perfection of God's word for every good work. Do we want to quicken the sinner? Then it is said, "Thy word hath quickened me." Do we want the sinner to be begotten again? "Of his own will begat he us with the word of truth." Do we want faith? "These things are written that ye might believe." Do we want a person born again? "Born not of corruptible seed, but of incorruptible, by the word of God." Do we want any one converted? "The law of the Lord is perfect, converting the soul." We have shown that the Scripture, the word of God is perfectly adapted to the constitution of man and answers the end for which it was given, (e. g.) for salvation justification and redemption. We hope when the smoke and debris of battle blows away, and you come to think soberly and without excitement that the truth will be comprehended and cordially embraced.

Eld. Frogge's Third Reply.

My brother wants to know why all men are not converted if the Spirit operates without the word. Why is it that they are not all converted by the word when they have it? Titus 3:5. Is there anything in this passage teaching that the Spirit operates only through the word of truth? Let me say to you that if men and women would cultivate the good thoughts and emotions which they have, they would all be converted. Rom. 1:16. The power of God in the gospel of Christ is the righteousness of God revealed. See Rom. 1:17, that is the direct influence of the Holy Ghost. "The word of God is quick and powerful, sharper than any two-edged sword." Heb. 4:12. This is true when it is wielded by the Holy Spirit. Jno. 15:3. Does it teach his doctrine? No; but teaches the direct influence of the Spirit. Matt. 13: Does he mean the book? but it is the idea. 2 Tim. 3:16. That the man of God may be thoroughly furnished unto every good work. I say it is perfect &c. I love this book; it is my book.

Ps. 119:50. Does he mean the word alone. 93rd verse. Is it the word alone? Is it restricted to the word? No. See Ephesians 3:14. 104th verse. Is it by the word alone? Ps. 19: "The law of the Lord is perfect converting the soul." Does it say the law alone? Acts 20:32. It don't say word only. Jno. 6:63. Does it say only? I have followed my brother through every one of his arguments, and he has failed to sustain himself in his position. Where is his proof? I say he has not given us one argument. But I have shown that we are saved by the whole Deity. Without holiness, no man shall see the Lord. Honest heathens are saved. I have shown that infant baptism is practiced as a sigh of the operation of the Holy Ghost in conversion. They (the infants) are corrupt, and depraved, and the Holy Ghost regenerates them; and baptism is the sign of the regenerating influence of the Holy Ghost.

We have shown that the gospel did not come to the Thessalonians in word only, but in demonstrations of the Spirit and of power, 1 Thes. 1:5. "God gives the increase." 1 Cor. 3:6, and Eph. 3:14, We have given you passages teaching that the Holy Ghost is given in answer to prayer— which shows that the Holy Ghost operates without the word. We have shown that, while the Holy Ghost operates through the word in a land of Bibles, it is not confined to the word. See 1 Thess. 1:5, 1 Cor. 3:6, Eph. 2:14. We have shown that the Spirit bears testimony to our spirits, that we are the children of God. Rom. 8:16. We now leave the arguments with you, and hope that much good may he done by our debate. It will not be long before I shall be called to go from my field of labor to the sun-bright climes above—and I think that my brother Brents is not far behind me. If I should be called home first, I will say to him that I will wait for him on the bright shore beyond, and will gladly give him my hand when he comes over and joins the sacred host above. For I must say he is a man of learning and piety.

The Brents-Pennington Debate
On the Identity of the Church

Between

T.W. Brents,
church of Christ

And

Elder Pennington,
Missionary Baptist Church

Propositions:

(1) "The Church known as the Christian Church possesses the Scriptural characteristics which entitle it to be called the church or kingdom of Christ on earth." Dr. Brents affirmed and Mr. P. denied.

2. The Baptist Church is the Church or kingdom of Christ on earth. Mr. P. affirmed and Dr. Brents denied.

A Report of the Debate

[Note: the record we have of this debate comes in the form of letters written by George Gowan to the *Gospel Advocate*. We present them here unchanged.]

The Petersburg Debate.

I have just returned from Petersburg, Lincoln county, where I heard one of the most interesting discussions I ever attended. The debutants were Dr. Brents of the Church of Christ and Elder Pennington of the. Missionary Baptist Church. Elder, P. I suppose, stands high among his own brethren as he received their hearty endorsement before entering into the discussion. He has gained much notoriety of late "in the regions round about" Petersburg because of his warlike proclivities. He seems to have been a veritable Ishmaelite, "his hand" being "against every man," smiting "hip and thigh" all who did not swear by his standard of orthodoxy. In one of the sallies of this champion against heterodoxy, he chanced to alight on Maple Hill in the vicinity of Petersburg where he utterly demolished "Campbellism" and where it is said he attributed doctrines to us which are disclaimed, by any sensible man among us. At the close of his remarks Bro. Hart who was present announced that he would at such a time and place reply to the gentleman's strictures.

After Some days Bro. Hart received a note from Mr. Pennington stating that on July the 13th at Petersburg he would commence a series of lectures too prove "that the church known as the Christian Church was not the Church of Christ nor any part of it," and if desirable he would divide time with any representative man whom the brethren might select. This, of course, had too much the semblance of a challenge to be ignored by the brotherhood. His suggestion was acted upon and a representative in the person of Dr. Brents was selected. The Dr. was upon the field of battle as early as the 11th and sought a conference with Mr. P. in order to arrange propositions to be discussed. Mr. P. although he had committed himself (exparte) to the discussions of the very sweeping declaration that "the Christian Church was not the Church of Christ nor any part of it," would not agree to test such negation in public debate.

The following propositions were however agreed upon.

(1) "The Church known as the Christian Church possesses the Scriptural characteristics which entitle it to be called the church or kingdom of Christ on earth." Dr. Brents affirmed and Mr. P. denied.

2. The Baptist Church is the Church or kingdom of Christ on earth. Mr. P. affirmed and Dr. Brents denied. The debate commenced Monday morning July the 13th at 10 o'clock and continued four days—two days being allotted to each proposition.

I took copious notes of the discussion and propose in future numbers of this paper to give the leading arguments and in fact, the Substance of all the speeches of both gentlemen.

It is needless to state that the cause of Truth was in safe hands with Dr. Brents at the helm. The brethren with one united voice were lavish in their praises of his presentation and defense of "our plea."

We have no congregation in Petersburg but in the regions adjacent I suppose the Disciples outnumber any of the denominations. Through the devotion and persistent efforts of Bro. John Davidson (now of Richmond) and Dr. Houston, a half interest in the Methodist Church has been purchased and we may reasonably hope for more permanency in the work in the future.

A deep interest obtained from the beginning until the close of the debate and many who had rarely if ever, heard any of our brethren were constant in their attendance.

To these the Dr. always made it a point to present in his own inimitable and powerful style the primitive gospel. Several of our preaching brethren were present, among whom were Bro. Dixon and Hart of the Cane Creek Congregation; Bro. F. W. Smith of Bunker Hill, Giles county; Bro. Tankersly and S. W. Morton of Marshall county. I doubt not that many others would have been present had it been generally known among the Middle Tenn. churches. I noticed representatives from the following congregations: Cane Creek, Richmond, Chestnut Ridge, New Hermon, Flat Creek, Liberty. Lewisburg, Friendship, Beech Grove, and possibly some others. Dr. Davidson, of Richmond, was the moderator chosen by Dr. B. and Mr. McLean a Methodist minister was selected by Mr. P. who selected Esq. Hamilton of Petersburg as the President Moderator. The rules laid down in Hedge's Logic were agreed upon as the Standard of order. But for an introduction, this is lengthy enough. There are many things which were brought out. during the debate, especially upon "Baptist Succession So called, which I deem worthy of reproduction in future numbers of the Advocate.

In my last, everything was in readiness for the work to begin. Monday morning, July 13th. at 10 o'clock found both speakers in their places, the moderators in their chairs and hundreds of anxious auditors, eager to catch every word of the prospective discussion.

But a word descriptive of the debaters, their methods, etc. I presume would not be amiss just here. Dr. Brents is too well and familiarly known to most of the readers of the Advocate to need much description. Suffice it to say that in the sphere of religious polemics, especially upon the controverted points, between our brethren and the denominations, he has not an equal, I suppose, in the church. These controverted points have engaged both his tongue and pen for most of his life, and although he has been actively engaged in secular and literary pursuits for several years past, yet the facility with which he handled the subject matter in debate, and his ready reference to the scriptures, proved him to be the possessor of a wonderful memory. His style in speaking is his style in writing. If you are familiar with the one, you know the other. His language is always well chosen, chaste and pointed. He never repeats except for emphasis. No confusion in his ideas is ever observable. He is a natural logician, a sound and convincing reasoner. It is hard to parry the force of the one or the power of the other. He is always dignified and courteous, both toward his opponent and audience.

Elder Pennington is a tall, slender, gentleman of 150 pounds. As to his age, I guess him to be on the sunny side of forty. He has naturally a good voice which has suffered much from a vehement and monotonous style of speaking. He never allows himself to stop speaking, even if he has to repeat himself a dozen times. He is certainly no novice in the art of sophistry, and has the happy faculty of making an audience see a point when he so desires. Although his elocution would be disclaimed by Bronson, still he is, beyond doubt, a forcible speaker. His idea of religious discussion, judging from his demeanor, is modeled after the old-fashioned debating club where nuns, and jokes and witticisms were the general stock in trade. He tells an Irish yarn with much grace, and can make a negro blush with his plantation dialect. He was soon driven, however, from this, his favorite-field, by the studied silence with which the doctor treated his attempts to provoke laughter.

PROPOSITION ONE

THE PETERSBURG DEBATE #1: DR. BRENTS' FIRST SPEECH

Promptly at 10 o'clock Esq. Hammond arose, read the propositions to be discussed and the rules of government agreed upon, and announced that Dr. Brents would now open the discussion. If I had the space, I would like to give this and the Dr's, closing speech entire. The broad solid arguments laid down in his opening hour's address amply supported as they were by scriptural proofs, were never successfully assailed during the entire debate. He stated that he was there to seek truth, to assist in investigating God's truth. That if in error, he desired to know it, and would consider himself most fortunate if, by any means he could exchange error for truth.

He said that it would be admitted by all that God had a church, an organized government on earth, and that this government is variously called, "the church of God," "the kingdom of heaven," "the body of Christ," etc. He then claimed that if the "Christian Church" possessed the same characteristics of the apostolic church it would be necessary to determine the time of its commencement and just how people were admitted into it and by this means whether or not our teaching is in consonance or keeping with theirs. He said that the prophecy of Daniel would not aid either of them, as it was an indefinite expression, "in the days of these kings" that would apply with equal approbation to the time of John the Baptist, Jesus, or to the Day of Pentecost. He then showed, both from Micah and Luke that Jerusalem was the place whence the word of the Lord and remission of sins should go forth and be granted to all nations. He proved that the kingdom could not have existed in the days of

John the Baptist, else John himself would have been a member of it. But Jesus said, "the least in the kingdom is greater than he" And after John's head had been cut off, we hear Jesus say: "Upon this rock I will build my church." Many other scriptures were produced, all pointing to the future as the time when the church should be established. An argument was drawn from the analogy which exists between the building of Solomon's temple and the establishment of the church. John and Jesus prepared the material which, at the appointed time and place, at God's bidding, dropped into its place and then vivified by the Holy Spirit, sent from Heaven, the great spiritual temple stood forth an existing, living, entity—a church. The law of pardon announced on this occasion was then analyzed and shown to be in exact harmony with the great commission, which contained, preaching, faith, repentance, baptism, remission and salvation. The question was then asked: "Do you know a people in all this country who give to inquiring believers the inspired answer which Peter gave to those on the day of Pentecost?" If so they have thus far, the scriptural characteristics. We teach baptism for the remission, of sins simply because God's book teaches it, yet for this we are denounced as heretics all over this country. In support of this doctrine a powerful argument was based on Acts 2:38, the commission as recorded by Mark and Jno.3:5. Not a single-writer of all the 76 who wrote during the first 400 years of the Christian era, but what taught that John 3:5 referred directly to Christian baptism. His address was listened to with marked attention by the audience and it was very evident that a solid and lasting impression had been made. His definitions were all so clear and his arguments so well supported by apposite scriptural proof that it was the verdict of disinterested and competent judges that this speech, not only could not be, but that it never was successfully attacked during the entire discussion.

THE PETERSBURG DEBATE #2: MR. PENNINGTON'S REPLY

It is my purpose to represent both sides in this debate fairly, but truth compels me to say that if Elder P's first address were stripped of its anecdotes, witticisms and personal allusions (which would not look well in print) there would be very little solid matter left. It was evident from the first that D. P. Ray's "Hand Book on Campbellism" was one of his indispensable aids. For four days, this book and Ray's Baptist Succession proved an unfailing source of inspiration to the gentleman. His first charge was that of inconsistency. He said we fought all kind of high-sounding titles, and then turned around and appropriated more titles to ourselves than anybody. A long list of these were given, accompanied with the admonition to "young preachers present" to carefully memorize them as we would have need for them all when we went "out to speak our "piece." The reader who is curious to learn these "titles" can find them on the first page of the body of "Ray's Hand Book on Campbellism." His next argument (?) against us was based upon the assumption that we had a human head or founder"—Alexander Campbell in the year 1827." And how do you suppose he proved it? Why out of his proofs? was a short letter of introduction sent by Henry Clay to Mr. Campbell on the eve of his (Campbell's) departure for Europe, in which Mr. Clay calls him Rev. Dr. Campbell and states that he is the "head and founder of a great religious community in the U. S. And that Mr. Campbell, upon the strength of this letter, without repudiating its statements, obtained audience with the magnates of England and Scotland, thus tacitly acknowledging the correctness of Mr. C's statement that he was "the head and founder" of the Christian church or else used what he knew to be a falsehood to further his progress in Europe. But this is enough for one letter. I promise you some rich things in my next.

THE PETERSBURG DEBATE #3

I beg of the reader a suppression of his smiles while pursuing the following syllogism deduced by Elder P. from the friendly little note of introduction sent by Henry Clay to Bro. Campbell.

"Mr. Campbell was either a gentleman or a scoundrel. (Might he not have occupied a middle ground?) If a gentleman, he would not have used a document which he knew contained a falsehood. But he did use said document. Hence, he acknowledged the truthfulness of the statement, (that he was the head and founder of the church) or else carried lies around in his pocket to subserve his own personal ends, and must, therefore, be set down as a scoundrel!!" Of course, the presumption was against the last alternative. Hence, Mr. Campbell stood at the self-acknowledged "head and founder" of the Christian church!

The above was delivered with a zest and self-asserting confidence that was really amazing.

His next proof of our human foundation was a quotation from John V. Segar about whom he talked loud and long. He, a prominent man among us, I suppose the words might have the more weight. He claimed that Segar wrote a biography of Bro. C. before his (C's) death, containing the statement quoted and that this book was in the hands of Bro. C., who never once objected to its statements.

Dr. B. had not the book at hand and consequently had not the opportunity of exposing his wretched manner of garbling his extracts in-this instance. Even grant-

The Brents-Pennington Debate

ing that prominent men among us have used the expressions similar to those quoted by Elder Pennington that doesn't prove that A. Campbell is the captain of our salvation. But as I have the word referred to, I will give you a glimpse of his manner of quoting. On page 34 of "Lectures on the Pentateuch," to which Segar's sketch of Mr. Campbell is an introduction. Mr. P. professed to quote the following: "Mr. C. became to be the great and acknowledged head of the church." Now let me give the quotation as it is in the book. "Mr. Campbell, aided by many able and devoted co-laborers had attracted to the movement of which he was the great and acknowledged head man; myriads of zealous and earnest sympathizers. His is not a quotation but a miserable perversion.

The difference between the two statements is clearly perceptible. One makes him the head of the church, the other head or leader of a great reformatory movement looking to the restoration of primitive Christianity.

On page 42, same work he professed to quote the following: "He (Mr. C.) is the talented founder of the Christian church." By referent to the book you will see that he quotes about one half the sentence; for the rest he has no use. Around this and other quotations he rallied at much length and with a mighty flourish of trumpets. Let me give the sentences from which his last extract is garbled: "In the newspapers which have lately alluded to him he is generally spoke of as the talented founder of the Christian church. Neither he nor those who have been stigmatized as his followers, have felt flattered by that 'founder.' He founded nothing that he called or they called religion" Here Mr. Segar says the "newspaper," immediately after Mr. C's. death says so and so of him and after this very statement is regarded by Mr. Segar as having originated with the secular and sectarian press and as being very offensive to him and the disciples, yet Mr. P. quotes this with much ado as being the testimony of a "prominent man" among us and as having received Mr. C's. tacit endorsement in that he never filed any objections to it. Well, I guess not, as he was dead before it was written. Indeed, there is nothing objectionable in the book, save as it goes through the twisting and transforming process exhibited above. It is hard for us to associate such palpable misrepresentations of the plain words of an author, with the spirit of fairness, candor or honesty.

He now stated that he had proved beyond a doubt that we had a human head, whereupon he set himself to work to prove from divers passages of scripture that Christ was the head of the church and as we had other than Christ for our head and founder, therein we did not possess the scriptural characteristics!

It is passingly strange that right on the heels of the foregoing labored effort to prove that Christ is the head of the church, (which nobody denies) that Elder P. should have based his next argument against us simply because we persist in being called after this same great "head of the church. "No," said he, "you do not possess the scriptural characteristics because you call yourselves Christians and that name is of heathen and not of divine origin!"

In reply to Dr. B's. argument on the establishment of the church on the day of Pentecost, Eld. P. replied that Christ had said "I will build my church," that it was not to be left to someone else but that he himself would build it, and that as he was dead on the day of Pentecost, he certainly must have built it before that time! All such passages as the following: "The law and the prophets were until John; since that time the kingdom of God is preached and every man presses into it." Again: "Woe unto you scribes and Pharisees, hypocrites! for you shut up the kingdom of heaven against men; for you neither go in yourselves nor will you suffer those that are entering to go in."

Dr. Brent's first Reply.

He said that according to the rules of all honorable controversy it was the duty of the respondent to follow the affirmant and to make at least a show of answering his arguments. But that in the present instance Mr. P. had studiously avoided all his arguments with a single exception and in that case, had set himself at work to establish a counter theory, instead of showing wherein his position was wrong. In vain did the doctor challenge him to test the strength of his arguments or the correctness of his interpretations. He then replied that A. Campbell established no new sect and that we acknowledged no person as our head but Christ; that there was a vast deal of difference between originating new truths and doctrines and discovering those already existing, and that this last was precisely what A. Campbell had done. His work was to eject heresies, reform the church by casting out corruptions in both doctrines and practices, which had been accumulating for ages, and to lead God's people back to the ancient land-marks of the gospel, thus restoring as nearly as possible the primitive faith, worship and practice of Christianity.

As to Clay's letter about which so much had been said, it yet remained to be proved that he had ever shown it to a single person in Europe and even if he did, it amounted to nothing as it was a note of introduction from a distinguished friend and politician, and was not intended to be an authoritative statement of Mr. C's, faith practice, or ecclesiastical position.

He replied that though Mr. Campbell might have admitted that the name Christian was originally given by the enemies of Christ, yet that such admission was far from proving that such a name was not to distinguish God's people, being, as it was subsequently appropriated, used and endorsed by his faithful followers and inspired apostles. He claimed that the name Christian is applied universally to all of God's people.

In 1 Pet. 3:14 the inspired apostle says, "If ye suffer for righteousness' sake, happy are ye:" in 4:16 be says, "Yet if any man suffer, as a Christian let him not be ashamed but let him glorify God on this behalf." Thus, Christian stands in the second passage where righteousness does in the first, Therefore, to suffer as a Christian, is to suffer for righteousness' sake. Is righteousness a reproach? If so Christian is also, or vice versa. He also dwelt upon the admission extorted from Agrippa that Paul had almost "persuaded him to be a Christian." Christ is the bridegroom, the husband, and as the church is the bride, the wife should be called after the husband. What would you think of a bride who refused to be called after her husband and preferred instead, the name of a particular friend. Yea worse she will not wear the name of her husband to whom she plighted her love, but desires rather to be called after the good old servant down in the kitchen! This is exactly what the Baptists have done. They refuse the name of Christ and prefer to be called by the name of one of his servants!"

THE PETERSBURG DEBATE #4

I promise the reader shorter reports of speeches towards the close of each proposition, as they consist largely, as in all discussions in a repetition and re-affirmation of former arguments and proof.

Dr. B. continued his reply by saying that Eld. P., was entirely without a name, as he rejected the name "Christian" as of a heathenish origin, and not fit to wear, and that the Baptist Revised version of the Scriptures had left the name "Baptist" entirely out of the New Testament and had substituted Immerser in every instance where Baptist occurs.

In reply to Eld. P's. statement that all of John's disciples were Baptists, the name he said was wholly official, like "Luke the physician" "Simon the tanner" and was never intended as a name to be worn by God's people. Besides according to the ablest lights of the Baptist church the name simply meant John the Baptizer, or John the Immerser; hence all his disciples were not simply Baptists, as the gentleman claimed, but they were all baptizers or immerses, men, women and all! Such was the absurd conclusion to which his claim led:

1. The name Christian is applied in the New Testament to the followers of Christ; the name Baptist never,—not even to the followers of John.

2 Christian expresses relation to Christ; Baptist does not.

3 Christian was applied to disciples of Christ at Antioch, the name Baptist is not so used until sixteen-hundred years this side of Christ and then it appears in the form of "Ana-Baptist" given in derision to a sect of dissenters, which fact kills the name according to Eld. P!

4. Baptist is the name of a sect, nothing more, but the name Christian has been applied to and can be appropriated by all of God's people.

5. For wearing the name Christian, men have been led to the stake and doomed to indescribable torture. No man ever suffered martyrdom for wearing the name Baptist.

In reply to Eld. P's. argument against the establishment of the church on the day of Pentecost, he said, that though Christ had been crucified at that time, he was not dead, but the crowned Lord and King in heaven; and that his declaration, "I will build my church" could be literally fulfilled, though Christ was not on earth, as he had left his "called and qualified agents—his apostles,—

whose express work it was, in co-operation with him, to establish said church, under his special direction and the guidance of his spirit on the day of Pentecost. Elder. P. quoted Matt. 18:17 to prove that the church was then existing because Christ said, "And if he shall neglect to hear them tell it unto the Church." To this it was replied that Jesus was here laying down a rule of action that should govern them in the future when his church should be established and when they would not have the benefit of his own personal instructions and care. Both John and Jesus preached the gospel of the coming kingdom saying it "is at hand"—draweth nigh. The great principles of the kingdom were preached and material for this coming kingdom was being prepared by inducing the people to acknowledge him as their future king, and to accept those principles which were to govern the coming kingdom. Hence, it could be truthfully said that the Pharisees "shut up the kingdom of God against men," "then is the kingdom of God come to you," and "since that time the kingdom of God is preached, and every man presses into it," etc. Its principles were being preached, accepted and rejected. No other view will explain such passages as "the least in the Kingdom is greater than he;" "on this rock I will build my church" "thy kingdom come," "who also waited for the kingdom," and also the fact that Christ's immediate followers knew not of its existence, if it did really exist. If it was established before Pentecost, it was a kingdom without a king,—a body without a head and without a spirit. As Jesus after his resurrection became the head over all things to the Church, was crowned Lord and King, and sent his spirit to give life and comfort to the body—the Church.

The old and the new could not have existed at the same time. Christ observed the old Jewish law till the day of his death. The sacrifices upon the altar continued till the very last with the Lord's full sanction. Not till he died was the veil in the temple rent in twain, thus indicating that the Jewish kingdom was at an end. Christ was the last great sacrifice, thus putting an end to the priesthood of Aaron, [Heb. 7:11-12] and taking out of the way the handwriting of ordinances, nailing it to the cross, [Col. 2:14].

Elder P. claimed that baptism was an ordinance of the church—was in the church, hence the church must have existed when it and the Lord's supper were placed in it by Christ. To this it was replied that baptism was not in the church, but one of the means appointed for getting into it. He who has put on Christ is in him—his Church.

"As many of you as have been baptized into Christ have put on Christ." No pardoned man, no Christian as such was ever commanded to be baptized.

There are many personal allusions and undignified expressions which I left out of Elder P.'s' speech, and which the Doctor treated with merited contempt, such as, "you are all a brood of ecclesiastical flat-heads," and many other equally untasteful expressions. In his next speech he will take some novel and original positions on the name and Acts 2:38. But we must wait a week!

THE PETERSBURG DEBATE #5

With much persistency, he held on to the statement garbled from Segar that Bro. C. was the "head and founder" of the church. The same fact was established he said by Millner the church historian. He knew Millner was correct; that he would not state a falsehood it would blast his reputation as an historian!" He said "there was a time when we couldn't manage this sect of Campbell's for there was a time when they didn't have a literature; but we can manage them now by turning their own guns against them. Jobs prayer, 'O that mine enemy would write a book' has been abundantly fulfilled!" He said that it would be more truthful to say that A. Campbell was a deformer than to call him a reformer. In reply to Dr. B's statement that A. C. originated nothing in the way of gospel truth but simply brought to light that which God had already originated, he said that the Dr. told the truth for once, for A. Campbell had come as nearly originating "nothing" as anybody he ever knew! And such contemptible quibbling as this was indulged in in the name of honorable controversy.

He then asked in a tone of apparent [triumph] "where in all the Bible has God authorized A. Campbell to reform his church?" The idea that God's church needed to be reformed is perfectly ridiculous, much less that A. Campbell should be the one to reform it. He said he thought that the church was the bride, the Lamb's wife and he supposed that the "old lady" (to use his own irreverent expression) "had got a little off the track, had ceased to be as virtuous as she should" and that A. C. was "sent to marry her all over again!" Said that he didn't know before is that God's church was so imperfect as to need reforming. He thought the church was the "pillar and support of the truth" but said he reckoned "the supports had gotten a little out of place and that Mr. C. was commissioned to fix them up again!" He charged that the Christian Church was founded by and the material made up of excluded members from the Baptist church.

The astounding revelation was then made that even granting the correctness of our desire to wear our Saviour's name we had most sadly missed it in calling ourselves Christians, for his name is not Christ but Jesus' Matt. 1:21 was quoted, "and thou shall call his name Jesus." "Here," says he, "is an angel from heaven announcing that his name shall be Jesus," then turning to the Dr. he said: "You have got the church married over again and as you want her to wear the name of her husband I guess you had better call her Mrs. Jesus as that was her husband's name!!" When Jesus died on the cross exclaiming "it is finished" Mr. P. insisted that he meant "the church is finished," therefore it was set up before the day of Pentecost. He argued that the Christian church was too young by 1,700 to meet the requirements of Daniel "in the days of these kings shall the God of heaven set up a kingdom," as "there didn't happen to be any kings about where and when A. C. established his church."

After much urging upon th part of Dr. B. Mr. P. finally crossed swords with him on Acts. 2:38. "O," says he, Peter answered the three thousand correctly but his answer is not applicable to alien sinners now. Those were not sinners who cried out "men and brethren what shall we do to be saved?" "'Tis true" he said, "they were guilty of one sin—the crucifixion of Christ, and were, therefore, baptized, not as you baptize them, for the remission of sins!" And to prove that the three thousand were not sinners he quoted the following from the fifth verse; Now there were dwelling at Jerusalem, Jews devout, men from every nation under heaven." "Hence these were devout men to whom Peter preached, and his answer cannot apply to alien sinners to-day." To the incredulous I would say the proof for the correctness of the foregoing report is abundant!

In reply to Dr. B's argument that Jesus would not have taught his disciples to pray "thy kingdom come" if it had been already established, Mr. P. said that the Greek word erchomai . (come) meant to spread or increase and should read in the passage "thy kingdom spread."

In proof of the church infallibility he quoted 1 Jno. 3:9. "Whosoever is born (begotten) of God doeth no sin because his seed abideth in I him.

Dr. Brents then said: "And lo! it turns out that I am debating with a Roman Catholic instead of a Baptist. The gentleman had better go to Rome where he belongs, than to be fighting in a covert way for the Baptists; for never did man come out more strongly in favor of church infallibility than he has done. Let him quit the Protestants, join the Pope's army and assist him in supporting and propagating this absurd dogma of infallibility." He then showed from the New Testament that many corruptions had crept into the church even in the days of the apostles and that they recognized the fact that it stood sadly in need of reform in certain instances. The church at Ephesus had left its "first love" and had "fallen" and its candlestick was in danger of being removed. The church at Pergamum was nearly ready for God to "make war against" it, and the church at Thyatira needed a "reform," so Christ in Revelation said, so if Sardis; and to the church at Laodicea, he said: "I will spew thee out of my mouth." Yet the gentleman says the church can't err and consequently needed no reforming, hence A. Campbell's work amounted to nothing. God's word never changes but men who constitute the church forsake that word both as individuals and congregations. Evidences of this are abundant.

The church is the "pillar and support of the truth" in that, the dissemination and defense of that truth depends upon the church. Truth absolute does not depend upon the church, but the church is built upon the truth.

God's faithful messengers must see that his truth is preached unmixed with errors. This work is perfectly consistent with the will of God. Special blessings are pronounced upon him who leads an erring brother into light again. This was precisely the intention and desire of the Campbells. Not to establish a sect or add to the long list of erring denominations, but to cut loose from sectism, discard all creeds, forget the conflicts and traditions of the past, to subordinate dogmatics to faith, and theology to religion. Such a work, though it was done a thousand years hence, would be perfectly right, accepted of God and blessed of heaven, even if its projectors were not called to such a mission by the miraculous voice of Jehovah. If Eld. P. were to attempt to effect a reformation of existing wrongs in his own fold by leading them more nearly in to the light of the gospel truth, his work would be acceptable to God.

Campbell was not excluded from the Baptist church nor were those who first took their stand with him on the Bible and the Bible alone. He and his congregation were permitted to quietly withdraw from the Redstone Association and join the Mahoning Association in which they remained in perfect harmony until that association: was induced to lay aside all ecclesiastical authority.

Because the Son of God was to be called Jesus, was no evidence that his name was not also Christ! The same God that named him Jesus; anointed and called him Christ; and he is now the risen Christ in heaven, after whom God's children should be called. Mr. P's. irreverent expression about the church being called "Mrs. Jesus" was passed by in silence.

Eld. P's. most novel and astounding position on Acts 2:38, was handled with gloves off. "Those three thousand who cried to Peter on the day of Pentecost were devout, pure, saintly creatures indeed. They were guilty of only one little sin; had only rejected the world's Redeemer, done despite to the wooings of his love and steeped their "devout"(?) hands in the precious blood of the Son of God!"

"What senseless and reckless positions men will take in order to boost a shaky human theory and escape the plain and simple teaching of the Holy Spirit!" "Guilty of only one sin you say, yet Peter speaking as God gave him utterance, said, 'repent and be baptized for the remission of sins." "Of the two, Pennington or God, take your choice."

The word erchomai occurs nearly six hundred times in the New Testament and never meant to 'spread." Hence Jesus never meant to teach his disciples to pray "thy kingdom spread.' Here are some of the examples: "We saw his star in the east and have come (spread) to worship him. Mat. 2:2 "Go search that I also may come (spread) and worship him. Mat. 2:8 "And it came (spread) and stood over where the young child lay;" "he came (spread) and dwelt in a city called Nazareth;" "Think not that I am come (spread) to destroy;" when he arose he came (spread) to the other side;" "John came (spread) neither eating nor drinking." So throughout the New Testament the uniform meaning of the word is the very opposite of spread; and refers to the coming of a definite thing.

THE PETERSBURG DEBATE #6

Mr. Pennington's Reply

It was hoped that the baneful tree, whose falling limbs for sixty years has proved more deadly than the poisonous asps of fabled growth, would be permitted to rest in harmless security in its sylvan quietude, but all our hopes were vain. Ruthless hands tore from that aged trunk another limb which did its direful work. A beauteous girl full of faith and hope and love, in the path of obedience was crushed by its fateful fall! The conclusion was: "Your theory sends this young lady to torment, therefore baptism is not for the remission of sins." And might he not have added, "And Peter, Paul and Christ were all mistaken."

"Mormons teach baptism for the remission of sins, hence the Mormon church is entitled to be called the church of Christ."

"Dr. B. buries a man to kill him and we bury him because he is already killed. Such doctrine as the doctor's is out-landish and heathenish."

In reply to Dr. B.s arguments on Jno. 3:5, and Rom. 6:4, elder P. ridiculed the very idea of baptism being typical of two things so entirely different as a birth and a burial. Said Christ never meant baptism when he spoke of being born of water" in John 3 5.

He met Dr. B's. statement that the gospel in its facts could not have been preached before these facts existed as such, by saying that there was not a particle of difference between preaching a thing that was to come and one already come. To use his own language, he said there was quite as much difference as between "tweedledee and tweedledum." The reader for himself can determine the extent of that difference.

He said that the church must have been finished before Pentecost for the Savior prayed the dedicatory prayer as recorded in the 17th. chapter of John, and that prayer is a counterpart of Solomon's prayer at the dedication of the temple!

The thief on the cross was saved without baptism. If it were so essential to salvation why did he not submit to it. He had abundant opportunity for thirty years, yet the Lord said to him, "this day shalt thou be with me in paradise." His final rally on Acts 2:38, was made by taking the words of Jesus as recorded in Acts 10:45, and tacking them on to the words of Joel in Acts 2:21 so as to read, "To him (Christ) give all the prophets witness that whosoever shall call on the name of the Lord shall be saved." "But how call," said he? "Why just get down on your knees and at it like good old fellows. Like we used to do at the good old Methodist camp-meetings where everybody got killing happy!" "Jesus said, 'ask and ye shall receive, knock and it shall be opened, seek and ye shall find.'"

In elder P's argument on church infallibility, as stated in a previous article, he quoted John 3:9, "Whosoever is born of God doth not commit sin." The church is composed of men born of God, hence it cannot err, was the conclusion drawn. To this it was replied by Dr. B. that the same John in the same letter had previously said, "If we say we have no sin we deceive ourselves and the truth is not in us." "If we confess our sins he is faithful and just to forgive us our sins and to dense us from all unrighteousness. If we say that we have not sinned we make him a liar and his word is not in us." 1 Jno. 8:9-10 Now must we understand from Jno. 3:9 that a Christian cannot sin, and thus make the apostle stultify himself?"

Prof. S. T. Green's translation of Jno. 3:9 was then read. The sense of that is that the Christian does not follow after sin continually. Sin is the exception rather than the rule of his life. And this rendering of the original is concurred in by all eminent critics.

The way elder P. wiggled out of this was amusing. He said that in 1 Jno. 1:8 10, he is speaking of the flesh, the body of the Christian sinning and in 3:9 of the spirit. "The flesh can sin but the spirit cannot."

Dr. Brents.

Christ said except a man is born of water and of the spirit into the kingdom of heaven he cannot go. All respectable authorities agree that this (water) refers to Christian baptism. Did our Lord tell the truth? If he did, then I'm no heretic for teaching the same. Did Peter, speaking as the spirit gave him utterance, mean what he said when he commanded the three thousand to repent and be baptized for the remission of sins? If he was right then I am right. Did Ananias know what he was about when he commanded Saul to "arise and be baptized and wash away thy sins?" If so, then I am right when I do likewise. Paul believed he was praying and was certainly penitent, but yet not saved. God sent a man to tell him what else he must do to complete his obedience and perfect his salvation. "Why do you tarry Saul? arise and be baptized and wash away your sins." What would Bro P. have done had he been sent to instruct Saul? You would have heard something like the following: "Pray on Bro. Saul you are on the right track now, the darkest hour is just before day!' Did Peter understand what he was about when he said "baptism doth also now save us?" Is my name to be cast out as evil for teaching the same?

God's commands commence where man's obedience ends. The heathen jailer who had never known a Christ was commanded to believe and his conversion ended in his baptism the same hour of the night. The three thousand who had already believed, were commanded to repent and be baptized. Saul who had both believed and repented was commanded simply to be baptized. Thus we see there was a strict and beautiful uniformity in the cases of conversion recorded in Acts. The apostles who preached under our Lord's commission taught the same on every occasion. The same conditions are expressed or implied every time. God's book is a sensible one addressed to an intelligent being who is not required to become crazy in order to be converted.

Certainly, whoever calls on the name of the Lord shall be saved. But God tells us exactly how to call, and gives us examples of calling on his name. "Not every one that saith unto me, Lord, Lord, shall enter into the kingdom of heaven, but he that doeth the will of my father who is in heaven." "And why call ye me Lord, Lord and do not do the things which I say?" Thousands on the day of Pentecost heard Peter preaching the gospel and they called on the name of the Lord, but how? They came, believing what he preached, and cried out in all the deep earnestness of their souls, "Men and brethren what shall we do? In the next breath Peter answered their prayer and told them exactly what to do, and they did it and the same day rejoiced in the fullness of the Lord's salvation. Joel's prophecy was fulfilled; they called and were saved. But they did not get down on their knees and agonize a week in order to salvation. Had elder P. been there and practicing what he now does he would have exhorted them to "get down and at it." "Start a song Bro. Peter, lead us in prayer Bro. John and the pitiful wails of, and the heart is conversion ended in his baptism the same hour of the night. The three thousand who had already believed, were commanded to repent and be baptized. Saul who had both believed and repented was commanded simply to be baptized. Thus we see there was a strict and beautiful uniformity in the cases of conversion recorded in Acts. The apostles who preached under our Lord's commission taught the same on every occasion. The same conditions are expressed or implied every time. God's book is a sensible one addressed to an intelligent being who is not required to become crazy in order to be converted.

Certainly, whoever calls on the name of the Lord shall be saved. But God tells us exactly how to call, and gives us examples of calling on his name. "Not every one that saith unto me, Lord, Lord, shall enter into the kingdom of heaven, but he that doeth the will of my father who is in heaven." And why call ye me Lord, Lord and do not do the things which I say?" Thousands on the day of Pentecost heard Peter preaching the gospel and they called on the name of the Lord, but how? They came, believing what he preached, and cried out in all the deep earnestness of their souls, "Men and brethren what shall we do?' In the next breath, Peter answered their prayer and told them exactly what to do, and they did it and the same day rejoiced in the fullness of the Lord's salvation. Joel's prophecy was fulfilled; they called and were saved. But they did not get down on their knees and agonize a week in order to salvation.

Had elder P. been there and practicing what he now does he would have exhorted them to "get down and at it." "Start a song Bro. Peter, lead us in prayer

Bro. John and the pitiful wails of, and the heartrending prayers of three-thousand penitent believers would for weeks, no doubt, have turned God's temple into a perfect bedlam. This is not the way the Lord saves those who call upon him.

"Mormons believe in the divinity of Jesus Christ, so do Baptists, therefore Mormons are Baptists, that's logic with a vengeance!" "Therefore, we are buried with him by baptism into death, that like as Christ was raised up from the dead by the glory of the father, even so we also should walk in newness of life."

When Christ was speaking to a man who was thinking of his Jewish birth, he spoke of baptism as a birth. When viewing it from another point of vision, Paul appropriately calls it a burial. There is nothing strange in comparison. In the first place, we don't know that the thief was saved at all, and second, no one can prove that he was unbaptized. He might have been baptized. His thirty years opportunity for baptism is a mystery to me, as John just commenced his ministry three and a-half years before.

THE PETERSBURG DEBATE #7

Conclusion of first Proposition.
Pennington.

The prophet said that when Christ's kingdom should come, nations would learn war no more. War has not ceased; therefore, the petition, "Thy kingdom come" did not refer to a definite thing, but the complete establishment of the church when wars will cease and universal peace shall reign.

"The doctor has a church with John and Jesus both excluded."

Baptism is administered by the authority of the church; hence the church must have existed, else John and Jesus could not have baptized.

In answer to Dr. B., that the "gospel of the kingdom" which was preached by John and Jesus, the twelve and the seventy went only to the Jews—"to the lost sheep of the house of Israel." Eld. P. quoted the words of Paul and Barnabas in Acts 18:46, as the words oi Christ, saying: "Jesus did go to the Gentiles, for he said to the Jews, 'you judge yourselves unworthy of everlasting life, lo we turn to the Gentiles.'

The three thousand on Pentecost only asked what they must do; they didn't say a word about what they must do to be saved.

Baptism is not essential to salvation, else Paul would not have thanked God that he had baptized none of the Corinthians.

Baptism is not salvation, but a picture of salvation.

In answer to Dr. B's. argument, based on 1 Peter 3:20-21, Eld. P. treated the audience to a lengthy reading from a dissertation upon that passage which he had published several years ago. It was indeed rich and will doubtless (?) become a classic in Baptist literature.

Peter says "eight souls were saved by water." Eld. P. says they were saved through water. Leaving out the parenthesis the 21st verse reads as follows: "The like figure [antitype] whereunto even baptism doth also now save us, by the resurrection of Jesus Christ." He argued that it was the resurrection and not baptism that saves us. He said that as it was the "answer of a good conscience" the good conscience must have been there before; hence persons are pardoned before baptism.

"It was not the water which saved Noah and his family, but the ark. They escaped from the water by entering the ark; all who were baptized in the flood were destroyed, and water will damn people to-day just like it did the antediluvians!"

God's plea of salvation is exactly like it was in the days of Abel. Abraham and Moses. They were all saved by faith in God. Isa. 51:8,1. Pet. 1:10 and Heb. 11:3b, were quoted to prove this.

The doctor's plea will let almost anything into the church. He will baptize any body that demands it, and says that-he believes. I reckon the doctor would have baptized those devils that believed and trembled.

If the statement, "Then went out unto him Jerusalem and Judea and all the regions round about Jordan, might have included the thief on the cross as one of the baptized. So, the same statement might also include infants."

Paul told the jailer to believe on the Lord Jesus and he should be saved; not a word about baptism. "He that heareth my word and believeth on him that sent me, hath everlasting life, and shall not come into condemnation but is passed from death unto life." John 5:35. "Everlasting life" is here predicated on faith alone.

"Therefore being justified by faith we have peace with God through our Lord Jesus Christ." Rom. 5:1.

"Thy faith hath saved thee, go in peace." Thus, we see that Jesus taught the same grand old system of faith.

"For by grace are ye saved through faith and that not of yourselves it is the gift of God: not of works lest any man should boast." Eph. 2:8-9.

"Knowing that a man is not justified by the works of the law, but by faith in Jesus Christ." Gal. 2:16. Paul taught the same old God-honored system of faith alone as opposed to salvation by works. Baptism is a work, therefore baptism is not essential to salvation.

Paul was a pardoned man before his baptism. The words of Jesus "for he is a chosen vessel" prove beyond doubt that Saul was then saved; Annanias called him "brother Saul" which shows that he recognized him as already a brother in Christ! "The scales which fell from his eyes represented the sins which had already been pardoned." Cornelius was saved before baptism else angels would not have visited, nor the spirit been given him. God gives the Holy spirit to all who ask it. "Ask and it shall be given," "Baptism does not procure a real but a formal salvation."

Brents.

"You do not desire to be called the church because you have changed God's order of faith and repentance; and because for such wars have not yet ceased, Christ's kingdom-has not yet come. The prophet meant that under this new rule that was to be established, nations should learn war no more. It was not to be upheld and propagated by the sword. Its principles were opposed to wars and swords, and under its gentle, loveable, peaceful way such unholy and reprehensible things should not characterizes subjects." "Eld. P. taunts them for leaving John and Jesus out of the church. Now I desire to ask him in the presence of this audience if he will take the position that John the Baptist was in the church?" Eld. P here stated that he had not nor would he take such a position. "Then in the name of common honesty, what are you berating me and trying to make me appear odious in the eyes of this people for doing exactly the same thing which you yourself have done?" "Ah, my brother, such tactics are unworthy the cause which you profess to plead."

You say that John was not in the church, yet baptism is performed by the authority of the church! Verily the legs of the lame are unequal. John and Jesus get their authority from God to baptize. It was Paul and not Jesus who said, "lo we turn to the Gentiles."

He must be hard pushed for argument, who would quibble over the inquiry of the three thousand simply because they do not ask what they must do to be saved. Peter's answer shows the object of their prayers when he tells them to repent and be baptized for the remission of sins. Evidently it was salvation from sin that they desired. How a man can find an argument against baptism in Paul's statement in first Corinthians, about being glad that he had baptized no more of them, is a mystery to me. He did not think that he had baptized none of them; but he was glad that he individually had done no more of it, and why? Because it was not necessary or Christ had not announced it? By no means. It was simply because there was a party in the Corinthian church that were inclined to accept him as its head and to be called by his name. Rather than that Christ should be thus dishonored, he was glad that he had given them no more occasion for this species of hero worship than he really had.

"Eld. P. ought to have studied his essay on 1 Pet. 3:20-21 a little longer. If he got anything intelligent out of it I failed to see it. He tells us that Noah's family were saved through water, yet it was the ark that saved them.

The original of the word "answer" occurs fifty-nine times, in fifty-five places of which it is rendered by "ask" or by some of its forms; in two, demanded; in one desired, and in one questioned. "To seek after" is given as the meaning of the word. Hence, "seeking" would be the more accurate rendering. How could a man better seek a good conscience than by obeying the Lord in baptism?

But my brother says "it is the resurrection that saves us and not baptism." Peter says baptism doth also now save us." "Peter or Pennington choose yes." Yes, but he says "the water destroyed the antediluvians and that it will to-day just like it did then."- Certainly it will if they are as wicked as the antediluvians were! Certainly, the people in the days of Abel, Moses and the prophets were saved if at all by faith in God. But that does not argue that the conditions of salvation are the same now as then. If so, my brother, you had better build you an altar and go to killing your sheep, kids and bullocks like they did.

Now as to those devils, they are your brethren. We did not claim them at all. They are "faith alone" folks and we don't claim that kind!

The multitudes that were from Jerusalem, Judea and the regions round about Jordan, did not include infants, for they were baptized "confessing their sins."

The gentleman, instead of answering my argument, comes along with a great long string of quotations, which he thinks prove the opposite of my position. This method of discussion in thus taking disconnected snatches of Scripture is better calculated to make infidels than Christians.

In most of the passages where it says that we are justified by faith, the faith thus spoken of is used in antithesis to the works of the old Jewish law.

In Rom. v, 1: "Therefore, being justified by faith, we have peace," etc., the gentleman found a strong tower for faith-alone doctrine; but if he had read on down- to the 17th verse of the 6th chapter, all would have been made plain. "But God be thanked that ye were the servants of sin, but ye have obeyed from the heart that form of doctrine which was delivered you, being then made free from sin, ye became the servants of righteousness." Thus, you see the apostle himself tells what he means by "being justified by faith."

"Not a word of baptism in the jailor's case, eh?" Of course not, in the verse you read. Had you not been afraid, and gone a little further, you would have found that he and all his were baptized the "same hour of the night." "Thy faith hath saved thee." In this expression, Jesus taught the "grand old doctrine of faith alone," so the gentleman thinks. The Lord could speak salvation of any kind and in any way while He was on earth. Special bequests could then be made, but His will is now left as a guide in the bestowment of His blessings, and we must go by it.

But "baptism is a work." Yes, and so is faith. "This is the work of God, that ye believe on His Son." So you had better tear faith out, too.

How does Elder P. know that the scales on Saul's eyes represented sin? The scales had already fallen, yet Ananias said, "arise and be baptized and wash away thy sins." But Paul was already pardoned. If so his sins were not washed away, for his last act of obedience did this.

God gave His Holy Spirit to His children, "whom the world cannot receive," are the words of the Book. Where repentance precedes faith, it is "repentance toward God and faith in Jesus Christ." But where the reference is to Christ as under the Gospel dispensation, faith always precedes repentance. "Know assuredly (faith) first, and then repent and be baptized," is God's order in the Gospel. Are you going to tear them asunder? "Cornelius was already saved." "Who shall tell thee words whereby thou and all thy house shall be saved. Yet you say, "already saved." God's word should not be contradicted.

Proposition Two

"Resolved, that the Baptist Church is the Church or Kingdom of Christ on earth."

The Petersburg Debate #8

Elder Pennington spoke in substance as follows:

"It is immaterial with me as to whether I succeeded or failed in the discussion of the former proposition. I had very little interest in that question; hence, it gave me very little concern. But all that I am, all that I have and all that I ever expect to have or be, centers in the proposition I am now to sustain. If I fail to sustain this, I fail in all, and all for which I've labored, and all my hopes are swept away.

"I now propose to prove that the Baptist Church is not only like, but that it is the identical church for which John prepared material, and the one which John himself built.

"All my arguments shall be grouped around the three following propositions:

"1. Christ built a church. 2. He built a Baptist church. 3. I will trace an unbroken line of Baptist succession from the Baptist church which Christ built, down to the present time.

"Kingdom and church are synonymous. The church is composed of baptized believers. We don't claim that the Baptist church is the church of Christ, because of our name. We base no argument on the name."

He then quoted Daniel: "In the days of these kings shall the God of Heaven set up a kingdom," etc., and the words of Christ: "On this rock I will build my Church." "Thus," says he, "we have a God-made, and not a man-made institution. The churches which Luther, Calvin, Wesley and Campbell started are all man-made institutions."

Elder P. then quoted all the prophecies and, references pertaining to John the Baptist as the forerunner of Christ, and as the one who was to prepare-the material for Christ's Church. He then said the character of a house is determined by the kind of material that enters into its construction. If the material is brick it will be a brick house; if wood, it would be a wooden house, etc. John the Baptist prepared the material out of which Christ built his church. It was Baptist material, because John the Baptist prepared it. Therefore, the church which Christ established was a Baptist Church."

"John was the first Baptist. The Baptist Church is a grand democracy without creed, confession or book of discipline. Baptist principles are the same as those taught by Christ and his apostles. Appleton's encyclopedia was quoted with much gusto as saying that the Baptist doctrine had remained the same "in all ages and countries." Look at the hundreds of denominations, and see how many of them have changed since their organization. But the Baptist church has never changed, nor has she ever needed reforming. -In America, in England, in France, in Wales, and in the forests of Bohemia, she has always been the same virtuous bride. It was never to be destroyed nor left to other people. Through all the dark ages it remained the same. The gates of hell did not prevail against it. The Baptist is the only church that has the blood of martyrs upon her garments.

"He shall reign over his house forever, and of his kingdom there shall be no end." (Luke 1:33) Christ said, 'lo, I am with you always.' Hence, he was with his church through the dark aces. As the Baptist church is the only one which can establish a line of succession through this period of the world's history, and as all others have had a human origin since that time, it follows that the Baptist is the church of Christ by inheritance!

This "kingdom cannot be moved," (Heb. xii, 28). A religious encyclopedia was quoted as saying that "the Baptist is the only religious denomination that can trace an unbroken line of succession back to the apostles" Elder P. then traced the history of the church down through New Testament times, and then quoted the first six verses of the 12th chapter of Revelation in order to show what God did with His church during the first twelve hundred 'years of the Christian era. He said that Christ was the "Son" that was born and caught up into heaven, and that the "woman" was the church. "And the woman fled into the wilderness where she hath a place prepared of God, that there they may nourish her a thousand, two hundred and three-score days." (Rev. xii, 6). "This woman, representing the Baptist church, was hid in the wilderness for safe keeping for 1280 days, which are equal to 1280 years, which corresponds exactly with the date 1286, ad., when the Waldenses or Anti-Baptists began to exercise influence in the world's affairs."

Brents.

You will observe the difference in our propositions. The gentleman affirms that the Baptist church is not only like, but that it is the identical church or kingdom of Christ on earth. Not a part of it, but it is the unadulterated simon-pure —the original thing itself. Now I desire the gentleman to inform us as to which one of the Baptist churches I am to fight? Is it the Old Baptist, the Separate Baptist, all the numerous Baptist branches combined, or the one particular Baptist zion to which he belongs? (Here Elder P. stated that it was the Missionary Baptist Church that is the "Kingdom or Church of Christ on earth"; Very well. My good Old and Separate Baptist brethren, you hear that? You who have been enjoying this discussion so hugely during the last two days, must now part from your brother's company. You are none of his. Let your farewell words be said. You are not the church nor a part of it. Only a base imitation or a downright fraud. He represents none of your manmade institution—only the church which God made! Yes. Christ built His Church. Wonder why he named it after John the Baptist? I really don't know what would have become of the gentleman if it had not been for D. B. Ray's Baptist Succession, from which he read his speech. He treated you to the very best that Ray can get up! Certainly Daniel said "in the days of those kings will the God of Heaven set up a Kingdom," but my dear sir, I deny the assumption that it was to be a Baptist kingdom. You assume without a shadow of evidence the very point in dispute. Most assuredly Jesus said, "upon this rock I will build my church," but he didn't say, "I will build my Baptist church," no; far from it, my brother. I accept your first proposition that Christ built a church, no dispute about that, but I deny your unwarranted and brazen assumption that "He built a Baptist church."

What if the woman in Rev.xii,6, did represent the church, and that church was hid in the wilderness as you say. The very point in dispute, that she was the Missionary Baptist church, remains still to be proved, my brother. He just assumes everything. A little proof would not be amiss here.

Ah! he doesn't base anything on the name. Yet we were heterodox in the former proposition, because we didn't have the right name! Well I'm glad I've made him repudiate his own. The most learned among the Baptists have long since abandoned it. One more step towards the right.

You base nothing on the name, but all on the Scriptural characteristics. That's exactly what I've been contending for, for the last two days. But not content with this, you must believe in Baptist succession, than, which there was never a more consummate farce. We shall see how you "succeed" however.

I accept the statements that John was to prepare material for Christ's church, and that the kind of house built is determined by the character of the material entering into its construction. I deny that John prepared Baptist material but claim that John baptized all of his material "for the remission of sins."

"And he (John) came into all the country about Jordan preaching the baptism of repentance for the remission of sins." Luke 3:3 and Mark 1:4. Yes, John preached baptism for the remission of sins, and you have done stated as a fundamental doctrine of the Missionary Baptist church that it baptizes none but those who have been pardoned—born again, and that it will not tolerate baptism for remission of sins.

Why sir, you would turn me out of your Baptist Zion before to-morrow night if I were to preach what John did. Yet he "is the first Baptist" and the one who prepared all your material by baptizing them for the remission of sins, No sir. I'm right here to stay and to see to it that your Baptist succession don't begin at John's end of the line. You wouldn't have me for preaching the same doctrine and you shall not have John. You would not have my brethren because they have been baptized for the remission of sins and I propose to see to it that you don't get John's material for the very same reason!

You say your church is a grand democracy, yet claim Jesus as your king—a strange freak in government—a democracy with a king! At the proper time, we will see whether the gentleman's church has a "creed" or not. The Waldenses practiced anything and everything, still we are told that Baptists never change. "He shall reign over his house forever, and of his kingdom there shall be no end." Certainly; but is it a Baptist house or a Baptist kingdom? "Lo I am with you always," therefore there is such a thing as Baptist succession! The "kingdom cannot be moved." Yes, but it doesn't say the Baptist kingdom!

A little more proof and less assumption would be in order, Bro. Pennington.

THE PETERSBURG DEBATE #9

Pennington.
My report of the discussion of the second proposition will be much briefer than the first because much of the ground gone over in the first was recanvassed in the second. Again, as elder P.'s little succession boat was so unceremoniously capsized before he had fairly launched it on the waves of Jordan, preparatory to his voyage through the dark ages, the audience was saved many tiresome readings from D. B. Ray's romance, which sad catastrophe and consequent result have tended materially to lighten my task!

After Bro. B. had so thoroughly robbed Eld. P. of all the material out of which he had constructed his church and commenced his succession, the audience was very curious to know how he would proceed. He had repeatedly said in the first part of the debate that the Baptists had no material baptized for the remission of sins, and would not accept that sort; and as the Dr. had conclusively shown that John's material out of which Eld. P. had constructed his church and started his succession was exactly that kind, curiosity was at its very highest pitch to know what he would or could do with the ruins of that magnificent Baptist edifice, whose every foundation stone had been wrenched from its place by Dr. Brents.

That suspense was soon relieved. Eld. P. stated in the beginning of his second address that for the present he would pass succession by and attend to "more weighty matters of the law!"

He stated that the Baptist church had seven peculiarities which differentiated it from all other religious bodies, and which peculiarities entitle it to the high claim of "the church or kingdom of Christ on earth."

1. Baptists recognize Christ as their head and founder—no other people do. He said that he could give the name of a human being as the founder of every church in existence except the Baptist church.

2. Baptists accept the Bible alone as their rule of faith and practice—this no other church does- They believe the Bible to be the Book of God, and accept all that it says.

3. Baptists teach that baptism and the Lord's supper are ordinances of the church, and preach repentance before faith.

4. Baptists immerse the regenerated—the man who is born again—no other people do.

5. Baptists teach that the Holy Spirit operates in man's conversion independent of the word so as to open the eyes of his understanding that he may be enabled to see, to understand and to obey.

6. We believe in the final perseverance of the saints.

(The remaining "peculiarity" never saw the light so far as that debate was concerned. The Dr. so completely routed him on the above mentioned six, that for reasons unknown the seventh was never given to the public. The imaginative reader is left to surmise what it can be. It may be that the Baptist church actually believes in the existence of a God or perchance that the moon is made of green cheese! These would have been quite as "peculiar" as some of the six)

Eld. P. then continued: "Abram was saved by faith alone" "Abraham believed God and it was accounted to him for righteousness." Salvation is the free gift of God. Hence the Baptist peculiarity of immersing none but saved persons. If of baptism, it is no more of grace.

The Dr.'s plan is on this wise: A poor hungry 'ramp comes along and asks for dinner. "Certainly," says the

Dr., "if you will cut me a cord of wood, I'll give you your dinner."

Baptism for the remission of sins operates just that way. A poor sinner desires to be saved. Salvation is the free gift of Cod, yet the Dr. says you must be baptized, and then you can have the free gift!

Elder P. then undertook to show that "Dr. B. and his so-called reformers" have a creed, notwithstanding their boast that they stand on the Bible alone.

He then read a creed which he said had been put forth by Moses E. Lard, one of our greatest men. Said that Lard forced it upon many of the churches in that part of Kentucky where believed and that he swore vengeance upon the churches and disciples who would not wear it. He also said that it was published and endorsed by all the leading papers of the disciples. He then read all the articles of the aforesaid "creed" and closed by a tremendous flourish with the words, "There is your creed with a vengeance, Dr., and you've got to swallow it."

Brents.

And it happens somehow that my brother has abandoned his succession business for the present. If he doesn't abandon it entirely before the close of this debate, I am very much mistaken. It is a feat which no sane man ought to attempt, and one which no man, living or dead, can accomplish. John's material he would not have if on earth to-day, and without it he never can commence his church.

Elder P. has now turned his attention to Baptist peculiarities and claims from them that the Baptist is the church of Christ. And the "Baptists recognize Christ as their head." Pray where is the church that don't do that? I certainly claim Christ as my leader. The Methodist and Presbyterian all do the same, and do tell me what is peculiar about that? It proves all to be the church of Christ if it proves anything. So away goes No. 1. But Baptists take the Bible alone, believe it to be the Book of God and accept all that it says! If there is one thing more peculiar about me and my brethren than another it is that we take the Bible alone as our guide; and who but infidels don't believe it to be from God and accept all it says? So there goes No. 2. Yes, but you teach that baptism and the Lord's supper are ordinances of the church. If you had said "ordinances of the Lord" we would have been nearer agreed. As it is, you don't differ in this from the other protestant sects of Christendom. So, No. 3 goes for nought.

But again, Baptists "immerse the man who is born again." Certainly, they claim that they do. The old Baptists and Separates claim to do the same thing, and our Methodist and Presbyterian friends claim to occasionally immerse the same character. In this you are not very "peculiar." So farewell to No. 4!

"Baptists teach that the Holy Spirit operate in conviction and conversion independent of the word." Yes, and so teach the Old Baptists and various other denominations. The truth of this "peculiarity" will be tested further on.

As to your 6th "peculiarity," the final perseverance of the saints," it is by no means peculiar to the Missionary Baptists, but is quite distinctive in the teachings of other Baptists and a so in those of the Old and Cumberland Presbyterian churches. All of Elder P.'s bluster about his seven "peculiarities" which marked their identity beyond all doubt, as being the church of Christ, amounts to absolutely nothing, as there is not a single item, whether true or false, but what is held in common by others.

The Bible does not speak of Abraham being justified in the sense that a sinner is justified in conversion, for Abraham was just as good a man when he is first brought to our view as he ever got to be afterward, so far as we can know. He was justified in the sense that God approved him. It was not faith alone that God approved. How would it read to say, "by faith alone Abraham when he was called, went?" "By faith alone he sojourned in a strange land" "by faith alone Abraham offered up Isaac." This would make nonsense. Let James explain the whole matter: "Was not Abraham our father justified by works when he had offered Isaac his son upon the altar? Seest thou how faith wrought with his works, and by works was faith made perfect?" Now listen: "And the Scripture was fulfilled which saith Abraham believed God and it was imputed unto him for righteousness." Could comment be plainer? It was not faith alone, but faith made perfect by works. So, does a living faith now lead to obedience. The faith that saves the soul is a living and active faith; one that walks and talks out; one that impels man to do whatever God commands.

Certainly, salvation is the "free gift of God." Who says it isn't? But does God give it to you whether you want it or not? God has seen fit to suspend salvation upon conditions which, when complied with, by no means purchase salvation. With all that man can do he is still an unprofitable servant. "If of baptism it is no more of grace" says my good brother. If God favors us with salvation upon submission to baptism as a condition of pardon, I suppose in that sense it would still be of "grace." But the tramp had to work for his dinner. Therefore, baptism is not for the remission of sins!

Now I'll have done a job of work myself. I tell a man that if he will dig me a cistern of specified dimensions, and wall it up with brick, I'll give him fifty dollars. He goes and digs the cistern, then comes and demands the fifty dollars. You have it dug? Yes. Have you walled it up with brick? No, I've just got it dug. But the contract was, you were to dig and wall it up for fifty dollars. He sues me. Is there a judge in the State that would make me pay it? Not one. God has commanded faith, repentance and baptism, and upon compliance with these conditions has promised you salvation. Can you claim it until you have done all that he has demanded? Surely not. And it turns out that we have a "creed" after all our effort to get rid of them. I will attend to this in my next speech.

THE PETERSBURG DEBATE #10

Pennington

"The Missionary Baptist church is the church or kingdom of Christ on earth."

Elder P. said: "I'm amused at Dr. B's. effort to turn my good Old Baptist, Methodist and Presbyterian brethren against me. Why certainly I don't cast them off. They are in God's kingdom, and will finally be saved in Heaven. My Old Baptist brethren are a little off. They have left the fold and are wandering a little, but will get back to us again. They were once with us and God will save them notwithstanding their little breaking off from the Father's flock.

We have articles of belief, but not a creed. The Dr. denies his creed that Lard wrote and fastened upon the churches. We'll see him when he chases that off. Dr. you are not as clear of creeds as you thought you were. Appleton says the 'ana-Baptists are the seed of the original church.' The seed is exactly like the thing itself. The Dr. berates me for saying that no man can come to God or understand his will unless he first be enlightened by the Holy Spirit. Here is what the Book says: 'No man can come to me except the Father which sent me draw him.'— John 6:44.

Most assuredly I believe that our religious friends, the Old Baptists, the Methodists, etc., will be saved. God has both a visible and invisible kingdom. We possess by virtue of inheritance the visible kingdom and other believers are in the invisible one.

Elder P. here concluded that it would be best to attempt his successive argument again. But since his utter defeat at John's end of the line, he concluded it the part of wisdom to start at some other point. Accordingly, he began to forge his claim at New Port, R. I., his first link being John Clark. All historians agree that Roger Williams was founder of the Baptists in America in the year 1539, but Elder P. would not have it thus, and proved from a tombstone in the New Port cemetery that one John Clark antedated him by one year. Of course, it would spoil the sauce to accept Roger as the first link in America, as he was not baptized by the sanctified hands of a Baptist preacher. He then professed to trace the church from Clark back through England, Wales, France and into the vales of Piedmont, through the German Baptists to the Waldenses. This end of the chain proved too much for him and his floundering was enough to excite the pity of the most callous hearted. His attempt was so intangible and incoherent that I find it utterly impossible to place it before the readers of the Advocate. It consisted of snatches of history researched from Ray's succession. He was so disconcerted at the Dr's flank movement in capturing John's material that his discomfiture was perfectly obvious to all. He never was himself again but with much repetition, time-calling and exhortation, managed to fill out his time.

THE PETERSBURG DEBATE #11

Brents.
"Now we are ready to examine that "creed" of which the gentleman has told you so much. And let me say now, and for always, that Moses E. Lard never conceived, wrote nor endorsed a single word, line or sentence of the document which Elder P. has flung into my teeth. The man who charges that said document was gotten up by M. E. Lard, fastened, as a creed, on church-

es, by him; or that it ever was endorsed by our leading papers, is guilty of perpetrating an unmitigated slander upon our brotherhood. I talk thus plainly that I may be understood. Such reckless charges made in the face of the facts which could have been known—and must have been known, in the very nature of the case, do not argue much for the candor of the man making them. Moses E. Lard copied that creed into his Quarterly, not to endorse it, but to give its writer one of the most scathing rebukes that was ever administered. The gentleman could not have seen this document, which he calls a "creed," without also seeing the name of its real author appended to it, and also the rebuke and terrible censure of Lard, yet he comes along despite this and boldly affirms that Lard is the author, that it was adopted by many churches and endorsed by all the papers!

The good brother says that he didn't exclude the Methodist, Old Baptist, etc., but they are in the kingdom. I now assert most positively that he has roundly surrendered his proposition. Yours "is the church or kingdom." Your own definition is that "church" and "kingdom" are the same. Are they in this Missionary Baptist "church or kingdom"? If so, all right; if not, all wrong. You have roundly surrendered, and so far as this proposition is concerned, we might as well dismiss and go home. Oh! you say they are in the invisible Kingdom, and not in the visible? Very well. As soon as conversion takes place, you claim that the spirit is in the invisible kingdom, and that the body remains out of the Kingdom until it joins the visible Baptist Zion. Before he joins the Missionary Baptist church, his body is in the devil's kingdom—the world and God has possession of his spirit. A kind of joint partnership, it seems? No wonder that the devil and Michael disputed over the body of Moses!

You say they are all in the invisible kingdom, and good enough for heaven, but are not quite good enough to eat at a Baptist table—a man can get to heaven easier than he can get into the Baptist church. If they are good enough for heaven, why are you going as a theological pugilist up and down the earth, smiting all who don't belong to your Zion?

Certainly, no man cometh to the Father except He draw him, but it isn't said that the Holy Spirit does this drawing by operating abstractly. If the gentleman had not been afraid to read the next verse, (John vi, 45) he might have become enlightened on the subject of drawing. "Every man, therefore, that hath heard or hath learned the Father, cometh unto me."

My brother, not content with his first attempt at Succession, thinks he can "succeed" better from the other end of the line. Of course, he has our sympathies in his miserable failure. No man ought to attempt such a feat as to trace an unbroken line of Baptist churches from the present back to the apostles. I will now let you hear from some leading Baptists on this subject. (Dr. B. here read six letters from as many professors of church history, in as many Baptist colleges and universities, in which they all charged the man who would attempt to prove succession, of imprudence, foolhardiness, or downright ignorance). Your own historians say that you or any other man are doing a vast deal of harm to the Baptist church in attempting such a feat as you have on hand. So, my brother, you had better go home, and quit injuring the Baptist cause in this country by chasing such a phantom as succession.

I will give my friend a much easier job to accomplish: If he will trace an unbroken line back to John Clarke's church in New Port, I will give up the question. Or, better still if the gentleman will give us the name of the man who immersed the preacher that baptized him, we, for the sake of peace, will give up the discussion. The brother is careering all through creation leaving missing links of a hundred years in his chain. That kind of work won't do. The chain is no stronger than the weakest link in it. Let him come closer home, trace the line to John Clarke, or Roger Williams, or prove beyond doubt that he has been baptized by a successor of the apostles. Get down to this kind of work; and quit skipping here, yonder and everywhere.

My brother says the Old Baptist are all right— are safe for heaven—because they once belonged to his church; then I suppose we are "all right" for the same reason, as he has repeatedly told you that we broke off from his church!

There is scarcely any doctrine but what the Waldenses held to and practice. They persisted in being simply called "Christians;" they baptized for the "remission of sins." Yet the gentlemen in his extreme eagerness to forge his chain, can hug them with all their heresies to his bosom. But grant that Elder P. could trace his line back to the Waldenses, he is then more than a thousand years from the apostles. And further than this he can never go. I propose to build a wall of fire 400 years deep, through which you never can pass. Dr. Wall says that every writer for the first 400 years of the Christian era, without a single exception, taught baptism for the remission of sins, and these very writers constituted the very "Baptist church" which you hid away in the year A. D., 300. No, sir. You can never stretch your link over this gap. You would not tolerate such doctrine as they taught, and you shall not claim them as your brethren. Thus, the Baptist chain with its end and middle links extracted amounts to absolutely nothing.

You have now heard all that my friend could say for his Baptist church, and you must determine whether or not he has sustained his proposition.

www.ingramcontent.com/pod-product-compliance
Lightning Source LLC
LaVergne TN
LVHW051622080426
835511LV00016B/2117